Experiencing Racism

Experiencing Racism

Exploring Discrimination through the Eyes of College Students

Richard Seltzer and Nicole E. Johnson

LEXINGTON BOOKS
A divison of

ROWMAN & LITTLEFIELD PUBLISHERS, INC.
Lanham • Boulder • New York • Toronto • Plymouth, UK

ROWMAN & LITTLEFIELD PUBLISHERS, INC.

A division of Rowman & Littlefield Publishers, Inc.
A wholly owned subsidiary of The Rowman & Littlefield Publishing Group, Inc.
4501 Forbes Boulevard, Suite 200
Lanham, MD 20706

Estover Road
Plymouth PL6 7PY
United Kingdom

British Library Cataloguing in Publication Information Available

Library of Congress Cataloging-in-Publication Data

Richard Seltzer and Nicole E. Johnson
  Experiencing racism : exploring discrimination through the eyes of college student
p. cm.
  Includes bibliographical references.
  ISBN 978-0-7391-3431-3 (cloth : alk. paper) — ISBN 978-0-7391-3432-0 (pbk. :
alk. paper) — ISBN 978-0-7391-3433-7 (electronic)
  1. Discrimination in education—United States. 2. Minority college students—
United States—Attitudes. 3. African American college students—United States—
Attitudes. 4. College students, White—United States—Attitudes. 5. Blacks—Race
identity—United States. 6. Race discrimination—United States. I. Seltzer,
Richard, Ph. D. II. Johnson, Nicole E., 1973–
  LC212.2.E97 2009
  378.1'9829—dc22   2009007789

Printed in the United States of America

♾ ™ The paper used in this publication meets the minimum requirements of
American National Standard for Information Sciences—Permanence of Paper
for Printed Library Materials, ANSI/NISO Z39.48-1992.

Contents

Acknowledgments

We are deeply indebted to the 939 students who wrote these essays and the nine other professors who assigned the essays as extra credit. Students spoke eloquently from the heart and for this we are profoundly grateful.

We would also like to thank several research assistants who collated, double-checked, and commented on essays: Rhea Nedd-Roper, Yolanda Curtis, and Shameka Cathey. Several friends and colleagues read through some or all of the essays and their comments were very helpful: Jane Flax, Robert C. Smith, and David Heffernan.

Our editors at Lexington Books, Michael Sisskin, Alyc Helms, and Lynda Phung were helpful and encouraging throughout this process.

Our families deserve a tremendous round of applause for their support through this process. We thank: Grace, Michael, Mathew, Lil, Bernie, Chris, Delores, and James.

Preface

Race is the great American obsession, the great American tragedy, and to some extent the great American success story. The Civil War was fought, in part, over the role of race, and elections have been won or lost because of a candidate's stand on racial policies. When we meet a new person, one of the first characteristics we note (probably right after gender and age), is the person's race.

This book, a collection of short essays about racial experiences written by college students, arose out of serendipity. One of us (Richard Seltzer) was teaching introduction to research in the Department of Political Science at Howard University. Several students did not do well on a test and began clamoring for extra credit. On the spur of the moment Richard said "write an essay on your worst racial experience." When the essays came in a week later, he was surprised because they were both well-written and interesting. The essays went well beyond the typical "Driving While Black" (DWB) experience that he was expecting. Students wrote about topics ranging from dating, sports, the police, and early childhood friendships to family issues, their lack of racial experiences, and intra-racial issues (light skin versus dark skin). The essays were passionate, thoughtful, and often surprising.

We decided to assign the extra credit essays over additional semesters and eventually got other professors at different schools to assign the essay for extra credit. The essays from whites, Hispanics, and Asians were also fascinating, surprising and covered a range of issues.

Essays were received from 939 students taking 26 different classes at 11 universities: Howard University, Middle Tennessee State University, New York University, Salisbury State University, Saint Louis University, St.

Mary's College (Maryland), Steven Austin State University (Texas), University of California at Santa Barbara, University of Maryland at College Park, University of South Florida, and Villanova University. We are profoundly grateful to the professors who assigned the essays as well as to the students who wrote them.

The 217 essays used in this book, chosen to highlight the range of experiences, were edited to retain the writers' style and conversational tone. Many essays were similar in content and were not used to avoid duplication. For example, we used only eleven of the nearly eighty essays that described bad experiences with police officers. In a few situations we quote from an excluded essay in order to highlight a point. These essays are marked as "not included." Upon request, we are happy to send copies of the excluded essays.

Some essays described experiences that took place outside of the United States and were excluded. For the most part, we also have excluded essays that recounted the experiences of others as well as experiences that took place many years ago (i.e., in the 1960s). There are some exceptions to this for essays that were truly compelling.

To protect confidentiality, as required by the Institutional Review Board at Howard University, we changed the names of all students in the book. If the student had an "ethnic" sounding name, another ethnic-sounding name was substituted.

It was not always obvious in which chapters to place the essays, and we had to make a lot of judgment calls. Consider an incident at a sporting event in which racial slurs were used and someone got hit. Does that essay belong in "Sports," "Racial Slurs," or "Violence"? Or, how about a child who is called a "nigger" in elementary school? Does that belong in "Racial Slurs," "Childhood," or "School"?

The essays came from elite schools as well as non-elite schools. Students came from forty-four different states and a dozen different countries. Women wrote 67 percent of the essays; the racial distribution of essays is shown in table 1.

Table 1.   Racial Distribution of Contributors

Race	Number	Percent
Black	368	42.9%
White	294	34.3%
Hispanic	138	16.1%
Asian	22	2.6%
Multi-racial	27	3.1%
Other	7	1.0%

However, the essays cannot be considered representative of racial experiences. For the most part, social science majors attending universities wrote the essays. Experiences from people of different backgrounds might be very different.

Another point of caution is that students wrote essays with the professor in mind. Some students were taking black politics or Hispanic studies classes. Several essays were probably written given the knowledge or perspective gained in these classes.

We organized essays into one of the following nineteen topics:

1. Childhood

These essays detail experiences at an early age. Several essays detail problems with friends at an early age that were often exacerbated by parents. Some parents did not want their children to play with children of a different race. In other essays, racial slurs were used by adults or other children. The extent to which the contributors remember these experiences with such intensity was somewhat of a surprise, given that many of these experiences occurred when they were very young children.

2. Family

Many racists learn their racism from their family. In these essays contributors talk about family members who made racially offensive comments or committed racist acts. The reactions of the contributors were equally fascinating.

3. Friends

In these essays contributors detailed experiences about friends or family members of friends who exhibited racist behavior. Some of these situations did not directly affect the contributor, such as when racist jokes were told among a group of friends of the same race. In other situations, one friend or family member of a friend directly insulted a friend of a different race. In other situations, some friends were not allowed to go to someone else's house or drive in the car of someone else's parent because they are of another race. In other situations, the friend made racially insensitive comments.

4. School

School environments can be very mean. Contributors detail how they were harassed and/or beaten at school because of their race. Several describe how students segregated themselves during lunch and outside of class. In some situations it appears that the school officials did little to try to stop the problem, while in other situations, school officials took a very active role.

5. Teachers and School Administrators

Teachers and school administrators also exhibited racist behavior. Some acted as if their students had no ability and should only take vocational-type courses and/or not apply to elite universities. Several other teachers made racially insensitive comments or exhibited other more overt racist behavior.

6. Dating

It is difficult enough to sustain a relationship with a partner under most circumstances. However, it is much more difficult when family members, the partners of one's "friends" and perfect strangers give the couple grief because the couple is interracial. Some of the contributors were essentially disowned by family members. Others were yelled at, grounded, generally harassed, or treated "as dirt."

7. Sports

Sports have often served to unite people of different races. Here we see where the opposite occurs through the use of racial slurs, not allowing others to play because of their race, and acts of violence.

8. Service and Shopping

In these essays we read about discrimination in the use of services and sales: taxis, restaurants, and retail stores. Some of the essays are by people who were accused of discriminatory behavior.

9. Discrimination

This chapter details discrimination that occurred in the workplace, housing, or in university settings. Some contributors were denied promotions or jobs and others believe they were denied scholarships or admissions because of their race. In other situations people were treated differently in prison, parking situations, or housing.

10. Stereotyping

People are often stereotyped because of their physical appearance. Many contributors recount situations where they were told they were admitted to schools only because of their race (and that they are not smart enough), they have certain athletic skills because of their race, their opinions don't count because they lack a certain characteristic, they must be racist because they come from a certain place, or they must be poor or a criminal.

11. Racial Slurs

Blacks, whites and Hispanics have been at the receiving end of racial slurs, as detailed in many of the essays in this chapter. In other essays, contributors detail how they were offended when someone of their own race used racial slurs. In some situations the victim treated it almost as a "rite of passage" and in other situations, the racial slur had an effect similar to being punched in the stomach.

12. Skin Color

People within the same race are sometimes very mean toward one another. Some would not date another person because they were of a different hue, some were told they were not dark enough, and some were treated badly because they came from a different culture (i.e., born in Africa). In other essays, contributors talk about how they were accused of "acting white."

13. Language

This chapter mostly relates to Hispanics who were treated differently because they did not speak English very well. Contributors or parents of contributors were insulted or discriminated against for this reason.

14. Other Ethnic

This chapter details the experience of Jews and Muslims who were victims of prejudice. We decided that they deserve their own chapter in order to highlight their specific problems and because, for the most part, they do not fit into the typical racial division in the United States.

15. Self-Image

Some contributors were very self-conscious because of their race. They discuss how they felt inferior or very uncomfortable around or because of others.

16. Violence

In this chapter contributors detail acts of violence that occurred because of their race. Some of these acts were directed toward an individual and others toward a group.

17. Police

Most of these essays detail police misconduct. Contributors were accused of crimes they did not commit and were generally harassed by the police. In some situations, the misconduct was violent. "Driving while black" (DWB) essays were reported by many contributors. To avoid repetition, only about one tenth of these essays are used in this book.

18. Is Prejudiced

Some contributors admitted to being prejudiced or their essays indicate that they held prejudiced attitudes. Many tried to explain their attitudes by detailing a bad experience. Most of these experiences were related to crime.

19. No Racism

About 5 percent of contributors said they never had a bad racial experience and discuss the reasons for this. The more common reasons for this include: times have changed; the contributor grew up in a nonracially diverse environment; the contributor grew up in a diverse environment; the contributor grew up in a progressive environment; or the contributor rose above such issues.

In addition to the nineteen chapters described above we have an introduction in which we discuss some of the objective reality of race relations in the United States as well as the academic understanding and debates about these issues. In the concluding chapter we summarize our findings and try to place this within the context of the academic literature.

Introduction

Since its birth, the United States' racial make-up has largely been biracial, consisting of a white majority and black minority. However, increased immigration and higher rates of intermarriage have gradually led to a significant multiracial population (Lee and Bean 2004). Therefore, at the dawn of the twenty-first century the question becomes: what are the *new* racial boundaries and how significant are they today? These questions are especially relevant when we consider the changing nature and dynamics of racism in America. Our traditional understanding of what it means to be racist, what it means to experience racism, and our notions of white power and privilege are being challenged in a society that is growing more multiracial; paradigms that applied to the black-white dichotomy are not applicable for other race relations. Specifically, a reconceptualization of how racism is experienced in America today requires an understanding of the diversity of experiences across racial and ethnic groups as well as within these groups and how such experiences shape the identities and attitudes of individuals. If indeed the black-white color line no longer characterizes the nature of racial/ethnic relations in the United States, what is the new color line(s) and how are these divisions reflected in our present race relations?

While the racial landscape of America has changed, many features remain the same. While the country is celebrating the historic election of the first African American nominee for president, in the shadow lurks the ongoing struggle of African Americans and other minorities to achieve racial equality. Although African Americans have made great gains and relations between African Americans and whites have improved, racial inequalities persist in income, employment, education, and healthcare, to name a few. Long-term joblessness continues to contribute to African Americans' difficulties in other sectors including home ownership, income, education, employment, and healthcare (Wilson 1987). As unemployment remains higher for African Americans and Hispanics than for whites, it is not surprising that both groups are less likely to have health insurance, an issue that is further complicated by the illegal status of many Hispanic immigrants. As the life expectancy for whites continues to rise, numerous studies have found that blacks and other racial minorities are less likely than whites to receive medical care and are therefore more prone to get sick and experience a longer recovery time.[1] According to the American Community Survey, the median income for black households has stayed at about 60 percent of the income for white households since 1980. The American Community Survey of the Bureau of the Census reports that in 2006 the median household income for whites was $51,429, $38,385 for blacks, $38,747 for Hispanics, and $72,305 for Asians. And while the gap in poverty rates has narrowed since 1980, it continues to be substantial. For example, the poverty rate for whites was 11 percent in 2006, compared with blacks (25 percent), Hispanics (19 percent), and Asians (8 percent). As many minorities struggle with poverty, they find themselves living in neighborhoods and communities that are often unsafe with limited job and educational opportunities.

Recent statistics show that barely half of African Americans and Hispanics are graduating from high school.[2] However, more minorities are attending college. In 2006, 28 percent of whites over the age of twenty-five were college graduates, compared to blacks (19 percent), Hispanics (12 percent), and Asians (50 percent).

It is perhaps in the criminal justice system that the starkest racial disparities exist. Mauer and King of The Sentencing Project (2007) report an incarceration of 412 per 100,000 for whites, compared to 2,290 for blacks and 742 for Hispanics. The rate for blacks is six times the rate for whites. When the data are further broken down, they report that 11.7 percent of African American men between the ages of twenty-five and twenty-nine are in prison or in jail.

The racial inequality puzzle remains as new divisions created by class, geography, and residence (e.g., urban, suburban, exurbs) further complicate the persistent questions of why racial inequality persists, what the role of racial discrimination is, *and* who the victims of racial inequality and discrimination are in an increasingly diverse society. The purpose of this book is to demonstrate through the individual experiences of whites, African Americans, Hispanics, and many other minority groups that our experiences with racism are common, *but* there is a diversity of race relations and racist experiences that are often structured by class, gender, geography, and residence. This diversity is not always captured in traditional social science research. The complex nature of race relationships depicted in these essays goes beyond our traditional understandings of what it means to be racist and *who* the victims and perpetrators of racism are.

THE TWENTY-FIRST CENTURY: THE NEW COLOR LINE(S) OR NO COLOR LINE AT ALL?

W. E. B. Dubois eloquently wrote in the *Souls of Black Folk* that the problem of the twentieth century would be the problem of the color line (Dubois 1903). The color line Dubois described was the black-white racial divide. However, as our nation has become more diverse, our understanding of race relations and racism has grown more complicated and eluded many contemporary social science studies. While racism persists in the twenty-first century, it is more subtle and impacts a more diverse population including Hispanics, Africans, Middle Easterners, Jews, and Asians just to name a few. Today, the racial landscape of America consists of multiple racial and ethnic groups (Lee and Bean 2004). Increased rates of immigration, intermarriage, and multiracial identification are changing American's color lines. Therefore, our understanding of race relations is no longer "black and white" both literally and figuratively.

So, how is it possible for racial inequality to persist when legal barriers to opportunity have been eliminated, access to opportunity is greater, and the vast majority of whites denounce racial discrimination? Decades of social science have shown that the nature of racism changes over time as it reflects changes in our culture and context. Therefore, an understanding of the *lived* experiences of racism shaping the cognitive frameworks that affect our views and attitudes is critical to understanding how and why racial inequality may persist. Experiences of racism are not just the stories of minorities but the stories of whites who are not always the perpetrators of racism but may also be victims of racism through their lens of interpretation. Likewise, what may be perceived as racism by some readers may not be perceived as racism by others. As we look at the individual experiences in this book, it is clear that racial experiences have affected individuals in ways that were probably unforeseen during the experience. Such experiences raise the question *does my race make a difference?* Whether we are the individual victim or individual perpetrator of racism and discrimination, one cannot deny that we have all experienced a moment when we ask ourselves:

- Did my race make a difference?
- Would I have acted differently if he or she was black/white/Hispanic?
- Am I a racist?
- Did I just experience racism?

How we react or respond in these moments changes us in ways that have yet to be explored in more traditional social science research. However, existing theories and paradigms for understanding race provides important frameworks for understanding the experiences depicted throughout this book.

Racial Attitudes and Contemporary Social Science Research

Social science on racial attitudes and race relations has typically focused on the black-white racial divide. Of course, this is largely due to the history of enslavement of African Americans and systematic legal discrimination that led to centuries of social and economic disadvantage. Other ethnic minority groups such as Irish, Italians, and eastern European Jews were able to assimilate and became "white," thus distancing themselves from black Americans. While many ethnic groups were able to successfully assimilate in American life, African Americans have not. Despite the fact that African Americans have adopted the customs, values, and practices of the majority population, they have not achieved successful economic incorporation (Lee and Bean 2004). The great hope was that once legal barriers were removed, African Americans would be incorporated into the social and economic fabric of American society. However, the removal of such barriers has resulted in partial, inconsistent improvement of African Americans (Lee and Bean 2004, p. 227). Much of the research on race relations has focused on increasing our understanding of how the American dream has eluded African Americans through the systematic practice and history of racism and discrimination. Social scientists have sought to understand how racial attitudes and stereotypes function.

One of the great issues that has marked social science research on racism is how prejudice and discrimination can be measured when it is often hidden and illegal (Quillian 2006). Beginning in the 1960s, legally enforced discrimination ended and overt forms of discrimination were denounced. Despite the progress of the period, the gap in racial equality persists and progress remains mixed. Thus, understanding the complicated dynamics of racism and discrimination continues to demand the attention of social scientists to understand the paradox of progress and decline in racial equality for African Americans.

A cornerstone for understanding discrimination and prejudicial practices is the understanding of racial attitudes. However, historically social science research on racial attitudes focused on the attitudes of whites while African Americans were rarely represented. Subsequently, social science research often resulted in an "unbalanced understanding of the nature of intergroup relations" between African Americans and whites (Monteith and Spicer 2000).

Contemporary social science research has sought to rectify this gap by comprehensive studies of white and African American attitudes (Kinder and Sanders 1996; Sigelman and Welch 1991; Schuman et al. 1997). Researchers have begun to pursue scholarship with more minority respondents in order to explore the attitudes, beliefs, and behaviors of minority group members with greater detail and cross-group comparisons (Dawson 1994; de la Garza et al. 1992; Gurin, Hatchett, and Jackson 1989; Hochschild 1995; Tate 1992; Zubrinsky and Bobo 1996). The increasing racial and ethnic diversity in the United States has lead to research beyond the cross group comparisons of African Americans and whites (Monteith and Spicer 2000). Social science research now includes seminal studies of Hispanics (de la Garza et al. 1992; Jones-Correa 1998; Welch and Sigelman, 1993) and Asians (Lien, Conway, and Wong 2004; Park 1995; Weitzer 1997). There is now also the recognition that economic and political competition occurs among minorities, which may lead to conflict (McClain and Tauber 1998; Franklin and Seltzer 2002).

Understanding racial attitudes and beliefs has been a complicated enterprise. Research has grown to include more minority groups, while research on racial attitudes rests on several competing theories first developed from studies of whites and their attitudes toward African Americans. These competing theories for understanding racial attitudes have led to multiple understandings of race. First, *Jim Crow Racism*, or biological racism, was rooted in long-held stereotypes of African Americans and the superiority of the white race. Many whites were able to justify their prejudiced beliefs on the perceived inherent biological differences between blacks and whites. For example, African Americans were believed to be inherently less intelligent, lazy, and irresponsible. However, since the 1950s there has been a steady decline among whites who subscribe to such views and this has been well documented in the literature (Schuman et al. 1997; Sniderman and Piazza 1993). Some scholars, however, caution that using questions asked in the 1950s and 1960s as measures of old-fashioned racism to detect changes in racial tolerance rests on the assumption that racism does not change over time (Bonilla-Silva and Forman 2000). For example, questions asked during the Jim Crow era and asked again thirty years will not fit the current racial climate or context (Bonilla-Silva 2000). Researchers assert there is a more subtle form of racism that results in less overt prejudice. This is termed modern, or symbolic racism (Kinder and Sears 1981). Symbolic racism is the belief that African Americans lack traditional American values of individualism, a strong work ethic, moralism, and respect for authority (Sears, Van Laar, Carrillo, Kosterman 1997; Tarman and Sears 2005). Social scientists also contend that "racial resentment" is rooted in the perception that racial discrimination is no longer a problem and that African Americans should work harder to overcome disadvantages. According to this theory, African Americans have received "special treatment" that they do not deserve. Symbolic racism and old-fashioned racism have been found to be highly correlated. Stereotypes of African Americans as being lazy and violating American values have been found to play a key role in understanding symbolic racism (Virtanen and Huddy 1998). Likewise a plethora of studies have shown that symbolic racism is strongly correlated with whites' opposition to racially targeted policies outweighing political attitudes, ideology, party identification, and attitudes toward the government and other traditional racial attitudes (Alvarez and Brehm 1997; Henry and Sears 2002; Kinder and Sanders 1996). Tarman and Sears (2005) find symbolic racism to be distinct from old-fashioned racism and the strongest explanation of whites' policy preferences.

An additional theory of racial attitudes is associated with a *sense of group position* or simply that racial attitudes are a function of protecting privilege or group interests. Therefore, whites who perceive that African Americans threaten their collective interests will be less likely to support policies in favor of African Americans (Kinder and Sanders 1996). These attitudes are rooted in the goal of protecting one's privileged position or status while suppressing subordinate groups (Sears, Van Laar, Carrillo and Kosterman 1997). For example, Kinder and Sanders (1996) find that a sense of group threat and disadvantage is strongly related to whites' views on race. However, Wilson (2006) finds in a study of affirmative action that whites' rejection of group-based preferences reflects a rejection of blacks and group-based preferences in general not just against blacks. Similarly, Krysan (2000) finds that policy preferences reflects evaluations of policy *and* target group. Thus, both studies demonstrate that whites' lack of support of race-based policies is not always rooted in animosity toward a minority group but is more clearly sensed as a threat to the collective interests of whites.

Much of the previous research on racial attitudes entails sophisticated quantitative studies that have allowed for cross-racial comparisons and multi-method analysis (Bobo 1997). And yet, there are few consensually accepted theoretical and conceptual models. The essays within this book show that the diversity of race relations and attitudes is far cloudier than has been portrayed in social science research. They do not fall neatly into existing theories of racial attitudes or how race functions.

THE GREAT DEBATE

Does racism still exist? Is it racism or something else? Scholars, policy makers, and politicians grapple with these persistent questions. Many scholars claim that laissez-faire racism has emerged in which African Americans are blamed for their failure to achieve economic standing due to perceived cultural inferiority (Bobo and Kluegel 1997). Kinder and Sanders (1996) have described the latest incarnation of racism as "racial resentment" of African Americans who have been given too much and could achieve economic parity and overcome discrimination and prejudice if they would only try harder. Bonilla-Silva and Foreman (2000) find through in-depth surveys and interviews that whites exhibit more racism, and that a new racial ideology has developed, which they describe as color-blind racism. The authors examine racial attitudes on various measures including affirmative action and discrimination against African Americans. The authors find that whites are actually more racist than what appears in social science surveys due to a new "racetalk" that allows whites to talk about racial issues in public venues in a way that allows for less overtly expressed racial resentment.

However, Bonilla-Silva and Foreman focus only on white respondents, and their measures of racism are vague and ambiguous. For example, while some respondents were against interracial marriage for themselves, it is questionable to argue from that they are racist. Krysan (2000) shows that white racial attitudes have changed over time. They suggest this reflects greater support for racial equality but less support for government policies to ensure racial equality. However, under private conditions whites were more likely to express less support for racial policies than traditional racial attitudes. This indicates that the context in which racial attitudes are expressed is significant. Picca and Feagin (2007) examine students' diaries of daily racial events and show that whites' racism is likely different depending on whether the context is public or private. However, like Bonilla-Silva and Foreman, the focus is on white respondents with little description of any possible positive experiences. The authors conclude that racism continues to exist because whites continue to benefit from racism.

Existing social science research has attempted to answer the question of whether racism still exists through sophisticated quantitative studies of *whites'* racial attitudes and levels of prejudice as expressed in support or lack of support for racial policies. Characteristic of much social science research on racial attitudes is that whites have always been portrayed as the perpetrators of racism. Indeed, many scholars have debated whether or not African Americans or other minorities can be racist given they are not part of a privileged class and lack "real" power and access to the existing power structure. And while the work of Feagin and Picca (2007) and Bonilla-Silva (2000) contend that whites continue to be racist, for social science research to move forward requires more cross-racial examination, not simply examining the views and attitudes of whites and the black-white dichotomy. Furthermore, existing research shows that racial attitudes are highly contextual depending on private-public setting, framing of the policy issue (Hutchings and Valentino 2004; White 2007), gender (Wilson 2006), class, urban-rural geographic setting (Carter, Steelman, Mulkey, and Borch 2005), and target (Hunt 2007).

THE PSYCHOLOGY OF RACE AND RACISM: IDENTITY, MEMORY, AND STEREOTYPES

Race is a socially constructed category based on fluid categories (Bonilla-Silva, 2000). However, as a social category like class and gender, there exists a social reality regarding race which influences society and its actors. Frederickson (1988) defines race as a "consciousness of status and identity based on ancestry and color." Social scientists view race as a social and cultural category rather than a biological category because it is often a defining characteristic of one's identity. Psychologists contend that the concept of "self" is critical to the psychological well being of individuals and specifically, "race and the social implications of phenotypic characteristics impact our understanding of self" (Mercer and Cunningham 2003). Race impacts how we view ourselves through interactions with others and our ability to categorize individuals into in-groups and out-groups (Kramer and Brewer 1984). As we categorize our interactions with others and develop meaning from these interactions we come to learn who we are in isolation and in relation to other racial groups (Helms and Talleyrand 1997).

Racial identity has largely been researched through the experiences of ethnic/racial minorities and much of that is experience has been structured by a past history and present experience of racism. Thus, what often bonds racial/ethnic minorities as respective groups is their collective experience with racism and discrimination. This sense of common identity and common fate is also known as race consciousness. Research has shown that African Americans have high levels of racial consciousness by identifying with other African Americans as a group through the common experience of racism (Smith and Seltzer 2000). However, as the black population in the United States grows more diverse with immigrants from Africa, Latin America, and the Caribbean, the notion of what it means to be black in America is also likely to change (Benson 2006). Black migrant groups go through a period of racialization and "adapting" to an African American identity but do not attach the same ideological meaning as do native-born African Americans. Indeed, some essays throughout this book demonstrate the tension many black migrants feel between their racial identity and their *national* and *ethnic* identity as they assimilate into African American culture.

The issue of identity and race is complicated for other minority groups as well. For example, Lee and Bean (2004) find that race does not provide an accurate label for Latinos and Asians. Many Latinos are often seen by others as white and Asian, specifically South Asians (Bangladesh, Pakistan,

Phillipines, and the like), have been categorized as "nonwhites" as opposed to "nonblack," thus reflecting whiteness as the racial norm in America (Bijlani, 2005). Hunt (2007) contends that researchers must examine beliefs of other racial groups in order to allow for analysis of cultural variations within ethnoracial categories (e.g., Korean, Chinese, Japanese within Asian category; Mexican, Puerto Rican, and Cuban within Hispanic category) and also differences by nativity/generational status, assimilation and acculturation.

Social scientists have grappled with how to measure identity and indeed, the essays within this book often show most people do not see race as their defining characteristic.[3] In fact, the term *ethnic identity* has come to dominate research literature in the area of racial identity measurement and resulted in a "loss of definitional clarity" regarding racial and ethnic identity constructs (Helms 1996). Some measures such as MEIM (Multigroup Ethnic Identity Measure) propose to measure a culture/racial identity model and others propose to measure an *ethnic identity* while using a racial identity framework (Cross 1978). Separating racial and ethnic identity has been increasingly complicated for researchers particularly as immigration and intermarriage has increased.

Historically, groups once seen as racial groups (e.g., Italians, Irish, Jews, Germans) are now considered ethnic groups. Such groups have reached equality with white Protestants in terms of education, income, and residential distribution and have assimilated as "whites" (Waters 2000). However, as "whiteness" no longer guarantees separate legal privileges, researchers have sought to determine the nature of white racial identity. Despite the increasing diversity of the United States, scholars contend that "whiteness" is still considered a privileged identity with access to private sources of social acceptance and power. McDermott and Samson (2005) contend that "whiteness" is conceptualized as being privileged, however there is little understanding of what whiteness means in terms of a racial identity. However, as the population grows more multi-racial the ambiguity of white racial identity is likely to become the center of discussion. Boundaries and definitions of whiteness are likely to change as are the racialized experiences of whites. Research has found that class plays an important role in defining the boundaries of "whiteness" and how white racial identity is experienced is different for poor and working-class whites (McDermott 2006; Gallagher 2001), through participant research, focus groups, and interviews shows that many whites are comfortable expressing racism to other whites they do not know because their "whiteness" makes them "kindred spirits in racism."

Class also has a profound effect on the identity of African Americans. Wilson (1987) argues that since the 1960s class is more important than race in determining the economic placement of African Americans. Smith and

Seltzer (1992) found that class was the biggest determinant in predicting differences in most attitudes between blacks and whites. Racial identity becomes important as a means for categorizing in-group and out-group members. In-group members are evaluated more positively than out-group members. Hewstone, Hantzi, Johnston (1991) find race is a persistent organizing principle for categorizing groups and one such way of categorization is through social stereotypes. Social stereotypes are commonly defined as "cognitive structures that contain the perceiver's knowledge, beliefs, and expectations about human groups (Hamilton and Trolier 1986). Social stereotypes are based on generalizations that are often exaggerated due to a lack of information from the perceiver. For example, individuals will tend to have more information about the group they belong to or "in-group" than an "out-group." Members of an out-group may be judged more harshly or negatively when an individual lacks information or experience with such out-groups (Blascovich, Wyer, Swar, and Kibler 1997). Likewise, Chatman and Von Hippel (2001) found in-group members may be judged more positively. The authors found that African American and white participants showed in-group favoritism biases in the employment candidate selections. African Americans' perception of racial bias still exists due to the "perceptual baggage" collected over time from the experiences and exposure to stimuli that affects how the behaviors of others may be perceived (Johnson, Simmons, Trawalter, Ferguson, and Reed 2003). Throughout the essays in this book, students repeatedly refer to the impact of stereotypes either in their own behavior or in attributing reasons for their racist experiences.

Historically, stereotypes based on "old-fashioned racism" (e.g., lazy, dependent on welfare, irresponsible, less intelligent) affected African Americans across all spheres including education opportunities, political empowerment, socioeconomic success, and housing (Jones and Luo 1999). And while old-fashioned racist actions may be less frequent, the stereotypes associated with African Americans may persist. Frazer and Wiersma (2001) found that in a study on decision making in employment interviews blacks and whites were hired in equal proportion. However the interviewers later recalled that the answers given to interview questions by blacks were significantly less intelligent despite the fact that the interview conditions were identical. Likewise, additional evidence found that in schools and the workplaces nonwhite candidates are often stereotyped on the basis of their name (Frazer and Wiersma 2001). Candidates for employment who have distinctive African American names are less likely to be called back for an interview (Bertrand and Mullainathan 2003). However, while many Americans believe that racial diversity is an important goal, they are reluctant to acknowledge the impact of race on individual decisions in order to maintain the façade of color blindness. Thus, within the context of decision making, individuals are often able to use nonracial language to explain their decision based on race (Norton, Vandello, Biga, and Darley 2008). Another important aspect of developing one's identity and the formation of stereotypes is memory. We use our environment and interactions with others to develop models of categorization to know how to interact with or approach others. The information we remember from our interactions versus the information we discard becomes a key component of how we form evaluations of others, in-group members and out-group members (Greenhoot, Tsethlikai, and Wagoner 2006).

There are many types of memories, including social memory, collective memory and autobiographical memory. Hanchard (2008) describes how groups "have recollections of stories told to them over generations concerning circumstances, people, and institutions that brought them trauma, humiliation, disgrace, violence and hardship." We often read and hear about the memories of Holocaust survivors and other victims of war and horrific trauma. Although, we may not individually experience a trauma, the collective memory of slavery may influence and shape the identity of African Americans generations later just as the collective memory of the Holocaust may shape or influence the identity of Jews. Through collective memory, memory can be shared across generations even though it is not experienced personally. Similar to collective memory is social memory, which pertains to how society chooses to remember past events. The collective memory of a community, generation, or other group may conflict with the social memory of a particular event; likewise, social memory and collective memory may conflict or augment our own autobiographical memories. Autobiographical memory refers to the personal representation of events, particularly everyday events and self-defining memories (Walls, Sperling, and Weber 2001). Both types of autobiographical memory are framed within the context of culture, gender, and the motivational and emotional aspects of the event's context (Walls, Sperling, and Weber 2001). Many of the essays within this book fall within the spectrum of autobiographical memory as students recall their worst experience with racism as a defining moment in their life. However, it should be noted that memories fade over time and change with new information and experiences. Many autobiographical memories are shaped by the existing collective and social memory a student brings to their experience. Therefore, the experiences recounted throughout these essays may not always be accurate depictions of the actual event.

The existing literature on race and the essays in this book demonstrate that race and the associated concepts of racism, prejudice, and stereotypes are complicated and continue to generate as many questions as answers. Indeed, the research discussed here is closely connected to the experiences of the students in this book. However, the depth and variety of the experiences explored in these essays show that there is still much work to be done if we are ever to move beyond the insidious impact of racism and prejudice in our society.

EXPERIENCING RACE: A DIFFERENT APPROACH

How does one define a racist moment or a racist experience? Locke (1992) defines racism as having "the power to do something based on prejudiced beliefs." This definition describes the act of behaving as a racist but it is different from being subjected to racism as explored in this book. Measuring the impact of direct and indirect racism on recipients is complicated (Watt 1999). Watt (1999) explores these experiences through storytelling. This allows a person to share the details of his or her experiences that adds depth and purpose to our understanding. Quillian (2006) contends that simply focusing on beliefs about prejudice and discrimination as conveyed through surveys, interviews, and discourse analysis misses how implicit beliefs about race influence judgments and actions. Indeed, it is these implicit beliefs in concert with explicit beliefs that reveal biases in real decision contexts such as labor markets and housing markets. Furthermore, these implicit beliefs may also inform the micro- and macro-connections between individuals and groups, particularly how the macro-context influences individual beliefs (Quillian 2006). Likewise, Condor (2006) contends that expressions of prejudice and racism tend to involve socially situated activity or actions between individuals that "involve cognitions and emotions in the heads of distinct individuals." Specifically, Condor (2006) contends that the ways prejudiced talk is conveyed, its purpose (e.g., bully, amuse, shock, claim a social or personal identity), and the intricate way it is woven in daily experience makes it difficult to challenge. Thus, we understand through the essays in this book the reasons students respond differently to their experiences.

The research on racism tends to use data sources that lend themselves to quantitative analysis such as surveys, or qualitative analysis using textual materials, interviews, and transcripts. However, recounting the individual experiences through more discursive approaches often captures additional information that may elude more structured research methods. Birzer and Mahdi (2006) conducted a qualitative phenomenological study of African Americans' experiences with perceived discrimination by using the reflections of African Americans. These reflections enabled the authors to contextualize meaning and understand how African Americans cope with experiences of discrimination. It is our hope that the essays in this book achieve the same goals. However, our lens is the diversity of experiences from various racial and ethnic minorities as well as whites. Similar to Watt (1999), we conduct a thematic analysis of 217 essays we chose to analyze. Initially, we attempted to conduct a quantitative approach of the essays;

however, this approach failed to capture the richness of the essays. Through a thematic analysis we are able to show a diversity of experiences that has not been captured in other social science research.

In fact, the central theme of this book is the *diversity of race relations*. Many stories are common to our own individual experiences while many others are not. In this book we show the variety of ways that race and race relations enter our everyday lives when we least expect it. Although we attempted quantitative analysis of these essays, the themes and interpretations were far too diverse. Therefore, we encourage the reader to use their lens of experience while reading these essays and make their own interpretations of what these racial experiences mean. We also encourage the reader to try to understand the lens of the authors of these essays. Our understanding and knowledge of contemporary race relations must be broadened beyond the scope of African American and white attitudes to encompass the experiences of a far more diverse population than has been portrayed in present social science research.

While scholars and academics have grappled with the concepts of race, racism, prejudice, and stereotypes for decades, at the heart of these issues and what is seldom looked at is how people define their racist experiences. How do they *know* they have experienced racism, how do they cope with such experiences, and how do such experiences change them? Through exploring personal essays, this book provides a snapshot of the types of racist experiences people have had, how they have dealt with such experiences, and what the common themes of racist experiences are that confront people of all backgrounds. The existing literature on issues of race, racism, prejudice, and stereotypes provides context to the "real world" experiences described by the writers of these essays. It is the authors' hope that readers will take the existing research and use it as a framework for thinking about these stories. However, the existing literature is paradoxical. While providing frameworks for understanding the experiences of the students, a gulf exists between the scholarly and "real world" understandings of race. This gulf points to the necessity of additional work and suggests promising directions for future research.

NOTES

1. Stein, Rob. "Race Gap Persists In Health Care, Three Studies Say," *Washington Post*, August 18, 2005, section A01.

2. Lewin, Tamar. "Boys are No Match for Girls in Completing High School," *New York Times*, April 19, 2006, www.nytimes.com/2006/04/19/education/19graduation .html.

3. According to the 2004 NORC-GSS, 35.9 percent of whites felt very close to their "ethnic or racial group" compared to 53.4 percent for African Americans.

1

Childhood

People often recollect their first experience with racism during childhood. When children attend schools with children of diverse cultures and backgrounds, social interaction with other children grows more common. During grades K–6, young people learn and develop a sense of their own competence. At the same time, negative experiences and devastating memories with teachers, parents, and peers can be particularly harmful (Walls, Sperling, and Weber 2001). In fact, from the ages of five to eight years old, children acquire information about their own identity and understanding other's differences. The first school years pose a critical time in the formation of a child's own racial identity and understanding of prejudice and fairness (Derman-Sparks, Higa, and Sparks 1980). Ellen describes her experiences in kindergarten: "I remember being enrolled in kindergarten classes at the school. I spent some of the most horrified days of my life in that classroom because I did not fit in due to the color of my skin."

Research has shown that children, like adults, use skin color and racial cues in making judgments about individuals, evaluating cross-race peers less positively than peers within their own racial group (Graham and Cohen 1997; Kowalski 2003). Therefore, while cross-race friendships are a way to reduce racial prejudice, such friendships are rare (Aboud, Mendelson, and Purdy 2003). One reason for this is that race is perceived as an in-group/out-group characteristic where a child either belongs or does not belong. It is not until later that similar interests, goals, and so on, become additional characteristics in which peers may judge each other (Nesdale, Durkin, Maass, and Griffiths 2005). In fact, children as young as three years of age exhibit racial prejudice; although researchers contend that young children are actually demonstrating a positive bias toward their in-group rather than out-group derogation (Cameron et al. 2001). However, institutional, structural, and social conditions can lead to the development of prejudice within young children (Cameron et al. 2001).

Peers are particularly important for students in grades seven through twelve, who are likely to recall events involving boy/girl memories or best-friend memories during this stage (Walls, Sperling, and Weber 2001). Anna describes events following a kiss shared with a boy who happened to be black. Moore (2002) explores how children learn and use the concepts of race within their peer cultures and interactions. Kids often replicated the racial categorizations seen from adults, so greater diversity encouraged greater awareness and power distribution, but the development of cliques was more often race-based. This is especially the case today when schools and communities are becoming more diverse.

Bias and the potential for cross-race friendships during childhood exist for both minority and nonminority children. Margie, Killen, Sinno, and McGlothlin (2005) find that minority children were more likely to judge the actions of fellow white children as more negative than children within their racial groups. However, this did not impact their judgments regarding friendships. In a similar study of white children attending racially and ethnically diverse and less diverse schools, white children were somewhat biased concerning friendships with minority children (McGlothlin, Killen, and Edmonds 2005).

The collection of essays in this chapter are indicative of just how early individuals experience their first encounter with racism or their first understanding of what race means. Many of the young people in this chapter describe common experiences. For example, Shameka and Donelle were called names by their fellow classmates due to the color of their skin. Other students such as Anna, Helen, and Bonnie describe how they were punished, ridiculed, or not allowed to play with children who were of another race. And of course, childhood is often the first time many young people encounter being called a "nigger." Andy and Darcy recall the first time they were called "nigger" and how this experience changed their life. These indelible experiences are reminders of how early experiences with race forever affect individuals in ways that are both positive and negative.

However, these essays are about more than name-calling and others' prejudices. In fact, throughout this chapter we see how race affects the perceived self-identity and self-image of children, especially young girls. More specifically, we see the very limited notion of what is considered beautiful and the recognition that if you do not fit this standard then you are considered unattractive. Chen (2000) finds that ethnic minority children often struggle with two or more cultural realities and one's ethnic identity and perceptions of their ethnic culture may change over the course of their life span. For example, Mona, who is Native American, describes how isolated she felt in her school because she was "dark." She describes crawling into her mother's lap, sobbing and saying, "I wish my skin was your color." Donnelle describes how she, "used to walk around the house with white T-shirts hanging on my head, pretending I had long, blonde hair," and Ellen pleas "Daddy, can we paint ourselves white?" These essays hint at issues that resurface again during adolescence in the chapter on skin color and Self-Image.

Students of mixed race often have a particularly difficult time fitting in. Reid (2004) finds that students from more than one racial background are more likely to experience trouble in school and are at higher risk of health and behavior problems as teenagers. Shameka, a fair-skinned African American student, describes how the tormenting name-calling (e.g., "mutt") forced her into the care of a psychiatrist to deal with this traumatic experience.

This chapter of essays demonstrates how youthful innocence can be shattered by a single hateful remark or action. More importantly, we see how a singular childhood experience can often set in motion emotional and psychological turmoil that affects one's life forever.

Shameka was a black student at Howard University. She describes how she was called "mutt" by white students in elementary school. She never told her mom, and the entire racial experience at school led to her having to see a psychiatrist.

When I was seven years old, I lived with my twenty-eight-year-old single mother in a two-bedroom apartment in Jenkintown, a small suburb outside of Philadelphia, Pennsylvania. The majority of the families in the neighborhood were Caucasian, middle- and upper-class families. I transferred from a school in the Philadelphia school district to a school with only one other black student in my grade. The other African American girl and I did not get along because she was very mean to me. I was always alone at the school during recess and ate alone in the cafeteria almost every day.

When I wanted to play with the white kids, they would tell me that I would have to buy them ice cream and/or give them my lunch money, and then they would play with me. Every day I began to buy them ice cream, and even give them my lunch money, which meant that I was unable to eat lunch. One incident in particular that sticks out in my mind was when I bought ice cream for this girl named Melissa. She said she would play with me at recess if I did. When I went out to the playground and approached Melissa to play, she said she didn't want to play with me because she didn't know what I was. As a very fair-skinned African American girl, with waist-length curly pigtails and nearly green eyes, I didn't realize that I would encounter these remarks. She laughed at me and called me a "mutt." She teased me in front of the entire playground until I cried.

Those two years spent at Jenkintown Elementary are the most vivid of my memory. I remember feeling so alone, and crying all of the time. I felt alienated from all of the other kids because they proceeded to call me "mutt" and bark at me whenever they saw me. My mother had no idea why I cried every night and broke out in hives the night before school from being so upset and nervous. As a young mother, my mom was so confused and upset, thinking that she was doing something wrong. I ended up having to see a psychiatrist to sort out my problems. This experience might not seem as bad as others might; however, it sticks out in my mind very clearly.

Donelle was a black student attending Howard University. Her classmates called her dirty at her daycare center.

The first time I experienced racism, I was five years old. I was too young to even know or understand what racism was. I was a military brat and we lived in Carson City, Nevada. My family was the only black family that lived in my neighborhood. I went to a before- and after-school care center. They would take me to kindergarten and pick me back up. Of course, I was the only black girl in the entire daycare. I didn't feel different though. I didn't feel out of place or beneath any of the other white kids. I looked at everyone as the same. One day I was playing with the other kids on the jungle gym, when the kids started asking me if I was dirty. They used to say that my mother didn't wash me, because my skin was so dark. I didn't understand what they were trying to say so I went home that night and my mother ran my bath water, just like she did every night. I got in and I started scrubbing and scrubbing and scrubbing, until my skin started to bleed. My mother walked in with a towel, ready to dry me off and saw what I was doing. She stopped me, and asked me, "Danty, what are you doing honey?" I told her the kids at school told me that I was dirty. My mother could not believe what I was telling her. She asked me if I had told any of the teachers. I said yes, but they didn't stop them. My mother was furious. She could not believe that the teachers at that daycare let those kids call me names just because of my color.

The kids at daycare, whose parents obviously taught them about those ignorant views, damaged me psychologically. At five-years old, I wanted to be white. I could not understand why I wasn't. I used to walk around the house with white T-shirts hanging on my head, pretending I had long, blonde hair. After a while, my mother explained to me that white is not better. Black isn't either. It doesn't matter what color a person is, because it is what is on the inside that counts. At five years old, those kids didn't know any better. They say that children don't see color, and if they do, it was taught to them. Those children's racist parents were teaching them that black kids are different. That's a horrible thing.

Darcy was a student at Howard University. On the first day of kindergarten a classmate called her a "nigger."

My first experience with racism occurred at a very young age. I was only five years old, and it was the first week of kindergarten. I was so excited to finally be able to attend school! For me school represented growth, freedom, and not being a baby. As the eldest of five children, I couldn't wait to be considered "a big kid" so that I could play with my older cousins and not be associated with the "babies"—my younger brothers and sisters.

I wore my favorite pink dress, and I was willing to endure the two-hour-long hot-comb straightening process for my hair that I usually avoided like the plague. For me, everything about my first day of school had to be perfect. I had a brand-new, brown, fake-leather (I thought it was real) backpack and matching Mary Janes. In my mind I was prepared to wow not only the students, but my teacher as well. Nothing could ruin *my* day, or so I thought.

Kindergarten was wonderful! It was even better than I had expected. My best friend Jason and I had convinced our parents to let us walk home together since we only lived two blocks away from the school. On the way home we saw one of our classmates a few paces ahead, so we ran to catch up. He turned around and immediately his smile faded to a scowl. "I'm not walking with that nigger!" he shouted. "She's not a nigger!" Jason shouted back

"Yeah, doo-doo head, I'm not!" I retorted.

Our classmate (to this day I don't remember his name) picked up a rock and threw it at me. Jason immediately picked up a fallen tree branch and whacked the young boy across his face. I followed suit and picked up a twig and began to smack the little prankster with all my might. I was crying, but that didn't matter. I wanted that stick to cut his flesh the same way his words had pierced my esteem.

From that day on school was *never* the same.

Ellen was a black student attending Howard University. The kids in her kindergarten class would not play with her.

Looking back over the past years of my life, the most crucial moments that I can remember were initiated during my childhood. Children have outstanding memories and minds that excel far and beyond what most adults give them credit for. My parents had recently remarried and we had to move so my father could finish school.

I remember being enrolled in kindergarten classes at the school. I spent some of the most horrified days of my life in that classroom because I did not fit in due to the color of my skin. My father had taught me how to read at the age of three so I was well above my class, but for some odd reason that was not enough; the other students and the teachers made sure I knew that I was different. The teachers still did not like me, I was still blamed for things I did not do and it seemed that nothing I did could be good enough because I was black. One day, during recess, I had asked the children to play with me. I was tired of playing alone and I really wanted to fit in. As usual, no one wanted to play with me so I played by myself. I ran around on the play set and made my own little mud cakes and pies. When it was time to go in, this little white girl named Erin was crying. She pointed her finger at me and stuck out her tongue. While they were playing, someone kicked her in her kneecap and this caused her to have a bluish and pink bubble on her kneecap. The teachers called me to the side and told me how bad I was for doing this to Erin, how I should apologize, and how much trouble I would be in once they told my parents. I did not get the opportunity to read because they had me in time out. The teachers would not listen to me; it was the little girl's word against mine. This was the same little girl who made sure that no one played with me and made sure that I knew I did not belong. There were so many harsh and rough times I had experienced that year, but that day things just seemed to all pile up and I felt like I could not take it anymore. I came up with a brilliant idea (so I thought at least at the time). On the way home that day, I said six words that would stick with me forever, "Daddy, can we paint ourselves white?" My daddy was furious when I asked this question and when we went home he and my mother took me through a series of books and articles that showed slavery and graphic photos of people being hung, beaten, and abused. They told me how proud I should be of who I was and whatever I would be. They wanted me to have an appreciation of who God made me to be. Unfortunately, in spite of their efforts, I went from wanting to be white to literally hating all white people except my daddy's friends on the track team.

Bonnie was a black student attending Howard University. Her friend's father berated her for playing with his white son. Bonnie's well-known father then intervened.

One of the worst and most memorable racial experiences that happened to me as a child was pretty confusing at the time. Fortunately, my parents were able to help make some sense of it. Unfortunately, that experience struck a nerve and required many years of healing.

I grew up in an affluent, predominantly white neighborhood in Texas. My father was a pretty popular person in our community. He was a successful high school football coach and had just recently retired from playing professional football.

It was a typical day after third grade. My friends and I were playing flag football in David's backyard. David was one of my closest friends since kindergarten. He was white and lived in a single parent home with his mother and siblings.

On this particular day, David was getting piled up on by everyone because he was the one with the ball. A few seconds later, the sliding glass door flew opened and an angry man's voice bellowed, "Get the !#*@ off of him!" Well, of course we all froze in our places. No one knew what we did wrong and who that person was.

Unbeknownst to us, that man was David's father and the next thing that he shouted was, "Who is that nigger girl out there laying on top of my son? All of y'all need to go home now!"

I promptly got up and ran home as fast as my little legs could take me. I was crying profusely and I told mom and dad what happened. My parents were shocked and appalled at what took place. My father grabbed me by the hand and took me back to David's house. When we got to David's, I stayed in the car because I was too scared to go back inside.

When the door opened, the man who screamed at me was standing there in awe because he was a huge fan of my father. He introduced himself and began quoting my dad's stats to him, showing just how much of a fan he truly was. To my surprise, my dad and David's father went inside and closed the door behind them.

A few minutes passed and then I saw David come from the backyard. I got out of the car and asked him who the angry man was and why he screamed at me. David told me that it was his long-lost father who he hadn't seen since he was four years old. David also regretfully told me that his father didn't like black people and that I wouldn't be able to come over and play with him anymore.

Just as he finished telling me the bad news, the front door opened. My father and David's father were standing in the doorway. David's father had his hand on my dad's shoulder and was grinning from ear to ear. My father called for me to come to him. As I turned the corner, the look on David's father's face was of a person who had seen the living dead. My dad asked me to explain again what happened and who did it. David's father immediately knew the football fanfare was about to be over. I did as my dad asked. In turn, my father snatched David's father's arm off his shoulder and proceeded to shout and berate him.

When the hailstorm was over, David and I were standing in between our parents even more hurt and confused than before. The next thing that I knew, my dad grabbed my arm and quickly escorted me back to the car. David's dad snatched him inside and slammed the door.

After my dad calmed down he sat me down and told me what happened. He explained that David's father was cool with him, the big-time football player, but wasn't cool with his son rolling around in the grass with a little black girl. Apparently, he wasn't aware who his child was and why he was there until it was too late.

As the days and years went by, the friendship between David and I inevitably became more distant and was never the same. His father continued to come in and out of his life more frequently than before. Sadly enough, his presence was seemingly instrumental in altering David's feelings toward black people.

I, on the other hand, was still able to play with whomever I wanted to play with no matter what their race. However, the scar remained in my heart. I was hesitant when going over to the houses of friends who were of different races. I preferred them to come to my house; it was safer and more comfortable for me.

That was a classic example of how hatred is taught and spread. Racial, socioeconomical, religious or any other differences among people shouldn't rule the world. Unfortunately, in my humble opinion, it clearly does.

Helen was a forty-one-year-old white student attending the University of South Florida. Her father was upset when he saw her playing with a black boy in kindergarten.

I was born in a small town in Georgia. After kindergarten, all the children would gather on the front lawn and play until our parents picked us up. I remember being very excited the first day because a boy named Joe was paying quite a lot of attention to me. He was chasing me around and I was running and screaming as he tried to catch me. I noticed my parent's car pulling up right as Joe caught me. He told me he had a surprise for me and he shyly handed me a small adjustable ring with a red plastic stone. I ran off to my parents, happy with my first gift from a boy.

As I climbed into our car, I could tell my parents were not happy. From past experience I knew the best way to handle this was to be very quiet and hope I wasn't the target of the unhappiness. I clutched the ring tightly in my sweaty palm and waited as my father started to drive. I didn't have to wait long. "Who was that boy you were talking to?" my father asked. "Umm, he was just running around. I don't really know him," I said, stalling to see what I should say. "He's a nigger." My father shook his head in disgust. "You don't talk to niggers."

I didn't realize it but that was the first year they had allowed black children to attend our elementary school. The parents were very concerned with the cross-playing. I heard quite a lot about it from that day on and eventually the kids learned to segregate while doing free play. I never talked to Joe again but I did keep that ring for quite a long time.

Anna was a white student attending Salisbury State University. When she was eleven, her black friend kissed her. Her cousins then beat up the black friend.

The worst racial experience that I can remember happened when I was about eleven years old. I couldn't wait to spend every day with my new friend. A boy my age had just moved in across the street from my mom. His name was Darrell.

My favorite thing at that point in my life was riding my bike in front of my house all day. Darnell also had a bike, and he loved to ride too. We spent almost the whole summer riding our bikes together in front of the houses. He was my best friend, and I was his.

Near the end of summer my older cousins came to stay at my house for a while. They were all boys and older than me, so they spent the days fishing and doing guy things. My cousins being there did not really affect the time that Darrell and I spent riding our bikes.

One day as it was getting dark, and my mother had called me to come in for dinner. I told Darrell goodbye and that I would see him the next day. Instead of the usual high-five that he usually gave me though, he kissed me. It was not just a peck, but a whole-mouthed kiss. I was surprised. I had never thought of him as a boyfriend, but as a friend that was a boy.

When Darrell had kissed me, my oldest cousin happened to be walking out of the house. He saw Darrell kiss me and ran over screaming. At the sound of his screaming, the rest of my cousins came out. My cousins all had a major problem with the kiss that Darrell had given me. Not only was a boy kissing me, which I could see why they would get upset about that, but Darrell was black.

My cousins had always talked about "black" people using racial slurs. Since I had been around it all my life, I never realized that they didn't like black people; I had just always thought that they were different names that black people were called.

I learned later that my cousins had been angry about me playing with a black boy the entire time that they were at my house, but my mother had told them to leave us alone. When they saw Darrell kiss me though, they would not stay out of it anymore. My cousins ran over and started to beat Darrell up in front of me, screaming at him the entire time.

When I screamed at the top of my lungs, my mother must have heard me because she came out and stopped my cousins. She took Darrell home to his mom. That was the last time I ever saw him. His knees were all scuffed and bloody like he had run through the briar bushes and his face was all puffy. I wanted to walk him home with my mom but my cousins were watching and I did not want them to beat him up anymore.

When I went to Darrell's house the next day he did not come out to play. His mom told me he had gone to live with his grandmother. She would not tell me where she lived, and asked me to please leave. I spent the rest of the summer wondering where Darrell was and if he was all right. I only wished that I could have seen him one more time to say that I was sorry for what my cousins had done, and that I did not hate him because he was black.

Mona was a Native American student who attended the University of California at Santa Barbara. Her family moved out of New Mexico because of racism.

I once lived in an area notorious for racism and as a result of my childhood experiences, my parents decided to move to California—a place rich in diversity. While I lived in Farmington, New Mexico, I was picked on and excluded as a child because I was a Native American in a predominantly Caucasian area. I happened to live on the "wrong" side of the street near the Navajo reservation and my skin color made it difficult to be accepted among other children. Not all of my classmates were racist, but there was still a sense of division and many of them had never been exposed to the Native American culture nor had they experienced a diversity of other ethnic and racial backgrounds. My mother was fair skinned and commuted to her work at the Navajo hospital. However, she had always been very active in Native American culture from childhood; she grew up on an Indian Mission and was eventually adopted by the Potawatomie tribe. In fact, I remember her using bronzer to cover up her light skin so that she wouldn't be noticeably different on the reservation. My father however, was full Seneca and I received his genes of dark skin, dark hair, and dark eyes.

The school I attended as a child was in a neighborhood nicer than my own, even though it was just a couple blocks away. It was literally, "on the wrong side of the street." The racism I experienced was not an outwardly hostile traumatic moment, but a continuous series of moments where I was treated differently. My mother described a time when I came home from second grade and she could tell something was obviously was wrong. I crawled into her lap sobbing said "I wish my skin was your color."

I remember being different from most of the children at my school and I didn't understand why I didn't have as many friends. One of the only girls I played with also grew up in the "wrong" area. As I look back, I realize she had the same dark skin. This was the breaking point for my mother and she realized she didn't want me growing up in an environment where people weren't treating equally.

Moving to California changed my life because for once, I was able to be proud of my culture and share it with other people, as they did with me. My teachers taught the importance of diversity and in fourth grade, we even had a "Celebrating Our Culture" dinner where the whole school and parents were invited. I was so thankful to see acceptance and the range of cultures now feels like the norm for me.

2

Family

Racism and tolerance, as well as coping with racism and prejudice, are often learned from family. However, there is limited research understanding how racism and prejudiced are transmitted to children (Hughes and Chen 1997). Throughout other chapters within the book, we discuss how minority parents help their children deal with racism and discrimination in society through a type of racial socialization and fostering group identity (Sarkisian and Gerstel 2004; Hughes and Chen 1997). However, how do children learn to cope with racist attitudes and prejudice within their own families? Barack Obama recently described this difficulty in his March 18, 2008 speech on hearing his white grandmother express her own racial prejudice and the resulting painful feelings he experienced. Many students in this chapter express similar feelings of hurt, anger, and disgust. The essays within this chapter describe complex relationships with family members and the generational differences that exist when it comes to understanding matters of race.

Interestingly, the literature on intergenerational transmission of racism and prejudice is scant and is even more limited regarding how individuals cope with racism and prejudice within their family, particularly when they receive messages from society that prejudice and racism are unacceptable. O'Bryan, Fishbein, and Ritchey (2004) state that it is generally assumed children's prejudiced attitudes simply reflect their parents' attitudes. However, additional research shows that children's prejudice is only moderately influenced by their parents. In fact, the transmission of prejudice and racism is somewhat more complicated as O'Bryan et al., discover. Mothers may have a greater affect on their daughters' attitudes, while fathers may have a greater affect on their sons. Weis and Hall (2001, p. 52) show that

11

women often attempt to "rewrite negative race scripts perpetrated by the men in their lives, as they attempt to interrupt such ideology through direct intervention with their children." In their ethnographic study, Wies and Hall (2001) tell the stories of many poor white women who often fought and challenged fathers and brothers on issues of race. Tatum (1994) describes how many white students often go through a period of guilt upon learning about society's pervasive racism. Subsequently when they consider times they have exhibited racist behavior they may become resistant to learning about racism and prejudice. However, as demonstrated in these essays many students find the courage to go against their primary socialization and become more accepting and tolerant of individuals from different racial backgrounds.

As with most of the essays within this book, there are many commonalities across the highlighted experiences. What is perhaps most interesting is that most of the essays in this chapter are written by white students. The experiences these students describe in this chapter are provocative and thoughtful as they describe how *they* have had to come to terms with racism within their family and how some of them "unlearned" their own prejudice. For example, Ken describes how a racist incident that happened to him as well as his father's attitude toward blacks made Ken racist for a very long time.

Other essays describe how students struggle with racism within their family and how they often feel embarrassed, guilty, and apologetic. Perhaps one of the most powerful essays is written by Karen, who writes about her experience learning that her family was involved in the murder of Emmett Till. Karen describes how she felt, "I had the worst sinking feeling in my gut. It really hurt to know that someone related to me, whether by blood or through marriage, could do something so hateful." Jessica, who upon hearing her grandmother use a racial epithet stated, "I was incredibly offended, gave my grandmother a horrible look and left the room to go watch television."

Aside from embarrassment and discomfort regarding family racism, some students describe how their multiracial background often presents challenges within their family. For example, Sharon was disappointed that her white mother could not see how she was affected by being ostracized at their predominantly white church and Daniel was insulted by his uncle for being part white.

The essays in this chapter demonstrate the complex dynamics surrounding family relationships and issues of race, particularly in terms of generational differences. Also, given the experiences highlighted within this chapter, there is certainly a gap that exists in understanding how youth come to accept or reject socialized prejudice. Throughout these essays are many examples of students who courageously confront racism within their own families and strive to unlearn prejudice. The ways in which students cope with racism and prejudice within their own households presents a provocative avenue of research for scholars of racism and prejudice.

Karen was a white student attending Middle Tennessee State University. She learned that her family was involved in the murder of Emmett Till.

Sitting at my history desk, I thought the class period was going to be a breeze. Our teacher put in a film about racial experiences and warned us that what we were about to see could be haunting. I thought it was going to be just another film to suffer through for an hour. As the narrator began telling the story, I really began listening when he mentioned my hometown of Clarksdale, Mississippi.

When I grew up in Clarksdale, it was a divided town. I know that sounds odd, but if you lived in the South, you would understand. For as long as I can remember, blacks and whites lived on opposite sides of the railroad tracks. If you talked to my grandparents, they would say, "Well, it has always been that way and I am not sure when it will change." It wasn't until we moved to Tennessee in the late 1990s that I realized how racially divided the Delta of Mississippi truly was and still is.

The film was on Emmett Till and the trials that were held in Sumner County. He was a young black boy visiting from up North. He went into a store and made a gesture to a white woman, which was unheard of at the time. Till's body was later found tied to a gin belt in the Tallahatchie River. I knew that my grandmother had learned to swim in this river. My cousin even has farmland around Sumner County. I went home that afternoon and called my dad to tell him about the film that we had watched. He said that he remembered the incident vividly and even named a man on the jury that he had once worked with. He told me to call my grandmother and talk to her about the whole situation and perhaps she could explain it in more detail. When I called my grandmother, there was silence on the other end when I asked her to explain.

She told me some things that I will never forget. She started off the conversation by telling me not to judge other people and that sometimes the past is better left alone. She stated that some people are so blinded by hatred that they do things without thinking about the consequences. I was shocked when she told me that the men accused of killing the young boy were the nephews of my great-aunt by marriage. She said that the young woman Emmett Till gestured at was one of their wives. After the body was found, the men were taken to trial. The jury reached a quick verdict of not guilty. She said that there was no surprise among the "white community," because in those days, white people could get away with anything. She remembered sitting at work and watching the black people load the buses to ride to the trial. She said that she felt ashamed about what the men had done.

After I got off the telephone, I had the worst sinking feeling in my gut. It really hurt to know that someone related to me, whether by blood or through marriage, could do something so hateful. I wonder if they thought about the ones that would have to deal with the consequences decades after their actions. I have never been so embarrassed by something that my family had done.

Ken was a white student attending Villanova University. Although he describes a violent act against him, his relationship with his father is particularly interesting.

My worst racial experience took place when I was in sixth grade. I was a heavier kid living in Ocean City, NJ. My dad was a hard-nosed alcoholic who kept me believing what he told me, as he was my role model at the time. We lived on the bay, and there was a Wawa (convenience store) down the street from us. This particular Wawa was in a black neighborhood that was right by ours. I was sent to this Wawa frequently. Living with an alcoholic dad as my only parent meant that I would have to purchase many meals from outside places.

One time while on the way back from Wawa, I was approached by three black kids who were larger and older than me. They started chasing me, and even though I was on my bike, I could not outrun them. They caught up with me, throwing rocks and such, and started calling me "fatty." They wanted my bike, despite the fact that it was not much of a bike. I denied them. One of them then proceeded to kick the wheel of my bike in, push me over and curse at me. Then they left. I was very upset by this, and slowly headed back to my house.

My father responded by calling them "niggers" and telling me that all blacks were bad and not to trust them. I am sorry to say that because of that incident, my young age, and what my father said, I was a racist child for many years. It was not until later in my life when I left my father and grew up that I realized that just because a few people of any race do harm to you does not make the entire race "bad." It was a terrible experience for me to say the least.

Sharon was a black student at Howard University. Her mother joined two white churches where Sharon and her brother were ostracized.

When I was seven years old, my single white mother became a fundamentalist Christian after having lived a very secular lifestyle. All of a sudden the friends I was accustomed to seeing around the house vanished. The

1980s rock evaporated into Christian contemporary. MTV and BET were banned. Halloween? You could forget about that. When I first started going to church I felt like a fish out of water. My brother and I were completely isolated from the rest of the kids, but we chalked it up to being unfamiliar with all the Bible stories and songs. After a year of isolation, and after seeing other new kids come and be accepted, we figured out it that it was our race that kept the other kids away and their parents from inviting us to all the church parties.

For the next ten years of my life this was a consistent theme. I would go to church every Wednesday for youth groups, Friday for home group, and Sunday for service. I remained "the black girl" of the congregation, and my brother "the black boy." It was plain and simple that despite how beautiful my Jessica McClintock dresses were or how radiant my personality, I was always excluded from the church social circle my mom forced our life to evolve around.

However, after five years, my mom finally woke up and saw how psychologically damaging this was to me. It was horrible that when discussing events to pray about, my race was referred to as "those people." When it was the L.A. riots, I was called a nigger so many times that I no longer considered myself biracial—I was simply black. Did I hate white people? Yes, especially my mom who took five years to change churches but only to pick another where there was not a single black member!

My new church was a little more tolerant. In fact, most of the members of it were hippies. Nevertheless, I was always an outsider. My brother and I were into hip-hop culture. The white kids wore the alternative clothes and wore makeup similar to Marilyn Manson's. We were never invited to their youth group nights or elite social gatherings, but they were constantly inviting every newcomer who walked through the door in a Nirvana tee shirt.

The people who did speak to my brother and me acted as though they were doing some sort of charity work, like they deserved a pat on the back because they are liberal enough to speak to a person of another race! My mother was asked all sorts of offensive questions, like "What would you do if a man was interested in you, but did not like the fact that your kids are black?" What did they want her to say, that she was willing to ship us off to a boarding school because a racist man in our congregation was interested in her?

My mother thinks our presence was part of the solution, not the problem! I think it created a wall between the Christian church, whites, my Christian walk, and sadly enough my mother and myself! There is nothing more psychologically damaging than going some place where you know you are not wanted because of your race while the people who despise your presence preach the gospel of Christ and His love!

Jessica was a white student at St. Louis University. She got upset when her grand-mother started to refer to "niggers." Her father talked to the grandma about this. Did you ever have a relative that should have been confronted? How did you handle it?

I am fortunate in the sense that I have not experienced too many racist encounters. Growing up in Imperial, Missouri, the diversity was slim, yet there were not many prejudices. My parents raised me to not just toler-ate other races, but also accept them. There was one incredibly offensive instance that occurred when I was about fifteen years old. I remember it to this day.

My family and I went to visit my grandparents in St. Louis City one afternoon. Chatting in the kitchen for a while, my grandmother started to tell us that the "xxxx niggers" were out of control and some lived right next to them. She went on to say that she wanted them to leave. They did not deserve to live in such a nice neighborhood.

Being fifteen, I had never heard someone use that word before. I was in-credibly offended, gave my grandmother a horrible look and left the room to go watch television. My brother came into the room and asked me if what she said offended me. I responded with yes, and began to cry. I told him that I did not understand how or why people could feel that way about a human being. Just because their skin is a different color does not mean that they are less of a person. He gave me a hug and told me that I needed to take what she said with a grain of salt.

I guess because I am not from the same generation, I do not understand how my grandmother feels about African Americans. My parents grew up hearing the same sort of slang words and they just let it go through one ear and out the other. I refused to do that. I would never bring this up to my grandmother, because I have respect for her. I simply just do not agree. I spoke with my parents and they explained that I did not grow up in the same environment that they did or my grandparents did. Society is more accepting today. My father told me that he would talk to my grandma and ask her not to use those words in front of me again, because it offended me. To this day, I have never heard her mention those words again. For that I am grateful. However, it does not change the fact that it was said. I know in some ways racism is getting better. I just wish it would stop some day soon. I simply do not understand.

Daniel attended St. Louis University. He was half-Tongan and half-Jewish. He was stereotyped for both parts of his ancestry.

I am a biracial child. My mother is an immigrant from the Tongan Islands in the South Pacific and my father is a first generation, Hungarian-American

Jew. I was mostly raised in the Tongan culture. Despite the fact that I have been cultivated as a Tongan male, I am always regarded as a little different by members of my mother's family. Ever since I can remember, I was always praised by my Tongan family whenever I could complete a task that was physically demanding, such as lifting a certain amount of bricks. In contrast, I was treated as a lesser individual because I was part white.

As I grew older and acquired more and more understanding of the Tongan language, I began to catch on to the fact that I was held in a different light by my family members. Once a boy across the table from me in Sunday school said something about me being white and I responded in Tongan. A fight between us followed. He won the fight. I remember my mom and the boy's father, who was my uncle, fighting over how I got beaten up. He responded to my mom by saying something along the lines of "Well if he wasn't a white piece of shit he would have won."

The next racial situation that I continue to find myself in continuously involves anti-Semitic comments. Most people are unaware of me being half Jewish and because of this, I am able to hear their anti-Semitic views. A couple of days after my dad died, one of my friends was talking at baseball practice and he said, "Hey you want to know the difference between a pizza and a Jew? A pizza doesn't scream when it's in the oven." At first I did not know how to react to this type of joke. It was so foul. The more I thought about it, the more I got angry because that joke was referring to my father, aunt, and grandparents. I remember thinking, "What has any Jewish person ever done to this kid to make him tell such hateful jokes?" As I went through high school and as I am going through college, I also realize that this attitude is widespread. This scares me because the more I think about it, if I were alive in the era of the German Third Reich I would be sought out and destroyed. They would make no distinction between me being half Tongan and half Jewish. However, despite my feelings toward my friends who make these very hateful jokes, I put my feelings away and bottle them up. However, I do disclose that I am half Jewish to my close friends so that they know not to make these jokes in my presence.

Karen was a white student attending Salisbury State. Her parents would not allow her black friend to come to her house because it would "tarnish" her reputation.

When my parents were kids, there was still segregation between people of different races. As they grew up, they saw a lot of hate and tension between the races. Toward the end of elementary school and the beginning of middle school I become best friends with a girl named Miya. She was black and I was white, but to us color was not important. As the years continued, we became closer and closer, until one day she wanted to come over to play. My parents said no. I remember getting into these long, drawn-out arguments over their deeply rooted issues.

At the time, it was unacceptable for my parents to let their children mingle with black children outside school. It was not the fact that they hated Miya, but the fact that they did want my reputation tarnished. My parents were not entirely wrong in their thinking because there were people that would label me according to the color of the friends that I hung out with. I was only seven or so, but I was fighting a two-hundred-year war on discrimination. I never understood why my parents, at the time, acted the way they did. Toward the end of middle school Miya's parents moved away to California. All of her friends held a going-away party for her. This was the first time in the five years since we had been friends that I was ever allowed to see her house. My parents were not deliberately trying to be racist; they were just protecting me.

Robin was born in Israel and attended the University of California at Santa Barbara. She confronted her uncle who had made a racist remark upon seeing an interracial couple.

I was born in Israel and moved to California at the age of three. Being a foreigner, by the age of five, I was already aware of the social hierarchy of dealing with different ethnicities. I remember feeling that I did not belong to the community into which we moved. The kids never played with me and always laughed at the smell of my foreign lunches. When my dad would come to pick me up from school, he would find me sitting by myself minding my own business. When asked why I did not play with the other kids, I remember feeling embarrassed and I believed that there was something weird and different about me. I was not good enough, pretty enough and smart enough. As my English got better, I started to make friends but I never forgot how I felt as a child.

Unfortunately, the rest of my family did not come to the understandings that I did. When I was fifteen years old, my uncle came to pick me up from school. As we drove home, there was an interracial couple holding hands and kissing in the street. My uncle said, "Look how disgusting that is! That is such a waste of a beautiful girl."

I looked at him in complete shock. I knew that racism existed in the world but I did not know that it existed in my own family. Not only was I not aware of it, but I also did not expect it. How can someone who had struggled to fit into an Anglo-American lifestyle and had personally been discriminated against because of his ethnic background, also judge someone based solely on the color of his skin?

Abandoning the family values that my parents had taught me, I looked at my uncle and said, "I guess you are not as smart as I thought you were. In fact you are completely ignorant and shallow. For the first time in my life I am ashamed that you are my uncle!"

Now it was his turn to not believe the words that came out of my mouth. He was furious with my comments, told my parents that he would never pick me up from school, and told them that they really needed to rethink the way that they were bringing me up. When my dad asked my uncle what had happened, he said that, "Your no-good daughter chose to bad-mouth her uncle for a black man!"

I explained the story to my parents and for the first time stood up to authority. I said that just because I was younger did not mean that I was not entitled to my own opinion. My uncle interrupted me and said, "But, black people are bad people; they are thieves and killers."

I apologized to my uncle for offending him. Those were not my intentions but I knew that by speaking to him that way, he would take me seriously. I told him that every racial group and ethnic culture has stereotypes but that we cannot live by them. I said the media tells us that crimes are predominately committed by African Americans. Furthermore, I said that people have stereotypes about Jewish people and not too long ago the entire world turned against us because they believed those stereotypes. Six million Jews was the price that was paid for living in a world that abides by stereotypes.

My argument had a lasting effect on my family and even though I cannot say for certain, I believe that racism no longer exists in my family. If it does exist, it only exists in the personal secretive beliefs of a particular individual. In other words, the issue of race is never argued over and everyone in my house has learned to accept that just because we all look different, and the media concentrates on one racial group more than another, does not mean that we are not equals.

Tracy was a Hispanic student attending the University of California at Santa Barbara. She has had several arguments with her stepdad about his racism.

Chicano families that I know of don't like to be called "wet bags," "beaners," or other related names but they *do* use the terms "Gringo" for Caucasians, "Negro" meaning black for African Americans, and many other slurs for other races. What makes them think that the other races would like those names if they themselves don't like what they are being called? As it is said, "Treat others as you would like to be treated."

Coming from a Chicano family (I prefer the term "Latino"), I've encountered certain racial incidents. My stepdad was born and raised in Mexico. He is very racist and stereotypical. It all began when we actually moved into our new home. It was a wreck. There was trash everywhere, holes in the walls, refrigerators locked, beds everywhere, cockroaches creeping around, and a stench that you could barely withstand. The only reason we were considering this house was because it was very economical.

Days later we were approached by many neighbors, wanting to welcome us. Most of them told us they were relieved that we moved in and that the tenants that lived there before were big troublemakers. My dad stated that it wasn't a surprise to him, seeing the kind of people they were. "Negros Cochinos," dirty blacks, he referred to them. I was so embarrassed; I didn't know what to say. The neighbors seemed surprised and just changed the subject. Some neighbors agreed with him and actually elaborated on the conversation. I always wanted to speak out but I was taught that I must respect my elders. So, I would just make an excuse to be able to leave. I thought that was the most uncomfortable moment of my life.

I was wrong. It continued. We would often drive around our neighborhood and the minute he saw an African American he would start cussing them out and speaking bad about them. He would stereotype them, saying that they were dirty, lazy, and dumb. He would generalize and say that they were all drug dealers and they probably did the drugs too. He would threaten us by saying that we better not end up with any of them, and that if we did we would only end up miserable. That was the last straw for me. I spoke out and told him what I thought. I accused him of being racist, he decried it and justified himself by saying that he was only telling the truth. "Por qué defiendes a esos *mayates*?," "Why do you defend those *mayates*?" he said. Mayates are insects that are said to come out of "shit," if I may use that word. They're supposed to be filthy and ugly. That really bothered me, but seeing that I wouldn't be able to win against him I decided to back down.

He still hasn't changed his mind and it seems like he never will, but I've learned to deal with it. I just know that I will not judge anyone for any reason, especially race.

Carlos was a Hispanic student who attended the University of California at Santa Barbara. Students at his school thought he was white. While on a school trip at the county fair, students humiliated his mother because of her broken English. He joined in.

I am a Chicano, but is it really through choice? My name might emphasize the fact that I am Mexican, my language might represent my strong Chicano culture, yet my image reflects my white culture. My light complexion and my "fair hair" confuse many when I say my name. They often ask, "What nationality are you? Italian? Spaniard?" From my clothes to my music of choice to the length of my hair, I am white.

Both of my parents were born in Mexico and both came to America roughly after the age of fifteen. I was raised in Los Baños, amongst our

Euro-American counterparts. Going though school, I was always the little Mexican boy who looked white, but had a Mexican last name. Our culture that we learned at an early age had faded into a white-washed Mexican culture. We were white, with white friends, white teachers, white neighbors, white everything. Although my white-washed culture at school was my predominant choice, once I stepped foot on our marble floors, I was Mexican. My language changed and my attitude changed. Even though our home was decorated in fine white furnishings, my mother stressed the fact that we were Mexican, and nothing was going to change that. So why was there a mask over our true identity?

In fifth grade we took a class trip to the county fair and my mother volunteered to chaperone. On the day of the field trip, my mom walked in the classroom. It was at that point that she realized that all the mothers were white and spoke English, while she had a very thick Mexican accent that limited her English. Not only did everyone speculate that she was my nanny, but everyone started to say very insulting things under their breath. I just played along, never establishing that she was my mom, but establishing that I had brought her along on the trip.

When it was time for lunch, my mom had the money and everyone wanted a corn dog, cotton candy, and soda. However, when my mom went to order, the attendant couldn't understand her broken English. My mom didn't know how to order a corn dog, or even say corn dog. I was stuck in the middle of a cruel joke. Should I explain to my mom what a corn dog was and help her order, or laugh hysterically with my friends? I laughed of course, and as my group pointed and yelled that my mom was a stupid Mexican who couldn't even say corn dog, I did the same. I laughed and laughed, humiliated my mom, humiliated myself, and humiliated my heritage and culture.

When I got back home, I don't remember my mom talking to me. She was typically a very verbal woman and would speak her mind all the time. Yet that day, she just walked into our white house and had a very disappointed face. It took several days for her to talk. She finally confronted the situation and lectured me about what had happened earlier. She said it was partly her fault for not allowing us any exposure to our Mexican heritage. I apologized of course, but I still wanted to be white.

3

Friends

Academic concerns were the primary reason for desegregation of American schools; however, a secondary goal was the promotion of cross-racial social interactions to help reduce racial prejudices over time (Lease and Blake 2005). In fact, childhood is considered a critical time for intergroup contact, since having a close cross-race friend in childhood is associated with positive racial attitudes and integration in adolescence and adulthood (Aboud, Mendelson, and Purdy 2003). Today, young people are more comfortable than their parents in dealing with individuals of another race. However, problems often occur when there is a lack of awareness of the norms and practices of other races or cultural groups leading to misunderstandings, hurt feelings, or worse (O'Neil 1993). For example, Betsy became upset when her best friend used the term "nigger" and could not understand why Betsy was so hurt and angry.

The research pertaining to interracial friendships is more thoroughly covered in the chapter regarding childhood. Overall, children go though developmental stages when peers and peer acceptance become more important as they get older. Adolescents often experience intimacy and conflict equally in close peer relationships with conflict often leading to stronger ties and greater understanding or alternatively, betrayal and interpersonal insensitivity (Pagano and Hirsch 2006). This may be especially the case with interracial friendships and is demonstrated in some essays within this chapter.

Many scholars find that cross-race friendships are not only fewer in number than same race friendships but the duration is often shorter and the quality may be lower. As a consequence, interracial friendships tend to decline with age with older children reporting fewer cross-racial friendships than younger children (Aboud et al. 2003; Hallinan and Williams 1989). School racial composition affects the development of cross-racial friendships. Joyner and Kao (2000) find that as a school's racial heterogeneity increases so does the likelihood of its students having an interracial friendship. Subsequently, children who have interracial friendships are more likely to possess such friendships as adults (Joyner and Kao 2000).

Some of the essays within this chapter describe their friendships as adults or as college students. Racial diversity on college campuses have long been a significant issue and goal of colleges and universities. Colleges and universities have adopted many initiatives to increase the racial, ethnic, and cultural diversity of their campuses. Cowan (2005) poses the question of whether or not such diversity has lead to a diversity of interactions with students of different races and cultures. As minority populations at colleges and universities increase so will the likelihood of more interracial interactions. The college experience can certainly change one's views of race as demonstrated by Judy's essay, "I am fortunate to have my friends at Villanova who have helped me gain a better perspective regarding racism in our everyday lives."

One of the major theories for understanding interracial friendships is the contact hypothesis. The contact hypothesis posits that the divide between the social lives of blacks and whites promotes ignorance, which feeds oversimplified and negative beliefs. Increased personal contact between racial groups can correct inaccurate assumptions (Jackman and Crane 1986; Sigelman and Welch 1993). For whites, the diversity of interracial contacts has a greater affect on positive racial attitudes than the depth of relationships/friendships. When whites experience a greater degree of personal contact with minorities, feelings of personal animosity are less likely (Jackman and Crane 1986).

Despite the importance of interracial contact in producing positive racial attitudes and facilitating friendships, interracial contact often consists of brief, superficial encounters (Sigelman, Bledose, Welch, and Combs 1996). For whites, encounters with African Americans and other minorities depends on where one lives, works, and worships. However, for African Americans it is early life experiences that occur in childhood that affect the likelihood of white interracial contact and developing friendships with whites. Nevertheless, one of the interesting features of these essays is how friendships change during childhood as children grow into adults and find new friendships and peer groups. Mary, a black student, starts distancing herself from her Jewish friend as she grows older while Judy, a white student, starts distancing herself from her white friends as she no longer appreciates their racism.

Elena was a student at Howard University. Her friend's mother would not let Elena go in her car on a school trip because she did not like black kids in her car.

I would have to say that my worst racial experience occurred when I was in the third grade. It came from a classmate, Lisa, who was a good friend of mine since kindergarten. It was around the middle of the school year when our class was focused on our Mission Projects. Lisa's mother was a part of the PSA, and she was taking some of our classmates to a real Mission about three hours away. When I heard of this, I asked Lisa if I could ride with her and the other classmates to the Mission. Lisa was nice about it and told me that she didn't mind, but she had to ask her mother first. The following day Lisa came back and told me that there was not enough room in the car. When she told me this, one of the girls riding with Lisa said that she was not able to go, so I could take her spot. Then Lisa said that her mother does not like black people riding in their van, because they put their heads on the windows and the grease from their hair gets on them.

When this first happened I was very upset because I really wanted to go to the Mission. I felt alienated and insulted, but I was more upset that I could not go to the Mission. When I went home after school that day, I told my mother and father what Lisa told me. My parents were furious and it was then that I realized just how inappropriate it was for her, or more so her mother, to make those comments. My parents ended up taking me to the Mission, but after that I never associated with Lisa or her mother.

When I look back at the incident, I see how that experience affected my views of white people. Before that experience, most of my friends were white, but after that I never got close to a white person again. I guess I thought that white people would be nice to African Americans, but they really don't want anything to do with us. To this day I don't have any white friends. Maybe this is because deep down I don't trust that they will truly accept me.

Betsy was a black student who attended Howard University. Her best friend used the term "nigger" and could not understand why Betsy was upset.

I was raised in a predominately white town for most of my life. I always knew that racism existed, but it always occurred in a subtle and covert fashion; blatant racism was rare. No memory is more vivid in my mind than the time I was betrayed by one of my closest friends in high school. I have heard the word nigger before, I have been told that I am a nigger, but I had never been in the presence of one of my friends who acted one way to my face, but behind my back was a racist.

In eleventh grade I attended a party that would end up being a nightmare. I, as usual, was the only black person at the party, surrounded by
white faces. I had gotten over the awkward feelings years ago and I used my
individuality as strength, to dominate the white masses.

My friend Pam and I (note Pam is white) were in a group of people
dancing to some music when the DJ changed the record to a rap song.
Immediately and without thought Pam yelled out, "Oh no, not another
one of those nigger songs, turn that shit off." It hit me hard. I expected
to hear the word nigger from ignorant and racist white people, but not
from one of my friends. After she made the remark everyone in the room
started laughing except me; everyone thought it was a joke except me;
everyone forgot that there was one black person in the room except me,
because it was me. Without delay I became enraged, I started to yell,
"What did you say and what is that supposed to mean?" Her reply was,
"Oh, I wasn't talking about you, you're not a nigger. Those people are."
She assumed because I was raised around white people that I wasn't
a nigger, but every other black person was. I was different. I was sorta
black to them. I couldn't possibly be offended because she was referring
to them and not me. It was then that I realized the magnitude of these
people's misconceptions of me—I was black and there was no sorta or
kinda about it.

I felt more disconnected with white people that evening than I ever had
in my entire life. No one could see the situation through my perspective;
no one could understand why I was in tears and screaming at Pam. She
shouldn't call any black person a nigger and she was a racist.

I was told later in school that I overreacted. I even heard rumors that I
was a racist because I made a scene at the party over the past weekend. Pam
and I rarely spoke after that, and a mental gap became even more ingrained
in my mind than before. These people could not and were not willing to
understand me. They only accepted me when they remained in the illusion
that I was more white than black.

*Bruce was a white student at the University of St Louis. His friends were con-
stantly making racist jokes.*

My worst racial experience is not one single occurrence. Rather, it was
a series of occurrences. After completion of the sixth grade, my parents
decided to enroll me in an all-boys prep school in St. Louis, Missouri. Although this was contrary to my wishes, I really had no say in the situation.
There were not many African Americans present. This did not seem out of
the ordinary for me, since I never had a class with any black students prior
to junior high school.

As I proceeded to make my way through the next couple of grades I began to notice the use of the word "nigger" more and more frequently. I knew this was wrong. I come from a very loving family who would never even think of using such ignorant language, but I did not dare say anything in the interest of being cool. The most blatant form of racism that I encountered, as well as participated in, is the telling of racially explicit jokes. A student at this prep school normally wouldn't go a day without hearing a new joke slandering blacks, Hispanics, and/or Jews. At first, I was taken back by the jokes. However, it is surprising how quickly one can become desensitized to something they previously thought to be extremely wrong. The funniest part of the whole situation is how one minute a white student would tell a racist joke and the next "suck up" to one of the few black students because the black student was good at basketball.

I believe one of the main reasons that these students are so hurtful toward people who were different is because of their lack of exposure to other cultures at an early age.

I knew what was going on was not right but I didn't have the courage to not follow the crowd. As I look back, I realize I was just as responsible for this counterproductive behavior as anyone else at the school and therefore this essay is about my racist ways as well. The one good thing to come out of these experiences is that I finally understand. Now that I am an adult about to make my way in the world, I am glad I have learned the ramifications of a closed mind. Nowadays, I ignore someone who holds hatred for no reason and I make it a point to treat everyone the same. This account of racial bias may seem somewhat trivial compared to other students' accounts but it made a lasting impression on me.

Mary was a black student at Howard University. She describes how other blacks made fun of her because her childhood best friend was Jewish.

I grew up in Pittsburgh where there is a strange and unparalleled racial divide. In Pittsburgh, there are only two predominant races—white and black! (In my eighteen years, I have encountered fewer than a dozen people of Hispanic or Asian ancestry.) The neighborhoods in the city are so distinct I can attribute racial and cultural titles to each neighborhood in the city. The racial divide in my city is razor sharp. We only mix in forced situations and institutions like schooling, public transportation, and shopping.

My first-ever best friend was a Jew. On my first day of kindergarten at an inner-city public school I simply approached the first girl I saw (who happened to be white) and asked, "Do you want to be my friend?" She stared at me with large, blue eyes. The question sounded so silly that we both laughed. We became friends almost immediately. We competed for best grades, best jokes, and the most points in sports games. We often made each other laugh until our stomachs ached. Our relationship was lots of fun. Ours was the classic relationship. We honestly encouraged each other's success.

We eventually wanted to spend time with each other outside of school. To us, this was nothing trivial. However, our youth and innocence made us incognizant to the larger picture. For Anna to come to see me and play in the streets of all-black East Hills was as astounding as me going to a blackless Squirrel Hill. It was a social statement, and in Pittsburgh this was a big deal. Our parents took the chance and crossed those yellow-lines and razor-sharp divisions.

When Anna walked through the door of my grandmother's home, my queenly, southern-born grandmother looked as if she'd seen a ghost. There was an awkward silence. Then my grandmother made conversation. I wonder, even now, if Anna was afraid. She most likely saw, heard, smelled, and felt many things that she'd never come into contact with before. Similarly, when I was invited to Anna's house, I did not feel comfortable at all. I noticed that her family was so busy that they neither ignored nor over-acknowledged me. I saw many symbols like the gold star charm on her pretty gold necklace adorning her house. There were lots of symbols and letters that were not legible to me.

Anna and I remained friends for years. We were aware of our differences, but as we grew older others constantly pointed them out to us. I remember hearing my mother whisper, "She thinks she's white." I knew that she was talking about me. But, I didn't see why my mother didn't understand that my relationship with Anna did not exist because I wished to be a Jew, or white, but because I just really enjoyed her company every day, just as much as the first day of kindergarten.

One day behind my back, I heard one of my classmates say, "She's an Oreo." Another time in physical education class the older girls at school ganged up and pushed me around. They said, "Why do you think you're white?" I could not understand why all of my black classmates were angry at me.

I began to distance myself from Anna at about the fifth grade. It seemed imperative. She seemed to develop the same callousness toward me. It is ironic that my first encounter with racism came from my own race. As I grew older, I began to see the lines more clearly. Racism in my city came from both sides of the fence. There is an attempt by whites to ignore the hell out of blacks, and in most instances, we do not interact. It was not until I went to college at Howard University that I became aware of the extended spectrum of the human race. In Washington, the attitude does not seem as overt. I was slightly scarred by my experience, yet I have learned a lot. As I saw new things in Anna's house, I see this attitude differently in the twenty-first century. I don't see racism. I see ignorance, pain, and confusion that can be simply corrected by allowing children to harbor friendships and ideas freely in youth.

Marianne was a white student attending St. Louis University. Her best friend was Asian and was taunted by others in school. She feels guilty for not standing up for her friend.

As a young Caucasian female in the world today, I do not have any personal negative racial experiences. This is not to say that I do not notice when others around are mistreated simply because of their race. In grade school in Nebraska, I witnessed harsh treatment against my best friend, Monica, for being Asian. Monica would frequently burst into tears in grade school, and I would find out later that this was due to the boys in our class heckling her for being Asian. They would comment on her "slanty eyes" and "stringy black hair." They would make fun of her parents, who could barely speak English and ran the only Korean store in town. Never being racially discriminated against myself, I could not understand exactly what she was going through, even though I knew the comments were hurtful. I did not recognize that it hit on something far deeper than the typical childhood taunting. These boys were cutting down who she was because of her culture and now she was being told that this identity was something of which to be ashamed.

At the time, I thought that these insults were just the same as being made fun of for being short or having glasses. Now, I wish I had been more sensitive to this issue. It was a direct attack on her identity. Her classmates' remarks had an overwhelming impact on Monica. She had depression and developed an eating disorder in high school, undoubtedly due to her not being satisfied with herself. This cynical self-image was probably a result of others telling her she was different, and that was bad.

Monica was a black student at Howard University. Her best friend accused her of getting into a college only because she is black.

I went to a predominately white private school, located just outside of Nashville in the richest county in the state of Tennessee. Only three blacks were in my graduating class of ninety-two. I had attended the school since my sixth-grade year and had not experienced any bad racial problems throughout those years. In the seventh grade a new girl came to my school and we became friends, so much so that by the eighth grade we were best friends and remained that way into high school. My best friend is half Greek and is a Greek Orthodox Christian. She often emphasizes that she too is a minority, although she looks just like any other white person. When applying to colleges, my best friend's number one choice was a small university located in southern Tennessee. It is very much like our high school when is comes to diversity. The same college made numerous phone calls to me and invited me on an all-expenses paid weekend to visit the campus. I attended.

Now on to explain what happened. I am a sarcastic and joking person and I decided to play an April Fools' Day joke on my best friend. I gathered my close circle of friends to make the announcement that I would be attending the school that my friend was accepted to, and already confirmed that she would be attending in the fall. As soon as the words were out of my mouth, my best friend started yelling, "I can't believe you would do this to me, I wanted to get away from all of this and you are ruining it." After saying this, she stormed off down the corridor before I was able to say April Fools'. I told my circle of friends that it was a joke and went off to find my "best friend" to explain the joke. However, she had gone into a classroom filled with our peers and had begun to tell the story of how I was only accepted to the school because I was a minority. She proceeded to tell everyone that I had low ACT scores. At this point, I was infuriated. How could my friend, who knew how hard I had always worked to keep a high GPA, and who always took honor classes with me, spew these lies to people? Due to our graduating class being so small, everyone knew what happened by lunch and the situation worsened.

What my friend failed to mention was that I had a higher GPA than she did and had only scored two points lower than she on the ACT. To see someone that I loved and trusted turn on me so quickly and sharply hurt me deeply. This would have to be the worst racial experience for me.

Lebrese was a black student at Howard University. She was not invited by her friend to go to a social event because of the friend's father's racial views.

I attended high school in the suburbs of Maryland where the predominately white student body was made up of five hundred girls. We had a mandatory uniform, which consisted of a blue dress, duck socks, and saddle shoes. Our Catholic school was rich in tradition with a focus on strength and unity. It's funny how an environment where we were being forced to look so similar can make you realize just how different you are.

One day after school at the end of my freshman year, I was walking toward homeroom with a group of my white friends. One of the girls was talking to everyone in the group but me about plans they had made earlier to have her father pick them up. They were going to her house for dinner and to go swimming. Knowing that we were all friends, I naively assumed that she had inadvertently left me out, so I asked if I could come. My friend looked at me as if she was truly at a loss for words. She stuttered and then told me I couldn't come over her house because her father didn't like black people. She finished by stating, "I mean, he's not racist; he's just had some bad experiences."

It bothered me that her father was prejudiced, but it was far from unexpected. What really hurt and concerned me was the fact that she truly believed that he wasn't prejudiced. I could not rationalize how she could instinctively know not to allow me to come because of my race, but believe him not to be prejudiced. I had certainly never given her any reason to believe that as a black person I would cause him to have any type of bad experience, so what else could it have been?

That day was the most blatant reminder of my position in the minds of so many of my sheltered peers. They truly could not see outside of themselves and their world to understand the mentality of a strong black female like myself. In my opinion this puts them at a serious disadvantage.

Judy was a white student attending Villanova. When two of her friends from college visited her in North Carolina, she became embarrassed because some of her friends from North Carolina made racially offensive statements.

Growing up in the south, there were many instances of racism that I have witnessed. I never really understood the severity of this until I came to college.

One instance of racism that has occurred in my life happened when two of my good friends from Villanova came to visit me in North Carolina. I was excited to have them see where I was from and to meet my high school friends. We went out with one of my high school friends, who made many racist comments during the evening. He told my Villanova friends how the "niggers" like to eat watermelon and fried chicken in the south. He also called this one girl a "mud shark" because she was white and she dated a black guy. My friend was revealing every stereotype in the book. At the time, I did not think anything of it because I was somewhat used to my high school friends making racial comments. However, the next day my friends expressed how appalled they were with my friends' statements. I quickly became embarrassed and ashamed because my friends were offended and uncomfortable. This incident happened over two years ago and my friends who came to visit me still talk about it. This incident had such an impact on my friends and I realized that it too had a dramatic impact on me as well.

Through this incident and others I have learned things not only about myself but even more about the person that I want to be. Coming to college and surrounding myself with people from different backgrounds and parts of the country has opened my eyes to all of the unpleasant aspects of racism. I am fortunate to have my friends at Villanova who have helped me gain a better perspective regarding racism in our everyday lives.

Nalini was a racially mixed student attending Villanova. She had a very uncomfortable lunch with the mother of one of her friends.

I am racially mixed; my mother is from Spain and my father is from Trinidad and Tobago, of Indian (Hindu) blood. I went to college for two years at American University in D.C. When I was there I had the opportunity to befriend people from all backgrounds, ethnicities, religions, and countries. In a place where no one is like anyone else, I was really able to find my niche for the first time in my life. Being a "mutt" all my life, I felt different. Everyone was different, so I have the advantage of being able to fit in with various types of people. My best friend is Swiss German and was born in Zurich. Her mother is from Germany and her father is from France. She is extremely open-minded but unfortunately, I cannot say that much for her mother.

Last summer I was having lunch with both my friend and her mother who was visiting from Switzerland. They started talking about a friend of theirs who is Indian. My friend was defending the guy, while her mother was constantly criticizing him:

"They do not know what respect means in that culture. Indians all follow the caste system."

"I do not like Indians anyway, I never have."

At that point I started to feel really uncomfortable, because my friend's mom knew that I was Indian—it was no secret. I had no idea how to even approach this. I also felt very uncomfortable because she had invited me to lunch, so I felt that it was not my place to start getting defensive. I decided it was best to ignore it and move on.

Then another topic came up. My friend's mom said, "Oh! Guess what? Today I saw a black man driving a Hummer! Can you believe it?" My poor friend was so embarrassed at that point that she just looked at her mother in disbelief. They started to argue about this black man owning a Hummer. My friend was saying that it was normal, and why should race have anything to do with the kind of car someone had? Her mother went on about how this could only happen under certain circumstances:

"He either stole it, or he is a drug dealer, or a professional athlete."

My friend brought up the possibilities that this guy could have been a politician, a businessman, or a doctor, and her mother just rolled her eyes.

"Forget it. No matter what you say, I won't like the black. I don't like the black, I don't like the yellow, and I don't like the red. I am not even comfortable with you having Arab friends, because you know they don't accept that over in Switzerland."

I felt that this was yet another comment, somehow directed toward me, and I wanted to see if I was on to something. So I asked, innocently, "Who are the red?" "The Indians," she answered.

Later that night I told my mom about what happened. I explained my frustration and that I felt like I could do nothing at the time. Even if I had tried to do something, it would not have made a difference. My mom advised me to call my friend, ask her about some of the comments that were made, and tell her how they made me feel. After I did this I felt much better. My friend told me that her mom meant no harm; she apologized, and explained that her mom is "a little backwards" sometimes.

Some people say that traveling is the best way to get rid of prejudices. Well, my friend's mom is probably the worldliest woman I know in terms of travel. What does it mean to be "a little backwards?" Does it mean you believe in a hierarchy of races? Does it mean you only dine with people of certain ethnicities? Does it mean you make racial slurs around those you feel comfortable with? Any way you look at it, racism hurts. It can be a comment, a joke, or something much worse. It can be directed toward your own race, or a completely different one. Racism is such a serious problem that it is overwhelming. I think all one can do is try not to lose faith in people, and take it one step at a time.

Ralph was a white student attending the University of South Florida. He was one of the few whites attending a mostly Hispanic high school in Chicago. A father of a kid that he was playing basketball with told his son to stop playing because Ralph was white.

Growing up in a predominantly Hispanic neighborhood on Chicago's northwest side, I have experienced racism from a perspective that many have not. In a neighborhood that featured such a heavy Latino culture that was very different from my own, I had to learn to adapt. There were parties and festivals that went on at all times of the year. Oftentimes I did not know the meaning or significance behind these celebrations, which often left me with the feeling of an outsider looking in. I learned to live with a feeling of not belonging. In my junior high class of 452, I was one of 7 white kids. I stood out. Most of the kids treated me no different than anyone else with the exception of one student and his father.

Juan and I played basketball together both for the school and in our spare time. Admittedly we were not the best of friends. We played together because we matched up really well and got the best practice from playing each other. One day after school Juan and I were playing when I heard a man's voice shout, "Stop playing with that white boy and come home." I had been called such names as "white boy," "cracker," "honky," and my personal favorite—"wonder bread"—for much of my time in school so it was not unusual for me to hear something like that shouted in my direction. With so few white people at my school, I knew that if I heard someone shout "white devil," it was meant for me.

"Juan you know that we don't play with people like him," his father said to him in a voice that was supposed to be a whisper but was loud enough for me to hear. I did not understand why his dad was acting like that so I asked Juan's father what he meant by "like him." Juan's father looked at me and smugly said, "Listen white boy, my son doesn't hang out with racist people like you." "Racist!" I shouted, "We've been playing ball for weeks. I ain't no racist." Juan's father then said that just because I am white I am racist because all the breaks in society went to me and my people and I had no idea what it was like to be a minority. With that, Juan said that he had to go and left with his father. We never played ball again.

At the age of thirteen I was told that I was a member of a privileged society that I had no idea even existed. I had racial slurs thrown in my direction every week and it felt odd that I was forced to take a Spanish language class in which there were only two other students that were not Hispanic. All of this and now I was called a racist. I did not understand Juan's father that day and I still do not. We were two kids playing basketball after school and we just happen to be of different races. Juan treated me no different than I treated him and yet with the harsh words spoken by his father, it was over. I was left questioning what would make him say those words to me without knowing anything about me except that I was a "white boy" in a Spanish neighborhood.

This type of bigotry happens everyday and somehow it seems almost politically incorrect for a white person to talk about being discriminated against. It is just as real as any other form of racism. Maybe one day that will change; maybe it will not. All I can hope is that Juan's father discovered that all white people are not the devil.

Beverly was a white student attending Villanova. She was embarrassed by the racist comments made by her friend's family.

I have always viewed the family of one of my good friends from high school as extremely nice, giving, and friendly people. They are a truly southern family at heart. Both parents grew up in extremely rural and southern areas. Over the years, I have spent countless hours with them since their daughter is a very good friend of mine. They usually make me feel very comfortable, like one of the family, but every once in awhile a racial slur or comment will be thrown out (usually by her father) without a second thought. Every time this happens, I never know what to say or do. It constantly surprises me because I always want to view this family with such high regard and genuinely enjoy their company.

One evening, when we were sitting around watching a TV show geared toward a black audience, my friend's father began to use the N-word to describe one of the characters. My friend then went on to call a small black child (this is hard to even write) a "Niglet." The father of course thought this was hilarious and the family proceeded to laugh. As I was sitting there, in complete awe of what was just said, I remember thinking "Why am I here right now?" Of course I was not laughing and I could tell the family saw that I was extremely uncomfortable. I have talked to my friend many times about her and her family's racist attitude, but I always feel like she brushes it off as not a big deal. I also always feel guilty about letting it continue without confronting the family, but it is a difficult situation to say something to a friend's parents, especially when you are a guest in their house. It's an extremely disappointing situation when it does arise because I know they are good people and would never out rightly be offensive toward an African American. I hope I will continue to approach the issue with my friend and get through to her that racism, though it might not be openly directed at a specific person, is always a big deal.

Eric was a white student who attended the University of California at Santa Barbara. His black friend was extremely popular because he was black.

When I was a junior in high school in Redding, California, a new student began attending whose family moved up from Berkeley. He was an African American student who, like me and many of my friends, was into jazz music. As students of jazz, we had grown up idolizing African American jazz icons such as Miles Davis, John Coltrane, Charles Mingus, and Ray Brown. In idolizing these artists, we came to identify ourselves with African American culture. We were all white so we did not have the chance to really converse or play jazz with many African American students.

This student was one of the better piano players I had ever seen at the school. He played and listened to a lot of jazz, and so he immediately identified with my friends and me, who were all heavily involved in the school's music department. However, almost immediately after he arrived, Joel was treated like a king in the music department. He was invited to every party and jam session imaginable, which was much more than can be said for any other new student that I had seen pass through the department. At first, I noticed that my friends would talk to him, then as soon as he would walk away, they would turn around and whisper giddily, "He's so black!" as if they had never seen an African American person in their lives. This struck me as odd, that the presence of an African American student could have such a cultural impact on our small world within the music department, and that people were truly amazed to see a black musician on campus.

Soon, I could sense that Joel was growing uncomfortable with his new-found fame, and he seemed to grow wary of the attention he was getting, probably not sure if it was really genuine. One day, he came up and struck up a conversation with me, probably because I was the only person with whom he could have a civil interaction without all of the praises he had received. "Why are these white people so crazy around here?" he asked. I shrugged my shoulders and offered my opinion on the situation. "I think it is because they haven't seen a black dude here in like two years." Joel laughed, then looked very confused, realizing that what I had said was probably true.

Due to the fact that we all loved jazz music and African American musicians, coupled with the fact that there indeed had not been a black student in the music department for some time, a bizarre kind of reverse racism started to take place. Instead of people being apprehensive of an African American student entering our social circles, they were ecstatic to the point of making Joel just as uncomfortable as if he were discriminated against for being black in a predominantly white school. This "positive" racism is still nonetheless racism, because it caused Joel to be treated differently simply based on the color of his skin.

Danielle was a white student attending the University of California at Santa Barbara. In sixth grade the mother of a new friend was very upset that Danielle had a black friend.

My friend Lynn and I have been friends since kindergarten. We always had play dates when we were little and I was always around her family. For a long time they seemed the same as my family. One day we made a new friend, Bree, who was brand new to the school. Bree and Lynn frequently came over to my house after school because our parents all worked and my house was closest to the school. One day Lynn's mom came to pick her up at my house and Bree was still there. Lynn's mom just got very quiet and hurried Lynn to leave. I did not really think anything of it at the time. Lynn showed up at school the next morning, and asked if she could talk to me alone. It was then that she told me that her mom said that she could no longer come to my house after school or do things with me if I was going to remain friends with Bree. At first I did not understand, and so Lynn basically had to explain it for me, "Bree is *black*," she said. "So," I replied, "why does it matter? It's not like she is any different than we are." Well, Lynn went on to explain that her mother had told her that all black people are thieves, are all part of gangs, and that her mother did not want her to associate with "people like that."

Lynn told me I had to choose—it was either her or Bree, but not both. When I told my mom, she asked how I felt about what Lynn's mom had said. I told her that Bree did not steal or hang out with gangs. She was my friend and I did not understand why Lynn's mom did not like her. I decided I would not choose. Lynn's mom would never know we were all still friends at school. She was at work, so that just limited the time we could all hang out together. Well, that worked for a while, but when Lynn's mom found out, she pulled Lynn out of public school and stuck her in an all-white private school. My mother tried to explain to me that some people just are not comfortable when people are different from them, and even though it was wrong, it was very hard to change someone's mind. I knew this was unfair, but all we could do was live with it. Lynn and I continued to be friends through high school even though she was rarely around. Bree and I grew to be very close and she has always been there for me when I needed her. She is an amazing person and has helped me learn more about racism. She even told me stories about how she had experienced it before, but as she says, "the bad things just make me stronger, no one knows me, and so I don't let them judge me, or even take it personally when they do."

I remember being very worried that Bree would not want to be my friend after I told her why all three of us could not hang out. But, while I think Bree was hurt by it, she did not take out that hurt on me. Racial experiences come in all forms, and while my experience was limited, and even though I was not being discriminated against, it hurt. Racism is in no way fair. I think that now, I thought so when I was eleven, and I will always think so, but it happens. I have a no tolerance for it now, and I never will. Lynn and I are still friends, but it is different now because I know how her parents feel about me and my other friends. I cannot help but wonder if she thinks the same thing about Bree sometimes.

4
School

Many schools across the country have become more diverse as children from various racial, ethnic, and cultural backgrounds are now sitting side by side in communities that were once homogeneous. However, a recent report by the Civil Rights Project at Harvard University (Frankenberg, Lee and Orfied 2003) documents what they term the "resegregation" of American public schools. The report concludes that the desegregation of black students is worse than it was thirty years ago. For example, the average white public school student attends a school that is 80 percent white.

While diversity has increased within schools, there is limited research measuring interracial contact within schools. Hallinan and Williams (1989) find that same-race friendships are far more common than cross-race friendships. Thus, while diversity in our schools has increased, interracial contact and cross-racial friendships remain limited. The essays in this chapter describe the isolation and insensitivity some students experienced as a result of feeling like a minority or being different.

The chapter on childhood provides a literature review focusing on how children come to identify and learn about race through the different stages of their development. The school, just like family, is an important socialization agent for understanding race. Lahelma (2004) describes the idea of "constructing different-ness in peer relations" and describes the "informal school" as a place for making contacts and meeting friends. In fact, memory research shows that when young adults are asked to recall their memories about school it is not the learning or successes and failures they remember, but their relationships with their peers. Therefore, those students who are outsiders or at the margins of school life can have a miserable existence. As Carmen describes from her experience, "Psychologically I began to hate

myself . . . Physically, I lost sleep and weight." Through such acts as bully-
ing, teasing, racist or sex-based harassment, students are able to define the
line between "us" and "the others," thereby establishing "different-ness"
(Lahelma 2004). Interestingly, these acts are not visible to teachers or other
administrators and are often not raised by the victims or the harassers.

One of the primary means for building cross-racial friendships within
schools is by facilitating interracial contact through extracurricular activities
(Clotfelter 2002). Mari describes how she was taunted and teased about
not being able to dance simply because she was white. As Mari describes,
"Even though the comments shifted from derogatory to praise, I was still
uncomfortable with the names they were calling me: Whitey, Cracker,
Wigger, and Pastey." On the other hand Janet describes a very positive
experience playing on her basketball team, "While in high school, I was
the only Caucasian girl playing on the basketball team. Never once was I
uncomfortable or threatened by this." However, Sherman (1990) finds that
at most athletic events segregation exists with whites and African Americans
sitting in separate sections to cheer their school's team. Verbal assaults and
racial slurs often go unaddressed and seen as typical adolescent behavior
(Sherman 1990).

Many of the students describe experiencing racism or racist sentiments
because of the color of their skin. The literature pertaining to color bias,
interracial racism, and intraracial racism is discussed in the chapters on
skin color and self-image. However, in this chapter we have essays from
white students who describe being harassed because they were white. For
some students, the racist experiences went beyond name-calling to absolute
torment. Gwendolyn, a white student was tormented on her school bus everyday by a fellow student. Jane describes the pain she felt as she witnessed
her sister Hannah being tormented by Hispanic students for several years
before being withdrawn from school.

These essays describe racist experiences that took place within the school
environment. The essays are painful reminders that the school environment
is not always the kindest or safest place.

*Gail was a Hispanic attending Villanova University. She describes how in second
grade, white kids made fun of her for hanging out with black kids.*

I was the only Hispanic girl in my third grade class of predominantly
white students. However, my skin completion is light, so the students must
have all thought I was Caucasian. It was then that I experienced my first
racial encounter. It still has a significant influence on my life to this day.

One of my best friends at the time was a boy named Hal. He was the only
person who could make me laugh, even when I was in the worst of moods.
It never bothered me that Hal was black, because I thought he was just the

greatest person alive. It didn't bother me that my other two good friends, Janelle and Trisha, were black either. So if it didn't bother me, why should it have bothered the white kids in my class? This is a question I could never figure out when I was in third grade; actually, it's a question I still can't figure out today.

My third grade teacher assigned me to a group project with four white students and they acted as if I wasn't even part of the group. "Why don't you go work with your stupid black friends?" The other white kids in the class also made fun of me for hanging out with black kids. I was confused and I felt isolated. Why should all the white kids hate me because I was friends with the black kids? It's almost as if they were trying to make me feel like I was a traitor to my race.

When I finally entered the fourth grade, everything was different. The white kids in this class accepted the fact that I wanted to be friends with everyone of every race because it just didn't matter to me. I found that they too associated with all different races as well. However, there was still that particular group of racist white kids that refused to accept anyone who was a different color.

If the goal of the white kids in my third grade class was to prevent me from being friends with my black friends, they certainly failed at their attempt. If anything, their obvious racism is what caused me to be even more open about my friendship with my black friend. I certainly felt isolated back then, but now I am finally able to realize that people who think this way are actually isolating themselves. They are the ones being hurt in the end.

Charlene was a black student at Villanova. She was living in a group home and was accused of stealing someone's purse at school.

I was placed in a group home setting at the age of fourteen due to abuse at home. I began to attend a suburban high school. My first day at this high school I received a lecture from the school principal who told me that even though my records showed I had no behavior or school problems, he would keep an eye on me because "most children who come from the village group home have underlining issues."

One day, as I was coming out of the shower from gym class, I noticed a small purse was lying halfway in the locker with the string outside of the locker. I opened up the locker, put the purse inside of it, and walked on to get dressed. A few hours later I was called to the principal's office because two students said I stole the purse. I told the principal what I did and thought that would be the end of it. He then called in the two witnesses who claimed they saw me take the purse. That was followed by a search of my locker. Finally, the two witnesses changed the story to say that the purse looked something like the small purse that I had on my shoulder. The principal then tried to convince me that maybe I picked up the wrong purse by accident and thought that it was mine. Finally, after hours of this, I just opened up my purse, removed everything in it that was mine and gave it to him. I now understand how people who are being interrogated by the police could sign a confession even when they are not guilty.

What happened over the next few days was nasty. I was called names, ignored, made fun of, and ridiculed by the teachers and students. Every time I came in a room students would grasp their purses or book bags as if I was going to steal them. Everyone had jokes at my expense. There were people in the school who believed me—the school nurse, the librarians, and the other village kids and staff people.

It later turned out that this planting of the purse was brought on by a two-dollars bet to see if I would steal the purse. The girls lost because I didn't steal it.

A couple of my friends from the group home offered to beat up the girls for me when the truth finally came out. I declined their offer because I didn't care anymore. I just wanted to forget it. The good part about this story is that I don't attach myself to material things anymore and I learned the important lesson of standing up for myself.

Lauren was a student at St. Mary's College. She recounts an experience when a girl in her fifth grade class was beaten up because her father was the head of the local KKK.

When I was in fifth grade, the local chapter of the KKK decided to have a march down Main Street. The town was bitterly split over whether or not they should be allowed. Some argued free speech while others argued that it was offensive. The head of the KKK had a daughter who was in my class. She was jumped and beaten up by about ten children—boys and girls. The kids decided to do this based on what they heard from their parents. Indeed, racist groups such as the KKK are terribly offensive, bigoted, close-minded, and ignorant. At the same time, teaching our children to physically harm innocent young people who have no control over the situation (such as this young girl) only serves to perpetuate the cycle of hatred. The parents who taught their children to use violence in order to combat racism only made a bad situation worse.

P.S. Growing up in a town where there was an active branch of the KKK was a terrible racial experience itself.

Carmen was a light-skinned black student at Howard University. When her classmates in third grade realized she was not white, they began to treat her very differently.

Most of my young life, I never thought of myself as different. Sure I was skintones lighter than my family and yes my father is white and my mother is black, but this is how my life is. Because I was a military brat, seeing interracial families was the norm. It wasn't until my mother was assigned to Fort Bragg, North Carolina. that I encountered my first appalling racial experience. I was in the third grade and my teacher sent the students home with a paper to be signed and brought back. Well this was a difficult task to accomplish since my parents had divorced and my mother was in field training. Obviously this was not going over well with my teacher since this paper was to be sent to our state government. It was to help the government view the racial and economic framework of the school districts.

By the time my mother came home the teacher was requesting her presence. Now note, up until now I was treated like a normal child by my peers and my instructor. I was viewed as the little white child with light brown eyes and the dark curly hair. Not to mention I still had my father's German, white last name. So that was it, I could be categorized—no confusion about having ethnic blood. I was just a simple white girl, in their simple white southern lives. That was until my mother came to my school. After the initial shock of meeting my mother, my instructor's attitude toward me changed drastically. From then on my white peers decided that I was of dirty blood, meaning that since I was not purely white I was not good enough to be their friend. It was even harder to fit in with my black peers. I had no comfortable space in my own skin. I was being accused of being a spoil of God's creations. To make matters worse, my perfect straight-A work seemed to be not good enough as it once was to my teacher. I was eventually moved to a "special" class that was for the students who were having an "educational brain delay" as I called it.

Psychologically I began to hate myself and the fact that my mother and I didn't fit into their mold. Physically, I lost sleep and weight. Finally after months of this torture, my mother switched me to the DoD schools, which are the school systems that are run by the government. After changing my last name, I've come to realize that being multiracial, (my father being German and Italian; and my mother being black and Puerto Rican), is not a curse but a unique quality that makes me the person I am today. I feel as a nation that is multiracial on a whole, we should attack this issue before it becomes brutal. No child should have to live like this or be ashamed of who they are.

Bethany was a student at Howard University. When she told a school administrator that a student made a racial slur toward her, other students accused her of being a tattletale.

The worst racial experience that I have had was an eye-opening experience. In Connecticut, I was the only student of color in my school for many years. Being the only black child, I had become accustomed to the questions about my hair, remnants of my southern accent, and any other distinguishingly nonwhite characteristic that I possessed. Though in a sense I was alone, I never felt inferior or disliked by anyone because of the color of my skin.

This view suddenly changed when one school day, I was walking in the hallway with a friend and two boys decided it would be funny to make racial slurs while walking directly behind me. In shock I turned around to say something in my defense, but was only able to get out "what did you say?" They chuckled and laughed and proceeded to walk by me. I felt that I had missed out on the opportunity to properly address these boys about what they had said to me.

I took action and told an administrator at my school. After telling my story I actually ended up feeling worse. It was as if I was being looked at by the authority figure that I went to as being too sensitive. I felt as if they thought the boys were just joking and I shouldn't have taken the incident so seriously. They made me produce a written statement of what occurred and I ended up having to defend myself and my accusations. I was in sixth or seventh grade at the time and don't understand why I had to go through all this to prove that this did happen to me. Why would I lie?

Subsequently, the boys did end up getting suspended, but ironically, I was looked at as the perpetrator and not the victim. That same day after the boys were suspended, someone who I thought was my friend shouted, "Why did you tell on Billy and get him suspended?" Once again I seemed to be at fault. All the times that I was told both in school and out of school that color didn't matter went out the window. I was now completely aware of society and the inevitability of race. This is not to say that I ever denied my blackness, but as a kid I assumed it was only an issue if you made it an issue. The fact is that society has made it an issue, and while it may not be visible at all times, it is definitely ingrained in many aspects of society.

Paula was a white student at the University of South Florida. She saw how some of her racist white classmates treated the Mexican kids in school.

I grew up in a small town in Florida. It was the kind of town where if you did something wrong, your mother and father knew it before you did. My elementary school was the only elementary school for miles. My high school was integrated with people of all races, but it was obvious which race dominated the hallways. The white boys in our school were some of the meanest boys I had ever met. They would constantly pick on the black and Mexican boys. They would even pick on the black and Mexican girls.

There wasn't one person in the entire school who didn't receive some of their disapproval. I never really let it bother me too much because I was just thankful they didn't pick on me. I wasn't the prettiest duck in the pond so if they wanted to, they could have worked on my insecurities too.

My dad took us to school because we had trouble making the bus on time. One day, caddy-corner to the road we needed to take, there were two large white buses with dark tinted windows. All around those two buses were police officers. Everywhere you looked, there were police officers. I started noticing that the men and women getting on those buses were Mexican. My dad explained to me that those buses were from immigration enforcement and they were there to take the illegal immigrants back to where they came from. I just kind of shrugged my shoulders and thought nothing of it the rest of the way to school.

It wasn't until I got to school that it really sank in. Those buses were taking the moms and dads away from kids I go to school with! It showed throughout the hallways of the school. There were hardly any Mexicans there and the kids I did see were crying or consoling someone else who was. As I walked to my first class, I saw a young Mexican boy crying by himself near his locker. I decided I needed to make sure he was okay. As I headed toward him, a small group of white boys beat me to him and they had another motive in mind. They pushed him up against his locker and called him some of the meanest names I had ever heard anyone call another human being in my life. They told him he should have been on that bus too, and that he didn't deserve to be in this country just like his parents didn't. I was frozen with horror but I couldn't speak. When it was all over, the boy just fell to the ground and sobbed. I ran over to him and just hugged him until he was composed enough to walk with me to the office. To make a long story short, the boys were expelled and I became a good friend to the Mexican boy.

At the time that this incident happened, I was so scared and I could not move. I didn't want those white boys to yell at me, so I purposely kept my mouth shut to keep from screaming at them. But now, I think I would handle a situation like that one a little differently. I hope I would put a stop to that behavior well before it got out of hand like it did. Nobody deserves to be treated like that. Nobody!

Gwendolyn was a white student who attended the University of South Florida. A black student on the school bus started calling her names and pulling her hair.

My worst racial experience occurred in middle school. I lived in Pinellas Park, Florida but was bussed to downtown St. Petersburg for school.

There was an African American girl named Tameka that rode the bus with me. She did not like me. I don't know why, she just didn't take to me. She had a huge attitude problem if something did not go her way. She was very proud and very intimidating. She refused to let anyone stand in her way or make her look bad.

One morning, I was riding the bus to school. I was seated in the seat directly in front of her. For whatever reason, she was especially mad and fired up on this day. So, because she didn't like me and I was right in front of her, she decided to call me mean names the whole ride to school: stupid, bitch, cracker, ho. I don't know that these were the exact profanities, but you get the picture. I chose to ignore her. Even though we were up in the front of the bus, the bus driver seemed to be completely oblivious to what was happening.

I ignored her because I was too scared to confront her. There were often fights between white girls and black girls at our campus. I knew that if I said anything back that she would try to wail on me and that she had more experience in fighting and could definitely take me out. I was also embarrassed that I was too scared to confront her about what she was doing. I was a "chicken." By ignoring her, it seemed to make her angrier. So, she continued to say more mean things. Finally, she became so upset that she couldn't get a response from me that she started yanking my hair. The first couple times I ignored it. Then I think that I told her to stop and she just kept on pulling it really hard and calling me mean things.

When we got to school, I immediately went to one of the administrators to tell them what had happened. She got called to the office, got in trouble and after that I never really had any more trouble with her. Later on we even become friends for a little while.

I hated telling on her. It was the only thing that I could think to do. I was truly scared that if I didn't I would get the same abuse on the way home from school. I really don't like tattletales or snitches, but at this time I felt physically threatened.

Danielle was a white student attending Florida State University. She saw a lot of racial attacks by Latina women against whites at her high school. She places this in context of the rich white kids at the school.

During my junior year of high school in Florida, I transferred to a different school in our county. My previous school was more country than this new school, and had a very different mix of races in it. The new school had mostly rich Caucasian kids. However, it also had a large population of Latinos as well. Eating lunch was a bit of a drag because it seemed that no matter where you went to eat, you were always running into these large groups of Latina girls. This was a large school, with a cafeteria and a courtyard that you could eat in, but it still seemed to lack room for those of us not belonging to any particular "clique."

These Latina girls always stuck together, and if you weren't one of them, you weren't welcome anywhere around them. If they thought you looked at them wrong, too long, or just in any way they didn't like, you were sure to hear about it. They would yell nasty comments, call you bad names, yell threatening remarks or threaten to beat you up unless you walked away from their area.

If you tried to go inside to eat, you had to deal with the snobby cliques who deemed the cafeteria "theirs." They too would make nasty comments until you would leave there as well. At least you could count on their threats only being idle ones, as they never would have really done anything for fear of breaking a nail or messing up their precious hair. The Latina girls rarely made idle threats. I saw many fights stemming from some white girl being in the wrong place at the wrong time. They weren't idle threats at all, and it wasn't just one girl who would come after you either . . . the whole group would! Back then, it was very intimidating to know these girls wanted to hurt you just because you weren't like them and they didn't like you. Lunches were the worst part of the day, which is surprising since most students will say that lunch is what they look forward to most during their school day.

Shortly after my senior year began, I transferred back to my old school. There I didn't have to worry about lunches or people picking fights with me because I was a white girl. Looking back, I think they were probably just insecure, and maybe a little angry at the way the rich, snobby white girls have treated them in the past. Maybe they thought we were all alike, even if they had never met you. This was a way for them to feel in control at a school in which they otherwise would not be accepted. I don't think it's such a big deal anymore. Then, though I must admit, I did let it get to me personally. Being the recipient of constant name-calling, threatening remarks, and just general harassment isn't how your school day is meant to be. No one, regardless of race, should be subjected to that kind of behavior at school, or anywhere else for that matter.

Emanuel attended the University of South Florida. His parents came from Nigeria, but he was born in Texas. He was treated miserably in his mostly white school.

My worst racial experience would have to be the six years I spent at middle and high school in New Port Richey. The school has a student make-up of either wealthy students or poor students and there were six to eight blacks at the school of two thousand students. There wasn't much tolerance for blacks. Being called a nigger was an everyday thing. I was desensitized to the word. I could have gotten into a fight every time somebody called me that but I would have ended up dropping out of high school or being expelled, and that's what they wanted. I don't regret the experience I had there because it shaped me into the individual I am today. It gave me a thicker skin.

I was used to being the only black in class. It gave me character. I had to create my own sense of identity. Now I can go into any social situation knowing that nothing can happen that I haven't already experienced. I was intimidated a lot by a small minority of students and ignored by the rest. I had about two to three friends that I talked to in high school. It made me a very bitter and angry person all throughout middle and high school, and even after I graduated. I always felt as if it was me against the world. I had classmates that would spit on me, and write "niger" on my locker and in the bathrooms. Since they couldn't spell "nigger" I knew that they were stupid and ignorant.

I remember a particular student by the name of Jeremy. He hated me because I was black and he always threatened to beat me up, but somehow I would always manage to outwit him or talk my way out of it. I had him in my government class, and I used to let him copy off of me in exchange for him not kicking my ass. Then he realized that I was the reason he passed the class and ultimately the reason he was able to graduate. He had already spent an extra year in high school. He ended up signing my yearbook as follows:

> Hey whats up I know that we didn't git along for a long time but once we started talking I thought you are prity cool thanks for your help in class if it wasn't for you I woudn't pass this class. Thanks, Jeremy

I wanted him to sign my yearbook, not because we were good friends or because I liked him. I knew he would probably end up working a construction job or some blue-collar job the rest of his life, but I wanted him to know I had something to offer. To this day I wonder if I changed him. I wonder if he still has prejudice in his heart or if he understands that you can't judge people by the color of their skin. I could have possibly taught him the most important thing he has ever learned.

I was never accepted in the years when we most long for acceptance. I had to search long and hard to find an inner strength to keep my head up. To make matters worse, the only black girl in my senior class used to say I was white. That really fucked with my head. At least one of my grandfathers never had to call any white man master. I was the closest thing to Africa she had ever met.

I had no athletic ability because I am afflicted with sickle cell anemia. However, I was on the football team in middle school for a year, which I consider to be an amazing feat. White folks knew nothing about the disease since it rarely affects them. It really threw them for a loop that I am black and not athletic. But fuck 'em. I wasn't put on this earth to play football; as matter of fact I hate sports. I think it's a mock slave trade because it distracts us from focusing on real goals. Why would I want to jump around or chase a ball for somebody's enjoyment? It takes our eye off the prize. When I went to the University of Florida in the summer I realized how corrupt and messed up sports really are. How could I be in a class with someone who had no clue about intermediate algebra? It was a foreign language to him but he knew how to run with the ball, so somehow he was accepted to the university.

All of my classmates hated the fact that I got accepted to the coveted University of Florida. Jimmy used to say it was because I am black and they had to have a certain number of black students. I guess his parents were opponents of affirmative action. They couldn't accept the fact that maybe I was smarter than them. I enjoyed rubbing it in their face. The last thing they would remember about me is going off to a college that they were yearning for. The tables were turned. It was sweet payback and a sort of redemption. I ended up hating that school, but they will never know that.

Mari was a white student attending the University of California at Santa Barbara. She was made fun of when she tried out for the dance squad.

Growing up, I found nothing to be more exciting than dance. There was no denying that I was born to dance! As soon as she thought I was old enough, my mom got me involved in a dance studio near my house. The studio was run by a black woman who had more rhythm than any soul I've ever seen on this earth. She taught the most advanced jazz dance. At the age of twelve, I was the youngest girl in her class.

My mom could not pay for me to attend private school and the public school near my house was not in my school district according to the Los Angeles School District. I was bussed to a school that was an hour away. White students were the minority. Flyers were posted around school advertising try-outs for the dance squad. Unfortunately my excitement turned to complete destitution when I walked into the gym where girls were trying out. I was the only white girl. Snickers, sneers, and laughs from black and Latina girls surrounded me. Comments were yelled out like, "Who let that priss in here?" and "Are you lost, cracker?" One girl walked up to me, smiled and pretended to pat my back and then snapped my sports bra. Another girl was getting laughs from her friends by mimicking me when I was doing warm-up stretches. I was on the verge of tears, ready to just forget trying out all together, but then I heard the audition song. We would be learning a routine to "Bugga-Boo," by Destiny's Child. My favorite song! I took it as a sign that I was meant to be there and to not be discouraged.

As I walked onto the gym floor I drowned out all the laughing and comments the girls were shouting at me. I danced harder than I ever had in my life. The song ended and there was total silence as I walked back up to the stage to watch the other girls. As the try-outs continued, girls in the stands started to mock their fellow black and Latina dancers by saying, "You better work it like Whitey worked it, damn!" Even though the comments shifted from derogatory to praise, I was still uncomfortable with the names they were calling me: Whitey, Cracker, wigger, and pasty. The next day at school, the list of girls who made the squad was posted and I was on that list. Practice started immediately after school, and the other girls who made the squad all had their differing opinions about me. Some continued to put me down while others smiled and simply asked, "How you got that rhythm, girl?" Either way, I was made certain never to forget that I was white, and they were not.

My mom and I moved after that semester so I don't know whether or not things between my teammates and I would have improved over time. I do know that being the subject of racial criticism is an incredibly painful experience. I have learned from my experience that no person of any color should ever be granted the right to pass judgment on another person. I also learned that just because I am white that doesn't mean I am impervious to racism. I have experienced the embarrassment and the ridicule associated with racial segregation. I am glad for what I have experienced because I am now more conscious and sensitive to racism. I can honestly say that I have become a person who refuses to participate in language or actions that would make someone who is not white feel discriminated against. It's like the old saying goes: Do unto others as you would have done unto you.

Janet was a white student who attended the University of California at Santa Barbara. There were a lot of racial fights at her high school.

I grew up in Stockton, California. My best friends have always been of multiple backgrounds: African American, Laotian, Puerto Rican, and Caucasian just to name a few. While in high school, I was the only Caucasian girl playing on the basketball team. Never once was I uncomfortable or threatened by this. I looked at these situations as a learning experience to increase knowledge of other cultures and people. It was difficult for me to see the difference in color because we all shared the same problems and experiences whether at home or at school.

I went through high school taking advantage of these opportunities for meeting new people by getting involved in clubs, student government, and sports. It was discouraging to me when I did not see others taking advantage of the same opportunities but instead were trying to dominate another group of students. Whenever there was a carnival, rally, or even during lunch, a fight would break out.

By my senior year, fights had become so regular that students were unable to use the restroom during class in fear that other students would start a fight. Racial lines were always being crossed among the Asians and the African Americans. I never understood the animosity between the groups, but they were the predominant groups with which the school had disciplinary issues.

Late in my senior year, the fights were becoming extremely violent and began to involve makeshift knives and other homemade weapons. The ethnicities involved in the fights were also starting to include Caucasians and Indians. The creation of "White Wednesday" really caught the attention of administration. This is when the Asian gangs would jump a white student or multiple white students just for the sake of their ethnicity. This made me extremely uncomfortable. It would not matter whether or not you had done something to them. In their eyes you had already done something by being born white. More rules were implemented about not leaving class and having a closed campus, but not much changed.

Thankfully in college, I have found people that are open to everyone's backgrounds and opinions. Unfortunately, the students at my high school have been unable to understand this concept of positive diversity.

Jane was a white student who attended the University of California at Santa Barbara. Her sister was treated very badly in school by Hispanic students.

My worst experience with racism actually happened to my little sister, Hanna, but it was painful for my entire family to witness. Hanna was going into eighth grade and was transferred (because of school districts) into a school where the vast majority of students were Chicano.

The children here were very cruel to her because she was white, with blonde hair and blue eyes. They were hostile and aggressive from the first day, although my quiet and passive sister had done nothing to incur their wrath. The boys were kinder than the girls, but they called her names that shamed and humiliated her. They called her "gringa" and "sticklet" (because she is so thin), and other names which they would yell at her when she ran laps in P.E. They also made fun of her for her fair skin. In class, they threw things at her head and whispered more names.

The girls, however, actually tormented Hanna. She was afraid to go to the bathroom because they would bang on the stall while she was in it, and loudly discuss how they were going to beat her up when she came out. Once or twice, a girl took Hanna's backpack and dumped its contents onto the ground, then made her crawl on the floor to pick everything up. They stole from her, but accused her of stealing from them. To make it worse, the teachers and staff simply looked the other way, and sometimes even joined in on the game. The lunch lady overlooked or simply ignored my sister, although she had stood in line longer than anyone, while the secretaries mocked her for going home sick (which she did often).

It was very hard for my family to see my independent, but shy and sensitive little sister become even thinner because she was always too nervous to eat. Once I picked her up from school and we both sat in the car and cried. She was constantly sick; she seemed almost dazed with horror. She was unable to remember simple details, and entirely forgot certain incidents in which the children at school had bullied her, until months later. My family is very gentle, and nothing in her life hitherto could have prepared Hanna for the treatment she received at this school.

Eventually, neither Hanna nor my mother could bear it any longer. My mother took Hanna out of school and home schooled her for the rest of the year. Hanna now goes to the high school my brother and I attended and is much happier there.

5

Teachers and School Administrators

The essays in this chapter describe the varied experiences students have with teachers and administrators and their experiences with racism. Most of these essays fall into a few common categories including stereotyping, cultural insensitivity, and open racism. While many are accused of being racist, most teachers gladly take on the role of bringing tolerance in the classroom through their teaching and interactions with students. Nevertheless, as the essays demonstrate many students recall painful racial experiences with teachers and school administrators.

Most teachers and administrators recognize the importance of tolerance, empathy, and openness in the general education classroom (Lahelma 2004). Teachers and administrators facilitate the student's process of coming into a school as a pupil and later becoming a citizen of the school's community. Throughout this process, students often navigate a complicated web of interactions including friendships, student/teacher relationships, student/administration relationships, peer relationships, and academics. Therefore, teachers and administrators have a primary role socializing citizens of the school and citizens of the world.

However, teachers and administrators are often not equipped with the tools and resources to deal with the growing diversity within their schools. Students come to schools with existing stereotypes and negative attitudes toward different racial, ethnic, and other social groups. Banks (2006) contends that without the proper curriculum intervention by teachers, racial attitudes and behaviors will become more negative and more resistant to change. However, teachers and administrators are often unaware of the cultural differences themselves (Vail 2005). Figlio (2005) finds white teachers are often more likely to say their African American students are more disruptive and have shorter attention spans.

Aveling (2006) contends that particularly for white teachers, a critical examination of their "whiteness" as privilege is imperative to bringing anti-racist teaching in the classroom. This finding also resonated in a survey of teachers and students conducted by *Education Week* where teachers and administrators agree that teachers must receive greater preparation to teach in schools with more racially diverse populations (Reid 2004). Indeed, many of the students describe how they felt their teachers or school administrators stereotyped them on the basis of their race. Brian assumed a teacher ordered him to play the role of the drug dealer because he was black. "No, I think I'll pass and move on to another group," Brian responded to the teacher. Perhaps one of the most interesting experiences is described by Betsy, a white student, who tells of an African American professor who stereotyped her as being rich and insulted her because of her beliefs.

Students also describe how many teachers set lower expectations for them simply because they are a minority. The implications of lower expectations are huge. *Tracking* or ability grouping became a primary means of organizing the learning of students beginning with the massive wave of immigration and the Great Migration of African Americans and peaking in the 1920s. Vocational tracks were provided to divergent groups, while mostly middle class children were provided an arts and sciences curriculum. Tracking became a way of Americanizing the new student populations and was perceived as being egalitarian and efficient (Ansalone 2001). However, racial/ethnic stereotypes and language barriers more often meant that minority students were placed on the vocational track while white students were placed on an academic track.

As immigrant groups assimilated, tracking became less popular within schools but in the 1960s as a result of the Civil Rights Movement, school equity became the policy focus. However, tracking is still very evident in schools today with a number of different models and with great debate. Today, students are tracked by a differentiated curriculum consisting of either vocational training (home economics, shop, and so forth) or academic training (AP courses, IB courses, and so forth). In the United States, approximately 60 percent of elementary schools and 80 percent of secondary schools use tracking within their schools (Strum, 1993). The track position of students may influence teachers and in many ways teachers have some role in maintaining the achievement gap between white and minority students by holding different expectations. Farkas (2003, p. 1135) finds that "generalized racist attitudes, either conscious or unconscious on the part of teachers and administrators" are a foundation for specific issues of student placement and instruction.

Many students describe how they were discouraged from taking certain classes or applying to certain colleges because of their race. For example, Ramona describes how her counselor dissuaded her from signing up for difficult courses as she states, "When it was my turn to sign up for classes, my counselor looked at my desired schedule and simply nodded her head and said 'you don't need those classes. How about cooking, do you like cooking?'" Juan describes how a counselor discouraged him from taking advanced classes until he meets a counselor that believes in his education. He says, "thanks to my counselor I never let anyone underestimate what a young Latino with passion can accomplish." Many students describe the insensitivity or racism of their counselors in this chapter. Constantine and Gushue (2003) find that although schools have been dealing with multicultural issues for some time, school counselors are not always equipped to handle many of the issues immigrant children deal with, including academic issues, psychological adjustment, and families that may not know English or may be unfamiliar with the U.S. education system.

Some students describe the open racism they experienced from their teachers. Ricardo describes the open racism of an art teacher toward him and his friends because they were Mexican.

These essays showcase a range of racist experiences as students describe how they were stereotyped and treated unfairly simply because of their race. Interestingly, these stereotypes are not simply "whites stereotyping blacks." Rather the interaction of race and class in these stereotyped assumptions is evident in some essays as well as intraracial stereotyping (e.g., black teachers stereotyping black students).

Andrea was a black student at Howard University. She describes how a high school guidance counselor advised her to apply to colleges with lower standards.

An unforgettable incident in my senior year of high school gave me the opportunity to witness the painful sting of hidden racism.

Any person who is a product of the U.S. school system knows that your last year in high school is not an easy one. From the prom to SATs to college applications, there is a lot of stress. I was Little Miss Involved, from varsity basketball, to National Honor Society, to senior class president. On top of all these obligations, I also had to find time to successfully complete several extensive college and scholarship applications. Trying to maintain this balancing act proved to be an arduous task.

To help alleviate the stress, guidance counselors offered special assistance to the seniors. During one particular session, my counselor asked my preference of schools to which schools I was applying. I said my top choices included the University of North Carolina at Chapel-Hill, Howard University, and Spelman College. His response was, "Well, what about a nice in-state school like Morgan State or University of Maryland, Eastern Shore?" He then said, "The schools you mentioned are nice, but they're really dream schools, aren't they? You would be better at one of the schools I named and they're probably more affordable for your mom."

I was astounded at his audacity. Here I was, with my high aspirations and standards, looking forward to experiencing a challenging environment. Yet he told me, (an honor student with a 3.89 GPA, graduating in the top 10 percent of my class, and not to mention the first black senior class president in my school's history) that my choices were basically out of my league. Furthermore, he assumed that my family would not be able to pay for my education. I have nothing against Morgan State University or UMES, but I knew that neither school would have offered as rigorous of an environment as my top choices. Maybe to the average nonminority student, this may not have appeared to be an alarming situation. But for me, it was devastating. I had worked hard throughout my years of schooling and had proven that I was just as smart and capable as any of my white peers. Yet, that brief conversation made me feel as if my work had been in vain. I guess even today, it doesn't matter how hard you work, people will still have their own preconceived notions of what you are supposed to do and what you are capable of. The ironic thing is that my counselor was not white. On the contrary, he was black! Unfortunately, he allowed other people's misconceptions to penetrate his own thought processes.

Tony was a black student attending Howard University. He was denied a ROTC scholarship at another college while other white cadets were given this scholarship.

I was raised in St. Thomas, Virgin Islands. My mother chose to bring me up in a Christian family setting. This was good because religion showed me the right way to live. It also taught me to treat people with respect, regardless of their race or ethnicity.

I enrolled at Georgia Military College in September 1999. Upon entering, I found out that I was short a couple thousand dollars because of tuition. Because I was an advanced ROTC student, I believed that the Army was automatically going to take care of my balance. That was not the case. I was supposed to apply for the ROTC scholarship, and then check for notification of receipt of the scholarship. Realizing that there was a scholarship that I was supposed to have, I went to the ROTC department and inquired about the money that was supposed to be posted to my account. The ROTC instructor that I talked to was Captain X. Captain X was a tall white man in his thirties. He looked up my file and found out that there was no application for me. Immediately I asked him if I was still able to get the scholarship. He told me no. He said that I was ineligible because of my SAT score and that the deadline had already passed. I did not question him about this because it is said that it is wrong to question your superiors in the military. I left the office gullibly believing everything he said.

I completed the academic term, and went on to Army training at Fort Lewis, Washington. During that year I found out that I could've applied for the scholarship anytime during the year. However, I was not mad because I believed that he simply made a mistake. It was during a conversation with my white comrade in the same class that I found out that I was racially discriminated against. During the conversation we had, I asked him how he was paying for college. Clint told me that he was on a full scholarship. I asked him about his scholarship, and he told me all the details that led me to the final point that Captain X intentionally misled me. Clint said that he got a call from Captain X who offered him a scholarship after the date that I conferred with Captain X. He was told that he was eligible. One of the eligibility requirements was to have a 950 SAT score. His was just above that while mine was a 1070. I felt bad because I believed that I was misled because of my race, even though I met the standards.

This was the first time I realized that racism still exists in America, and that I was a victim. I never followed up on the issue.

Randy was a black student at Howard University. His high school teacher made a racist remark during a film presentation.

My worst racial experience occurred during my junior year in high school in an introduction to psychology class. We were watching a video that was describing different aspects of cultures around the world. An African tribe was one of the featured cultures. The video showed the African tribe jumping up and down doing some sort of community ritual. While the ritual was being displayed, my teacher said in a very loud voice, "Hey Randy, that's your people." Being the only African American in the class, there was no question that the comment was referenced to me. Judging by the tone in which the comment was said, it was obvious that the teacher had said it intending to get a laugh from the class. However, no one laughed; they just turned and stared at me, looking for my reaction. Aside from a few mumbling curse words, I was left speechless.

Immediately after the experience I felt humiliated and outraged. I told my parents about the event, who then told the proper school officials. I don't remember exactly what happened after that but I think I received a half-hearted apology from either a school official or the teacher himself and was told the usual line that it would never happen again. What struck me the most about the entire event, however, was not the comment itself, but that it was said by a teacher whom I had previously considered to be a friend. In addition to having taken a class with the teacher before, the teacher had been my freshman basketball coach. We had formed a fairly congenial relationship and it was partly because of this relationship that I had signed up for the psychology class in the first place. When he said the comment, I was left speechless, not just because of the ignorance of the comment, but because of who said it.

Joshua was a white student attending Stephen Austin State University. Views of white students were attacked in his Introduction to Sociology class.

After my first year at SASU I decided to take some summer classes back in my hometown of Dallas, Texas. I took a math class and a sociology class at the community college there. There were only two other white males in the class. Our teacher was a white female, about fifty years old.

One day we discussed poverty, welfare, and unemployment. We learned that all white men have good jobs while all minorities are unemployed. Not true. We were also taught that minorities cannot get jobs due to white employers only hiring white workers. From that we went to the subject of reverse discrimination. Nobody in the class liked the subject of reverse discrimination except of course for the very few white males in the class. It was nice to hear that white people also lose jobs because companies have to hire a certain amount of minorities. Once we got past all that, we started talking about corporations. The teacher explained that only white men are heads of large corporations, and that they hold back minorities, including women, from succeeding in life.

Hearing about that got pretty old. The teacher all but came out and said "the world would not be in poverty if someone else besides the white man were in charge." She said that the white man had done nothing to help minorities or poverty stricken families.

Finally, a white guy in the back of the class said something. He asked the teacher how she could blame poverty and unemployment strictly on the white man. She got very offended that he decided to defend himself, which is strange, because the first day of class she said all opinions were welcome and would be taken with respect. That didn't happen. For some reason it was okay for the black or Hispanic students to speak up about injustice in their lives and communities, but when a white person decided to do that they were wrong because they are white. So, after the student spoke up, they talked for a while until it reached a pretty heated discussion. The teacher asked the student to leave the classroom because he was being out of line. Well, the other students in the class never got kicked out for voicing their opinion.

The strangest thing about it was that the teacher was white. She kept bashing her own race. She always said, "I'm ashamed to be white." What in the world is she teaching sociology for? That statement shocked me. I had never heard anyone say they were ashamed of to be part of their race.

After that whole experience with that sociology class I totally looked at college and professors differently. I realized that not all professors are right and have all the answers. Until that happened I honestly thought that professors did have the answers. Learning that changed the way I learn now. I question things more instead of just simply believing anything. I have learned a lot more by doing that. Plus, I pay more attention in class. This experience made me realize that racism can go all ways. It was actually a very good experience for me. It was very uncomfortable being blamed for unemployment and poverty, but in the end it was a great learning experience.

Brian was a black student attending Howard University. His teacher tried to place him in a role-playing situation as a drug dealer. Do you think he was right to object?

In tenth grade I was a student in a victims' rights class in my high school in Las Vegas. The teacher had students participate in a number of role-playing activities to illustrate certain concepts. One day one of the role-playing assignments involved interaction between a drug addict and a drug dealer. There were also other miscellaneous characters in the scenario. My teacher ordered me to play the drug dealer. I told her, "No, I think I'll pass and move on to another group." She aggressively retorted back, "No you won't. You will play the drug dealer." This led to a few minutes of "back and forth" and she eventually ordered me to go sit in another classroom. I told her that I would not do that and instead would go to speak to the dean.

I explained the situation to the dean and made a point to inform him that my teacher had never asked me why I did not want to play the drug dealer. The dean, who is a white male, immediately knew why I refused. I was the only black student in the class and I was not particularly thrilled about my teacher's attempt to force me to play a stereotypically degrading role in a class assignment, especially when there were other roles in other groups still available.

I never once thought of my teacher as racist and I still do not. I never thought she was attempting to discriminate against or humiliate me. She simply did not understand. It never crossed her mind that the situation might have been uncomfortable for me. She also never thought to ask me why I was so persistent in my refusal to play that particular role. She saw it as a simple role-playing assignment and a student defying her order.

Adrianna was a black student attending Howard University. When she was denied membership in the National Junior Honor Society, her mother intervened. Adrianna discusses the climate of subtle racism.

I encountered my worst racial experience as an adolescent in middle school. This one experience was very discreet and may even be looked upon as subliminal. It involved the faculty, students, and parents of my middle school in New Haven, Connecticut.

As a thirteen-year-old seventh grader, my main priority was school. I was very concerned with getting an education. I was very urban because of my demographic origins, but I was open-minded to new ideas and diverse surroundings. I had never received a detention, suspension, or expulsion in my entire academic career and I was held in fairly high esteem by many of the students and teachers. As the daughter of a school teacher that had taught for sixteen years, my mother expected nothing less and she made all of my teachers very aware of that fact.

I was a very active participant in school and club activities. I had served as class representative for grades five to seven, assisted the eighth-grade yearbook staff, was involved with the Girl Scouts, participated in dramatic plays and dance productions, and I was affiliated with the principal's advisory board. Above all of this I was an honor student and that is what made the experience so appalling.

The students were very segregated, not by force but by choice. The teachers did not influence how we mingled during social time; they only interfered during class. In general we "hung out" with our friends, which normally surfaced into groups of the "black kids," the "white kids," and the "other kids." Of course groups were broken down into smaller cliques. As children, we all recognized this, but it was never an issue. We hung around people we were comfortable with and that was the way it was on both sides.

The National Junior Honor Society's recruitment period was something that was not common knowledge. Many of my friends and I didn't even know what the Society really was. From past experiences, we thought that it was an organization that was only for a certain group of children. In our ignorance, we thought it was some kind of nerd social club for the "white kids."

You were nominated for the Society solely off of your cumulative GPA as well as your character, school participation, and scholarship by a selected group of faculty that had worked with you or taught you in the past. During my seventh grade year, the process had come to pass and yet another induction was underway with neither myself nor any of my other honor student friends invited to become members.

My mother was a curriculum facilitator at another middle school at the time and she was very aware of the Society. One day she came home and asked me when I was going to be inducted. I told her that I didn't even know if I was nominated and I commenced to ask her what exactly the Society was. I was surprised that she knew about it. She taught at a predominantly black school. My mother became enraged when I told her I didn't want to be a part of the society because I did not want to have to stop hanging out with my friends to go hang out with the "white kids." I got in trouble for making this heinous comment, but my mother was aware that I was ignorant of the facts.

She immediately recognized the problem and was at my school, meeting with my principal the next day. My mother discovered that I had been voted against by every teacher on the selection board. They all claimed that I had a behavior problem, an attitude problem, and that I would not uphold the standards of the society. My mother blatantly told them that they had no right to say that when they never contacted or notified her of any detentions, suspensions, or reprimands for behavior I had received. She basically forced them to show her proof of the allegations. When they could not, she demanded that my name be revisited and that they choose another selections committee. She insisted that she would get the superintendent (whom she knew personally) involved if they were not willing to comply. Her constant pushing of the issue in a very organized and active method proved that she would not take no for an answer. Although they thought of my mother as a crazy parent who would not accept the truth about her child, I was inducted the next year.

At the time my friends thought my mother was crazy, and I was extremely embarrassed that she came to my school almost every other day, challenging the judgment of my teachers behind closed doors. My teachers were probably a little perturbed at the fact that someone was pressuring them to change their ways. As I look back now, I do not feel I was discriminated against out of pure race discrimination, but I feel these events took place because of ignorance and conformity to status quo. Many of our teachers were from the suburbs. They did not understand our style of dress, the language we spoke amongst our friends, the music we enjoyed, or the personal connections we made with one another and because of this I think we were perceived as a slight threat to what was held in high regard with respect to proper style, dress, language, and attitude during that time. They were only familiar with the attitudes and tendencies that came from the children who resided where they lived—in the suburbs.

To this day I am exceedingly happy that my mother felt the need to step in and demand change. Now that I understand the significance of an accomplishment such as being a member of that Honor Society, I am grateful she took the time to teach me its value. The most important lesson I learned from this experience is to keep your eyes open and find out as much information as possible for yourself. If you know the facts, no one can tell you different. Undercover discrimination is the worst kind. We cannot allow the ugly face of racism to creep into any learning institution of this society. If we do, then we are defeating our purpose to move forward. Integrated environments will never succeed without proper education and exposure. As time has progressed things have gotten much better, but there is still much work to be done.

Sharmaine was a black student attending Howard University. Her ballot for the homecoming queen in high school was not announced because the school did not want all the nominees to be black.

My worst racial experience was not that bad in comparison to others I have heard. It was more embarrassing than anything else. When I was a junior in high school in Pittsburgh, I was nominated for the Homecoming Court. Those who were nominated were announced over the intercom, and then the entire junior class voted. It was known that those who were nominated walked onto the field during the half-time show of the Homecoming game and the queen and king would be announced during the homecoming dance.

I was sitting in class when the ballots were received. My name, along with four other girls and five other boys, were on that ballot. However, once the announcement aired, my name, along with one of the other African American boys, was not called. I immediately went to my principal, who was also African American, and asked him what happened. He simply stated that I did not have enough votes. When I told my mother, she contacted him, along with our class cosponsor, and was told that I was dropped from the ballot because I am black.

It turned out that everyone on the ballot was black, except for one Caucasian male and one female. Because my high school was predominately black, it did not look good to have all black nominees on the ballot.

This hurt for several reasons. First, I was not told privately, but had to find out along with the entire school; secondly, people that I once looked up to and that are of my own race discriminated against me; and lastly, the administration knew my parents personally, yet they still chose this method.

Nevertheless, my parents and I raised a lot ruckus, and I was still able to walk on the field during half-time. It was something that I did not need to go through, but I am blessed that that was the worst racial experience I've had.

Ricardo was a Hispanic student attending the University of California at Santa Barbara. He believes his black teacher in high school was racist toward Mexicans. Do you think this was a fair assessment?

"That nigga is a racist-ass mutha fucker," my fellow Mexican friends and I would say to each other about certain teachers at our school. We thought we would be screwed out of our grades saying things like, "this fool is gonna fail us just cause he don't like Mexicans, huh?" What else could be thought when the teacher showed mercy and cut slack to endless black students in the class? I never thought that there would be racism in a school where the minorities, blacks and browns, were the only students, but there was.

My school is located in an area know as "the 'hood." Endless numbers of financially struggling minorities live next to gangs and drugs and all the other associated things. Racism is alive despite all the hard work that goes into annihilating it.

My drawing teacher was an old man. He would try to be one of those teachers that the students felt they could relate to. He would try to be cool with us saying stuff like "Yeah, I'm one of you guys." My friends and I did not buy that. We knew he was only cool with the black kids because they were black and he was cool with some Mexicans because they were "mayateros"—one of many terms we used to identify the Mexicans that acted like they were black. By that I mean how they dress, how they talk, and how they assimilate themselves with black culture.

My friends and I sat in the back, away from the teacher, mainly because we felt that he was treating us like we didn't know anything. We believe he would fail us without even giving us a chance to show what we know.

I was transferred into his class halfway through the semester so it was even harder for me from the get go. He said, "You have to do all the work that we have already done." In shock, I couldn't believe what he was telling me! Adding insult to injury was that he expected me to get the work from someone else. Luckily, I had my friends in the class who helped me out.

This teacher was racist and there was no getting around it. Before my counselor transferred me into his class she told me that I would most likely fail his class because he "was hard." My counselor was a Mexican woman, and we got along pretty well so it was her way of telling me that he was a racist black man.

As I was intending to catch up with the class, the teacher didn't even care or even ask how I was doing. He just didn't care. I, thinking I was somewhat witty, thought that I could sort of teach him a lesson. He thought that my drawings were bad, and they were because they were all rushed. He never suspected a guy like me, a Mexican that looks all gangster, to be any good at drawing or anything for that matter.

So after I finally caught up with the assignments, my drawings began to improve of course. They were so good he decided to give me the most improved student award that he had. I was too good at drawing for him to overlook, but we still didn't like each other. I didn't like him because of how racist he was and because of how much he favored the blacks in the class. He didn't like me because to him I was just another Mexican.

Ramona was a Hispanic student at the University of California at Santa Barbara. Her advisor during her freshman year of high school did not encourage her to excel. A later advisor was very helpful.

I moved to the United States during seventh grade not knowing how to speak or write English. By the time I started high school, I knew how to speak and write English. I knew that I wanted to go to college and to achieve my goal I would have to take "hard" classes. I decided to sign up for honors English, Spanish, and math. When it was my turn to sign up for classes, my counselor looked at my desired schedule and simply nodded her head and said "you don't need those classes. How about cooking, do you like cooking? Or you can be in the Health and Human Services classes." I was stunned at the words of my counselor. Is it because I'm Mexican? I asked myself. She signed me up for easy classes. I was confused. I wanted to tell my family but they didn't know the system. It is hard to get Latino families involved with their children's education.

Later that year I found out about Puente, a program designed to help Latino students go to college. I met with the Puente counselor many times to talk about the program. All he asked was for my sister to be there and for me to fight for what I believed and wanted. Just because I had been in the United States for three years and had an accent did not mean I was not smart. He took a different approach to my desired schedule; he advised me to take regular English and from there he would see if I would be capable of taking honors or AP classes. I surpassed his expectations. I was enrolled in AP English and later in AP Literature. I was glad to have found such a counselor that understood and cared about me as a student.

Betsy was a white student who attended the University of California at Santa Barbara. In a black studies class she had a teacher who put her down because of her race and political beliefs.

While I was in high school, I also attended the local community college in order to accumulate a few extra units for high school, while also fulfilling some of the general education requirements of the University of California system. During the second semester of my senior year in high school I signed up for a black studies course.

During the first half-hour of class the professor used terms such as "stupid white men" and "white rich bitches." I wrote off his derogatory terms toward white people as having derived from a bad experience or the study of conflicts between black and white people. However, I became extremely offended when he asked if there were any "dumbass, hick, Bush lovers" in the class, referring to those of us who supported President Bush. Being a conservative Republican and raised in a military household, I was more than willing to support my side of the situation. As soon as I raised my hand, signaling my support of our president, he began tearing me apart. Little did he know that I have been raised among many of the people that he's fighting for. I've seen many sides. It's hard to support a family of six on a military salary and my mom went through a divorce that caused the repossession of many of our belongings when I was little. I've been on welfare, I know what food stamps look like, and I know what foods apply to WIC vouchers. My mother worked hard and saved money, eventually pulling us out of the situation and getting off of government aid as soon as she could.

Before I could explain my perspective, the professor accused me of being a "typical white, spoiled brat" who knew nothing of the world outside of my "pillowed nursery" in white suburbia. When he asked if I supported the war, I replied with a strong yes. He went on to say that he could "sign my pretty, little, white ass up" in the services and send me over to "get a sense of what hell" my parents were putting our servicemen through. At this point I informed him of my experience with the military and went on to remind him that the men fighting for our country and our values in Iraq had signed up to be there; and it was their choice to risk their lives protecting Americans, whether or not they supported them.

The rest of the conflict between me and my professor resulted in my dropping the class. He clearly stated that we would be writing papers on welfare the second week of class and that he basically expected papers that reflected his view. Not only did the unfairness of the class cause me to drop it, but also the inexcusable amount of derogatory remarks, direct insults, and generalizations of white people. One would assume that in a class that discussed the fight to end racism he would refrain from using the same tactics in class. I was amazed by the lack of professionalism that he displayed as a professor, not to mention the poor fight that he was making against racism. I was also shocked by the fact that in a class that was 80 percent white, I was the only one that had a problem with what he was saying. The entire issue made me more angry than hurt. It killed me to drop the class because in a way it seemed that he tried to be so rough with us in order to make us feel belittled by him and his race, and he was trying to put things into a perspective he assumed we needed to see.

Juan was a Hispanic student who attended the University of California at Santa Barbara. His high school counselor discouraged him from taking advanced classes.

I was always a bright kid, somewhat lazy but still smart. During my freshman and sophomore year I took regular classes, meaning no honors or AP and did fine. I had no problems with any of the material. In fact, it was so easy that I saw my grades suffering because class was so boring and not challenging at all.

In the end of my sophomore year, I found out about AP classes from a friend, and thought the added work and challenge would make class more enjoyable. That week I met with my counselor to set my schedule for my junior year. I mentioned to her that I was interested in taking AP English next year. She informed me that the class would be too difficult and I should really stick to regular classes, but I insisted, and she informed me that I needed to get letters of recommendation from teachers stating that I was capable of handling the rigorous courses. I thought that was odd but I agreed.

I talked to the same friend that told me about the classes and she said that the counselor's request was outrageous. My friend had never heard of anyone having to present letters of recommendation to get into AP courses. I realized that there were no outside factors my counselor could base her request on. The reason I was even questioned was because I looked like most of the students that attended the school. The school was in a low-income, predominately Latino community. Most of the residential students that attended the school were automatically placed in the easier courses, which included the hands-on classes like shop, wood, metal, and the like. I realized I was being judged by the way other Latinos were viewed on campus.

I was extremely upset and made a meeting with my counselor. My counselor tried to convince my mom and me by telling us that I had been placed in easier courses and the advanced placement courses might be a bit too difficult, which would hurt my grades. I got angry and demanded for my counselor to pull up my recent grades and test scores and explain what she was basing her assumptions on. My grades and test scores spoke for themselves. Despite this proof she still insisted that I think about it and not make any hasty decisions.

I researched programs in neighboring high schools and came across SAS, the school for advanced studies. I applied and was accepted. I enrolled in AP English, and got an A. Since then, I've taken five AP courses in two years and have gotten involved in cross country and track and field. I graduated with a 3.8 GPA and high honors. I am now attending the University of California at Santa Barbara.

Now that I am able to reflect upon this incident in my life I can see that my counselor was actually a motivation to me. Thanks to her, I forced myself to take AP courses and do well. I'm glad I did not ever doubt my potential, but I get saddened whenever I think how many other students just like me who were persuaded to take the easier classes and didn't get a chance to compete with their peers. Thanks to my counselor I never let anyone underestimate what a young Latino with passion can accomplish.

6

Dating

During the Civil Rights Movement, interracial dating was perhaps the most widely expressed justification for opposition to integration in housing, schools and public spaces. In fact, the Savannah-Chatham Board of Education filed suit to reverse *Brown v. the Board of Education* arguing that school integration would lead to interracial dating and sex (Romano 2003, p. 158).

Scholars contend that barriers to interracial romance and dating are simply another means for maintaining a racially stratified society (Lewis and Yancey 1995). An understanding of interracial dating and *who* is likely to engage in interracial romance is important for understanding the possibility of racial assimilation. "If Americans are unwilling to enter into romantic relationships with members of other races, then racial assimilation is unlikely," (Yancey 2002, p. 179). Yancey further proposes that the inability of African Americans to assimilate into the dominant culture is due to the low numbers of African Americans who intermarry. The fear of "miscegenation" has been and remains one of the major causes of racial antagonism. It was not until 1967 that the Supreme Court overturned Virginia's miscegenation laws, which prohibited any white person from marrying a black who had even a "single drop" of black blood. In 1967, thirty-eight states had similar laws.

There has been a sea change in attitudes. In a 1958 Gallup poll, only 4 percent of American whites approved of "marriage between blacks and whites." By 2007, this percentage had increased to 75 percent. In a 1997 *USA Today*/Gallup survey of teens (Peterson 1997), 57 percent of those who go out on dates said they had dated someone of a different race. On the other hand, 13 percent of teens said they would never date someone

of a different race and 24 percent of whites said they would have trouble
with a white person dating a black person. Twenty-three percent of blacks
indicated they would have difficulty dating a white person. Joyner and
Kao (2005) found that interracial relationships decline with increasing age
among young adults and speculate this may be due to families and friends
affecting the development of such relationships and a preference for same-
race relationships in the consideration of marriage and life partners.

Some researchers contend that because American dating is considered
more casual and not necessarily connected to marriage, there is greater acceptance of interracial dating as opposed to interracial marriage. Therefore,
individuals who engage in interracial dating may not necessarily be as likely
to become part of an interracial marriage. Nevertheless, some findings
show that men and those who attend interracial schools are more likely
to interracially date than women. One reason for this is the superior social
position men have within society that enables them more flexibility in their
dating habits (Yancey 2002). Women are likely to be penalized more for
their dating habits.

When dating outside of their race, white women often encounter more
objections from family members than women of other racial groups
(Tucker and Mitchell-Kernan 1995). The stereotypes of the threatening
black man or the violent and sexually aggressive black man persist in addition to the idea that African Americans are inferior to the white race (King
2004; Solsberry, 1994). Indeed, historically black-white intermarriage and
relationships have remained the most controversial and are also the most
identifiable (Reiter, Krause, and Stirlen 2005). Although attitudes toward
interracial dating have grown more tolerant there is evidence that young
people on college campuses are still likely to be segregated and have few
interracial/intercultural friendships (Martin, Bradford, Drewiecka, and
Chitgopekar 2003; Todd, Mckinney, Harris, Chadderton, and Small 1992).
Others contend that interracial dating is still less acceptable than interethu-
nic dating and race remains a defining barrier despite the perceived increase
in tolerance (Martin et al. 2003). However, as indicated in these essays, individuals who grow up in diverse neighborhoods or have a diverse network
of friends are more likely to date interracially or interculturally (Martin et
al. 2003; Yancey 2007).

While African American/white couples are the most visually identifiable
interracial couples, other interracial relationships are increasing rapidly.
Many scholars of interracial relationships have used the "exchange theory"
to explain interracial relationships between whites and other minority
group members. According to this theory, members of a lower status groups
are more likely to marry members of a higher status group. This theory suggests a hierarchical ordering of groups with whites having the highest racial
status, followed by Asians, Hispanics, and blacks (Yancey 2002). Neverthe-

less, while this theory has received great criticism Asians and Hispanics are most likely to marry someone of another race while African Americans are the least likely (Wang and Kao 2007). However, African American/white couples seem to garner the most attention and are the most stigmatized of interracial couplings despite the growing numbers of interracial relationships between Asians and whites, Hispanic and whites, etc. (Reiter, Krause, Stirlen 2005). In fact, Yancey (2003) finds that interracial relationships between an African American and white individual often has a powerful affect on shaping the racial attitudes of the white individual because the couple often faces such strong hostility.

Social and family barriers continue to affect interracial relationships. Vaquera and Kao (2005) find that interracial couples were less likely to engage in public displays of affection due to social barriers that still exist pertaining to interracial dating. Family objections to dating across cultural (especially racial) lines can be very influential and its effect has been well documented (Kouri and Lasswell 1994; Lampe 1982). One example of this is Fran who describes how her mother's dating of a black man set off a war with his uncle and grandparents. While African Americans have historically been more accepting of interracial couples, some research shows that African American women may feel they are competing for a marriage partner and thus resent the competition. Because there are more "marriageable" African American women than African American men, this accounts for the negative attitude held by some African Americans when white women marry African American men (Solsberry 1994).

In this chapter we have a variety of examples of how interracial dating caused conflict among friends, families, and contacts on the street. The "villains" were white, black, Hispanic, and Asian.

Jane was a white female student from Middle Tennessee State University. She describes a party where a white male won't kiss a black female when they played spin the bottle.

I am originally from Michigan. When my family moved to Tennessee, we found that there were a lot of changes, especially regarding how people viewed each other. When I was growing up, my parents taught me that I should treat all people with respect, but I would soon realize that not everyone thought the same way.

When I was a freshman in high school, my brother was a senior. One night, he invited me to attend a party with him. I was excited that he even asked, so I agreed to tag along. While at the party, someone brought up the idea to play "spin the bottle." There was a black girl there who came with a few of her friends. When it was one guy's turn, the bottle landed in her direction. He said that he wasn't going to do it because "that is just sick." He told everyone that he would never do something like that. The girl just simply smiled, and then everyone resumed the game. It was then my brother's turn, and it too landed on her. My brother didn't think anything about it, and he leaned in and kissed her. The other boy that refused to kiss her started to get upset and told my brother that he couldn't believe that he would do it. My brother looked at him, said that he didn't care what color she was, that he wasn't some racist redneck, and they should learn to have some respect.

The whole night made me very uncomfortable, but I guess the girl wasn't too bothered by it. She understood that the ugliness and prejudices of some people will never go away. It is just a part of life. Someone will always dislike something. It doesn't have to be their skin color, but simply what they wear, what color their hair is, or where they live. However, we all can help to minimize the hate by trying to understand their points of view and knowing that we are not perfect in any way.

Dennis was a black male student at Howard University. He describes tensions over dating a black woman from Guyana.

I fell in love with a girl on my job that was from Guyana. The majority of the people that worked on my job were of West Indian descent. I really felt uncomfortable working close with them, because they would speak in a language that I could not comprehend. It is called Patois, which is a form of broken English. Sometimes I feel that they would talk about me, because every time I would make a mistake, they would laugh and speak their language.

I met Rhea through a mutual friend. She would stare at me as I performed my duties on the job. I told my friend Julio who is of Spanish descent to put in a good word for me, so that I could get a chance to know her. Julio told me that she said I was cute and that she wants to get a chance to know me too. After work I would generally wait for her so that I could walk her home. We were now considered a couple.

Usually when we had our break I would walk her to the store. This is where the racial tension escalated. As we walked, people would gaze at us. All of the Guyanese (West Indian) boys would give her an evil look, and all of the African American females would give me an evil look. We did not care what people thought about us; we continued to kiss and hold hands in public. People on the job disapproved of me going out with her, because I was an African American and if her parents found out she would be punished. Our relationship had to be secretive.

Rhea one day said she had something important to tell me. She told me that she could no longer see me because of my ethnic background. In her religion and custom, her family believed in set marriages and that I was not good enough or light enough for their daughter. What baffled me about the whole situation is that she and her entire family are darker than me. I was deeply hurt by what she told me and had to bring this relationship to a close.

Eve was a black-Korean female student attending the University of Maryland. Her white boyfriend got in a fight with a black man over their holding hands. One interesting factor in the fight was who broke it up.

I am a twenty-one-year-old half-Korean (mother) and half-black (father) female living in Prince George's County, Maryland. My boyfriend of four years is a white male. Before I met my boyfriend I never experienced any type of racial experience that I was aware of. I honestly never thought I would. My dad used to tell me stories about how he was a young boy growing up in Gurdon, Arkansas, and how he had to go around back when entering a store, use a water fountain that said colored, etc. I'd listen but I could never really grasp the whole experience.

Since dating my boyfriend, I was able to distinguish certain looks of disapproval or almost shock because we are an interracial couple. One day my boyfriend and I were driving on I-95 holding hands in the car. I got the feeling that someone was staring at me, so I looked to my right and there was a black male in a blue SUV staring directly at me holding hands with my white boyfriend. He looked at me with disgust. I tried to act like nothing was wrong, but my boyfriend could tell something was wrong. The black gentleman exchanged curse words and every curse word had the word "white" and "nigger lover." So then it went to the next level. Both of them were trying to run each other off the road while I sat on the passenger side. Let me remind you we were in my car. We pulled off the highway, followed by the black gentleman in the SUV. The cars stopped at a light and the black male yelled out of his car window, "I'm going to kick your white #%!$ because you white people can't fight." I was sitting there thinking, "Please let the light turn green." The black male got out of his car and so did my boyfriend. I got out and tried to tell my boyfriend to let him go because at this point my boyfriend had him in jujitsu (head lock). However, he rammed the other guy's head into my car about four times. Then three young black males ran up. I thought, "Please don't let this be a riot," but they actually came and pried open my boyfriend's headlock on the guy. They finally got them separated and some rent-a-cops came by. My boyfriend got in the car, told me to get in, and we drove off.

Fran was a white female student at St. Louis University. Her mom fell in love with a black man and Fran describes the reaction of other family members.

Three years ago my mom fell in love. She was happy and looked forward to a future with this man. The only obstacle to their relationship was the fact that she is a white woman and he is a black man. Their different races caused occasional stares when they walked down the street holding hands, and our neighbors often questioned who "this black man" was and why he was at our house. However, my mom was able to ignore these prejudices and enjoy her relationship. This enjoyment was sustained because she did not tell her parents or brother that she was dating a black man. Members of our extended family are notorious for hating all minorities, so my mom only told them that she had a new boyfriend who had a good job and was a good family man. They were thrilled for her.

However, the tranquility of my mom's secret was destroyed one afternoon when she and her boyfriend went to Six Flags. My mom was unaware at the time that her brother's best friend was also at the amusement park that day and reported to her brother that he saw her "kissing a nigger." A couple of days after this trip to Six Flags, my mom's sister-in-law called to confirm whether this was true. My mom came out and said that the man she was in love with was black. Then her sister-in-law informed her that she was going to destroy the family unless she broke up with this man.

My mom ignored this threat and a few weeks later followed through with a planned visit to her parents' home. My brother and I went with her and we promised that we would not mention her boyfriend unless our uncle or grandparents questioned the relationship. When we arrived we were ignored. My grandparents offered a cold greeting, but my uncle would not look at us, let alone speak to us. We tolerated this coldness for an entire night and day, but by the second night it was no longer going to be possible to ignore the conflict that lurked. My uncle had been drinking the entire day and already before dinner, he was drunk. He tends to be at his worst when he's been drinking, so we knew what awaited us.

My mom, brother and I sat down at the patio table with my aunt, uncle, grandparents, and cousins as we waited for dinner. My mom was greeted by my uncle saying, "Hey there, nigger-lover." My mom, wanting to avoid conflict, immediately got up from the table and went inside, but my brother and I stayed. He turned to my adult brother and said, "You know your mom's a whore, right? Any woman who sleeps with niggers is a whore." My brother quickly came to my mother's defense and a heated argument erupted. My uncle repeatedly, with a beer in his hand, threw out the words "nigger" and "whore," making my mom and her boyfriend sound like the two worst people to ever live. Meanwhile, my grandparents, aunt, and cousins sat in their chairs, sipped their drinks and acted as if there was nothing wrong with the scene that was unfolding.

My brother got up from his chair and shortly thereafter, he and my uncle were only inches apart as they yelled in each other's faces and threw back their fists, ready to make the argument physical. At that point, I came between the two men in an attempt to prevent the punches that were ready to come. My brother walked away to go tell my mom that we needed to leave immediately. I lingered behind and my uncle grabbed my arm and said, "You don't understand how gross this is, Fran! She's so wrong for doing this. He's a nigger, you have to tell her that this is wrong!" I released myself from his grip and ran inside to pack my things. Within the next hour my brother, mom and I were driving home, vowing that we would never return again.

Since this weekend in the Ozarks, my mom has ended her relationship with her boyfriend, for reasons other than race. After months of silence, she has started speaking to her parents and sister-in-law again. However, she stood her ground and insisted that she could not forgive their behavior until they apologized, and finally they did. My mom did not speak to her brother for almost two years and now their contact is limited to the necessary conversations they must have at family functions. My uncle has never apologized or expressed remorse for the way he behaved that weekend, and I believe that if he had a chance to relive that weekend, he wouldn't do anything differently.

I find my uncle to be a sad human being. That weekend I realized that even though I despise racists, I did not feel anger toward him. I only felt confused and sad. I wonder how one person can be so full of hate that they can despise another person solely because of their skin color. How can somebody possess such stupid and blind hatred? I concluded that my uncle was probably one of the unhappiest people I had encountered in life, and to compensate for all of his unhappiness he had to blame other people. He chooses to blame black people. There's no excuse for my uncle, and for that reason, there is no way ever to forgive his behavior until he apologizes and changes his racist mentality.

My uncle's behavior upset me, but my grandparents' behavior infuriated me. My mom is more willing to make excuses for them. She claims that their racism will never cease and that we have to accept it because it's a "generational thing." I believe that as times change, people must change, and even though my grandparents were born almost eighty years ago, there is no justifiable reason for them to maintain the nasty prejudices that they grew up with. Furthermore, no prejudice should make it permissible for them to sit on their patio, casually sipping drinks, as their daughter is insulted.

I don't think this racism has destroyed our family, like my aunt warned it would, but it has divided and weakened us. I think it is impossible to overcome this weakness as long as the racism exists, because even though my mother no longer dates a black man, the hate is still present and it has left numerous scars on our family.

Aisha was a multiracial student attending Howard University. Her date to the senior prom had to cancel because of pressure from his Filipino parents.

Being a child of mixed race, I have encountered many instances of discrimination. I'm from the small town of La Junta, Colorado, which is not known for its open-minded citizens. Though my brother and I compose most of the limited black population, I had not encountered many instances of racism that I could not overcome. That all changed with the senior prom. My good friend Terry, who happened to be Filipino, invited me to attend with him. We had grown up together. I had played at his house, he had played at mine, and no mind was ever paid to the race of either one of us. That is, however, until his traditional, conservative parents thought that there might be a romantic spark between us.

I was so excited when Terry invited me to the prom. I knew there was chemistry between us, and I was sure that my senior prom was going to be the best night ever. One night, I got a call from him and he sounded like he had been crying. He told me that his parents had planned a surprise trip to the Philippines the same week as prom, and he wouldn't be able to go. The sound of his voice told me he was lying and I was heartbroken. I didn't understand why Terry didn't want to go with me anymore, but I knew I couldn't force him to I hung up the phone in tears, only to hear it ring again immediately. It was Bobby, a mutual friend of both Terry's and mine. He heard the tears in my voice and said he was sorry, he knew all about it and couldn't believe it either. Though I know it was hard for him to say, Bobby broke down and told me that Terry's parents did not want him to go to prom with me because I was black. I hung up the phone, feeling heartbroken, humiliated, and empty.

At the time, I couldn't understand how Terry's parents could be such hypocrites. They had been discriminated against, for their broken English and exotic looks. How could they inflict the same pain they'd experienced on me? As I look back now, I realize that minorities worldwide do the same. The colorism within the black community and the discrimination amongst different minority groups all come from a deep-seated pain. If all you know is that pain, then that is all you can inflict. You don't know that you don't have to tear other people down to build yourself up.

I thought I would never forgive them for the hurt and embarrassment they caused me, but I went to my senior prom, with a great friend, and had an amazing time. I sought comfort in those who were accepting of me, and eventually rebuilt my friendship with Terry. Though I moved on, I will never forget the loneliness and disappointment I felt when I received that phone call. I draw from that incident hopes that I never create the same feelings in anyone I come in contact with. I thank Terry's parents for teaching me a lifelong lesson.

Candace was a biracial student attending Howard University. The parents of her boyfriend threatened to disown their son if he continued to see Candace.

Growing up in America as a biracial individual sometimes can be very difficult. It seems that people in America see that you are either colored or not. Since I am mixed with African American and Caucasian, I have experienced discrimination from both races at least once in my life. The experience that I would consider the worst was when I had a Caucasian boyfriend and his parents disapproved of our relationship because I am half African American.

I was in Germany at the time because my parents are military, and we were stationed over there. My boyfriend's parents were also in the military. We met at the school on base the summer before we graduated from high school. We started out as just friends, which his parents were okay with. As long as we were just friends they did not have a problem with it.

As time went on, we became closer, and he asked me on a date. After our first date, many others followed. He never told his parents that our relationship had escalated from friendship to dating. I was always curious about why he never mentioned it to his parents because I had told my parents. I kept insisting that he needed to tell his parents about us, which I regret doing because of the results.

He told his parents about us, and after that everything began to change. His parents never let him see me. The only time we got to see one another was at school. Every time I would call him, his parents would hang the phone up on me. I was not allowed over his house anymore, and he could not come to my house. If his parents found out that I would be at an event for school, he was not allowed to attend. Basically, his parents did everything in their power to keep us away from each another. His parents even threatened to disown him if he continued to see me. They told him that it was unacceptable for him to date someone with any African American in them. Eventually, the pressure from his parents was so great that we had to stop seeing one another.

This event affected me the most because at one point in time, his parents accepted me as his friend, but they made me feel as if I was not good enough to date their son because I am part African American. Why was I good enough to be his friend but not someone to date? This event made me feel less of a person. For a while I just wanted his parents to accept me for who I was and not judge me based upon my race.

Susan was a black student attending Howard University. While she dated a white guy she had to deal with the racial "jokes" of his friends.

I was living in Tennessee and dating a white guy from my job. We were pleased with the relationship but some of his friends were not.

When my boyfriend and I first got together, I knew his friends weren't the nicest people; they were childish and liked to play around a lot. So, when the little remarks began, I would brush them off as playful behavior, but they never stopped. My boyfriend did confront his buddies about their comments on numerous occasions, but as expected, they always claimed it was all in good fun and that they really liked me.

The incident that I remember distinctly happened after punching out for work. A group of employees, including my boyfriend and his friends, decided to go out to eat at a restaurant. My boyfriend's buddies continually made subtle racist remarks and jokes the entire evening. One said, "That is the oddest couple I have ever seen, an attractive Negro woman and an ugly white hick." Later one said, "Hey man, later tell me what it's like to be with a black girl, I might want to try." The other friends would say, "Wonder what your children will look like. Don't you think if you ever got married your kids would be confused about what they are?"

Eventually my boyfriend and I did break up, but it was not because of his friends. Now that I look back on the situation, I really don't think his friends thought they were doing anything wrong. They really thought that the comments they were making were funny, which I cannot say is any better than doing it intentionally. To not be sensitive to other people's differences is wrong. I realize there is and always will be racism hidden beneath the shield of sarcasm, harmless teasing, and jokes.

Simone was a white student attending Howard University. She was verbally attacked at a movie theater by blacks for being with a black man.

As a white woman, one might think that I have never been discriminated against because of the color of my skin—gender maybe, but not skin color. This would be a mistake. It does not always go over well with black women when I walk down the street with a black man. Many times we have been stopped and asked if we are "together" or just friends. I have always found this shocking.

When I was seventeen or eighteen, I went to see the Janet Jackson and Tupac Shakur movie *Poetic Justice* with my roommate and self-proclaimed big brother, Lance, who happened to black. We went to a Saturday matinee at the Grand Avenue Theatre in Milwaukee, Wisconsin. As we settled into our seats, some woman a few rows behind us started talking loudly, "Well, would you look at that. Some skinny little white bitch thinks she can just walk in here with one of our finer specimens. Of all the nerve."

I turned around to see who was saying this and saw that not only was this woman and her cohorts staring me down, but other people were looking at me in disgust as well. It suddenly occurred to me that I was the only non-black person in the room and the majority of other patrons were women.

The hostility that was projected at me was thick, and I told Lance that maybe we should go and see the movie at a different theater. He assured me that everything was fine but I could tell he was tense. He had grown up as a gangbanger on the south side of Chicago and although he was now out of that scene, he always felt ready to "handle his business" if he had to. This made me even more nervous because I felt as if I had absolutely no control in the situation. The taunts and threats from behind continued, including the throwing of various food items and coins at me. Lance finally turned around and told the women to knock it off or there would be trouble. He was told, "It's okay, baby, we got nothing against you. It's just that little white bitch you're with." Lance said that if they had something against me, then they had something against him. He promptly turned back to the screen and put his arm around me. Fortunately, the film was a good one and everyone was soon sucked into it, forgetting about me, until it was over and I left as quickly as I could.

I consider this my worst racial experience for two reasons. The first is that I had never before felt animosity and hostility from such a large group based solely upon the color of my skin. It was only because I was white that this situation even occurred. The second is because I fear this is the most racist I have ever felt. Did I project acrimony on them because of some racist attitude of my own? If so, it was unintentional and regrettable, but there is no denying the ill will cast upon me by the group of women behind me. The small lump on my head from being struck by a quarter was the proof of that.

Bree was a white student attending Salisbury State University. When her father found out that she was dating a black man, her father fought relentlessly with her.

All my life I have done everything my parents have asked of me. I always got good grades, didn't do drugs, and I dealt with their crazy curfews and rules. My father said there were only three things I could do that would ever make him truly mad at me. The beginning of my senior year I began dating a boy named Brandon. Sounds normal, yet one of the things my father never wanted me to do was date someone outside my race. Brandon is mixed, his father is black while his mother is white. I am half-Portuguese. I hid our relationship for a while. I had to lie to Brandon as well. He finally asked me why we never went over to my house. One of the hardest things for me to do was to look in his eyes and tell him why our relationship was so secretive. That day the picture I had of my perfect family died in his eyes as I watched him cry. Yet, for some reason he stayed, and because of that I will always look up to him. He never gave up on us.

As months passed on you can only imagine how hard it was to keep my forbidden relationship a secret. One day my mom finally asked me what was going on with Brandon. I broke into tears and told her everything. She looked at me with disappointment in her eyes, told me to pretend we never had this conversation, and walked away.

A few months later Brandon showed up on my porch because his best friend's mother died. I saw my whole world crash around me. After I finished consoling Brandon, my father ripped me aside and asked me what was going on. I couldn't lie to my father anymore. After I told him everything, my father told me I needed to leave his home and I wasn't welcome anymore. As I packed up some of my things, I listened to my parents fight and my mother cry. I was leaving with a few of my things and my mom stopped me and begged me to come home after I was finished working. This was only the beginning.

For the next two years I was a stranger in my own home. No one would talk to me. I would come home and go straight to my room and not leave until the next morning. I won't lie. The thought of ending my life crossed my mind a time or two because I was so depressed and alone. My father hated me, and why? Only because I had finally found someone that made me happy.

Your senior year you should be going out having tons of fun with your friends, but I was not going anywhere because I now had to pay for everything on my own. My father said I could live in their home, but that is the only support they would give me. At eighteen I became semi-financially independent. I have never worked so hard in my life. I worked everyday. I ended up attending a community college. I had a lot of debt. Many of my friends asked me if this was all worth it. I loved him. How can I know what love is? I'm only nineteen years old. If love is knowing that you can depend on someone day in and day out, waking up and wishing they were there next to you, never being able to get them off your mind even when you want to, and finding yourself feeling safe in their arms, then I was in love.

I made many attempts to mend the torn relationship with my father, but continually got turned down. So I stopped. I couldn't take his rejection anymore.

A month before leaving to attend Salisbury University I received a phone call from my father asking me to meet him for dinner. At dinner he apologized to me for all that has happened in the past two years, but for some reason I couldn't forgive him. He said he would just pretend that Brandon and I were not going out because he refused to change his view on the matter. All this time I never asked him to compromise his morals or who he was. I just wanted him to understand this is what I wanted for me, and see that these were my morals and views, and that I was unwilling to change as well.

I went off to college and my father did agree to stop holding my education over my head. We are better now, I mean we talk, but he will still not accept my relationship with Brandon.

We have now been dating for two-and-a-half years, and besides all the struggles I have gone though, I feel as though this has made me a stronger person. Brandon is a good person and he makes me a good person. I am happy with him and don't regret all I have done to get here. I hope one day my father will finally open his eyes and look past the color of someone's skin to see that we are all the same inside because I fear that if he doesn't, one day he may lose me forever.

Deanna was a Hispanic student at the University of California at Santa Barbara. When she met her boyfriend's family, they treated her like dirt.

I had always dated Hispanic guys until about a year ago. It is not because I have a preference in ethnicity; it just always seemed to work that way. About a year and a half ago I began a new relationship with a white guy. His name is Bryan and we met at the beach. As our relationship progressed we felt that it would be great if we met each other's family. He got to meet my family first. My parents are very open-minded people. They had no opposition to our relationship. My family made sure that he felt comfortable when they were around by being as hospitable as possible.

The next weekend we went to meet his aunts and uncles. I had heard great things about them. The drive to their house was about three hours long. While on the road, Bryan told me about his family. He explained that they were an upper-middle-class family. I gazed at him confused, unsure of what relevance that comment had. I realized what he meant as I walked into his uncle's household. Everyone was next to the door, ready to greet us. They got their first glance of us and they immediately turned their backs and walked away. I was not sure what was going on. They excused themselves and left the house without a single explanation.

Bryan's cousins stayed behind. His tall, skinny, plastically enhanced cousin was the only one who spoke to me. She looked away as she spoke to me. I am not accustomed to that. She told me that if I was going to have sex with her cousin, not to do it in her bedroom because she had just gotten the room exterminated and had no need for Mexican infestations.

I grabbed my coat, asked Bryan to accompany me to the door, and left the house. I was not willing to be humiliated by some strangers. It wasn't until the next day that Bryan explained to me what happened. His family is racist. They think that all any Latina or Chicana wants is money, and will manipulate white men in order to take their money. I was appalled. I did not break up with Bryan; he's a good guy. Bryan and I have not spoken to his family since then.

Betina was a Hispanic student at the University of California at Santa Barbara. Several black girls tried to provoke a fight with her for having a black boyfriend.

My first boyfriend was black and his name was Anthony. He lived in my apartment complex and I hung out with him and his black relatives a lot. His family never appeared to have any bias, prejudice, or racist feelings toward me. The only problem between us was that we went to different middle schools. I was always scared that he would have another girlfriend that was smarter, prettier, and black, but he assured me that was not the situation so we had a pretty good relationship.

One weekend Anthony asked me if I wanted to go to the Monterey County Fair with him and his family. I said yes. We were having a lot of fun when I began to notice that a lot of black girls were glaring at us as we made our way around the park. Anthony said they went to his school.

All of a sudden I heard one girl say, "She ain't black," and another girl then said, "She just wants to be [black]." The girls (all black) began following us everywhere we went and they kept eyeing my boyfriend, calling out his name, and whistling at him.

I was so angry because the girls hadn't been acting that way toward Anthony until they found out that I was his girlfriend. I thought that the girls were so evil and mean and then it got worse. Later the girls were walking right past us, (for what seemed to be the millionth time), and one of them bumped into me real hard. She then turned around and said, "Do you have a problem chola?" Some of the other girls started getting rowdy and the one girl put her fists up as if she was ready to fight me. Luckily Anthony told everyone to settle down. We then went our separate ways. Anthony just held my hand and told me, "Those chicken heads are dumb!" Consequently, I agreed and we just enjoyed the rest of our time at the fair.

It wasn't until days later that I found out that the girl who tried to start a fight with me was an ex-girlfriend of Anthony's. She wasn't happy to see Anthony with another girl and she hated Mexicans. To her, I guess I was the enemy on two different levels.

I was taught to never look at race as anything more than race itself. I am a Mexican American female born and raised in California. My mother always taught me to never consider myself inferior to anyone else because of my race or gender. She always told me that I could do anything I set my mind to and to never let anybody tell me differently. Likewise, my mother was also not like the strict, traditional Mexican mother. She was a college graduate and worked to support two daughters as a single mother. Therefore, my mom was well aware of times changing and encouraged me to reach for the sky.

I thought it was ridiculous that a girl would want to beat me up because I was Mexican and stole her boyfriend. I never brought it up again with Anthony but from then on I tried to be aware of the black girls he talked to because I didn't want a repeat of what happened at the fair. I was really afraid of those black girls. Now I realize that it was so stupid because we were all only twelve or thirteen years old. However, it does prove that racism can play out even in children.

Pamela was a white student who attended the University of California at Santa Barbara. The family of her Persian boyfriend belittled her because of her race.

When I heard the phrase "white trash" as a child, I never fully understood exactly what it meant. I constantly joked about the term and thought nothing of the stereotypical definition. Fortunately, I have been blessed with a stable upbringing in an upper middle class neighborhood, and I never believed I would be compared to the phrase I took so lightly.

During my third year in high school, I began dating a close friend of Persian ethnicity. As things began to get more serious, I visited his house more frequently and was introduced to more members of his family. I have always found it difficult to gain comfort in the presence of his relatives. I constantly feel as if I am being carefully looked at and spoken about in Farsi, which is a language I don't understand. Some of my boyfriend's eldest relatives, such as his grandfather, have displayed very hurtful reactions to my presence, my looks, and my personal beliefs. In their eyes, a young white Catholic girl is not a perfect match for a Persian Jew.

About a year into our relationship, I was taken to Los Angeles to meet my boyfriend's grandfather for the very first time. We were hardly introduced when he began to speak to my boyfriend in Farsi. I wasn't sure what was being said, so being very accustomed to this type of awkward situation, I stood to the side and smiled. My boyfriend responded with a light chuckle and then the conversation ended. As we left his grandfather's house I curiously asked my boyfriend what was said at the beginning of our visit. He was reluctant to reply, but after a great deal of begging, I was shocked to discover that his grandfather had asked if I was white. He told my boyfriend that white girls are only for play, and that he must find a good Persian girl for the future. I was deeply hurt by this comment. Not only was I insulted, but I was also made to feel inferior and similar to a toy used for their temporary amusement. I literally felt like trash meant to be discarded after a certain period of time. These feelings have persisted throughout my two-year relationship with my boyfriend, and I know that they will never change. Though I love being included in a different culture and familial experience, it is difficult to feel ashamed of my own family traditions and know that I will never truly be approved of.

7
Sports

Most professional sports in the United States were racially segregated until the 1950s. Major League Baseball was completely segregated until 1947 when Jackie Robinson began to play for the Brooklyn Dodgers. Before then, blacks were forced to play in the Negro League. Robinson was not only a great baseball player (with a hitting average of .311), but also a major figure in the Civil Rights Movement. There were a few black professional football players in the 1930s (most notably Paul Robeson). However, blacks were excluded from professional football between 1934 and 1946. Professional basketball began to integrate in 1942 when ten black players were added to the rosters. It is argued that basketball integrated first as it was mostly an urban game.

There is debate about the extent to which racism still exists in professional sports. Some recent findings include: blacks are more likely to receive penalties in the NBA than whites (Price and Wolfers 2007); white players in the NBA earn 12 percent more than black players (Wallace 1988); whites are more likely than minorities to be in positions of control such as quarterbacks in football or managers in most sports (Washington and Karen 2001); and salary discrimination occurs in basketball, football, baseball and hockey (Kahn 1991). On the other hand, Brown et. al., (2003) found white and black student athletes in college were equally likely to identify as athletes and to believe that racism is not a major problem on the playing field. However, there has been some research at the gradual absence of young African American players in Little League Baseball (Comeaux and Harrison 2004). While some argue that the increased interest in basketball and football contributes to fewer African Americans who want to play base-ball, others suggest that the lack of African American baseball programs in African American neighborhoods contribute to this decline.

Sports became a way of uniting both fans and players. Many prejudiced white fans began to reconsider their attitudes when they found themselves rooting for sports teams with black stars. Byrd and Ross (1991) found that participation in junior athletics lead to decreased racial prejudiced within schools. Racial integration in sports became a model for racial integration in society (Demas 2007). However, racism and racial divisions remain. In 2007, Don Imus was fired by MSNBC for referring to the Rutgers women's basketball team as "nappy-headed hos." Debate continues about the use of American Indians as mascots, whether Barry Bonds or Michael Vick are the latest "poster boys" for "bad blacks," and whether the media unfairly focuses on fights among black basketball players.

Sports are supposed to be the great equalizer. The metaphor "a level play-ing field" is used to justify the fight for equal opportunity. In this chapter we see how racial adversity still exists in football, baseball, softball, basket-ball, hockey, soccer, lacrosse, and water polo (For more on race and sports among youth, see Gatz, Messner and Ball-Rokeach 2002). Racism occurs among players, coaches, fans, and referees and among people of different races. Ken describes how he felt after being called a "nigger"; "I felt betrayed to a certain extent, or alienated. Here we were playing as a team, toward one common goal—to win. Yet, I was the only one of my teammates to encounter such a spiteful personal attack." Their racial experiences are per-haps a microcosm of racial dynamics in professional sports and society as a whole.

Paul was a white student attending Villanova University. He describes a racial fight on the basketball court.

I lived in a predominantly white community. There is one aspect of my life where I interact with races of all types—when I play basketball. At first, in grammar school, I played on teams with a bunch of my white friends and our team would play other teams, some being all white, some being mixed, and some being all minorities. At the games where the other teams were all of different race, racism was evident, and the feeling could only be described as uncomfortable. All the white parents sat on one side of the court, and the other team's parents sat on the opposite side. While the games did not get too intense, the separation was visually evident. As I got older, the games became quite intense and also personal. Every time I stepped onto the court, I felt like I was playing for more than just to win, but for respect. Each time we played an all-black team, the crowd would harass us extensively, not because we were playing against their favorite team, but because we were white, and in their area. I'm not saying that this is bad; it's just the way it is.

All of these feelings that had developed over the years exploded last summer. Each year, the city of Buffalo hosts a popular three-on-three basketball tournament. It is a social event for nonplayers as well. Three of my friends and I formed a team. When we got to the game, the court was already packed. There had to be four hundred to five hundred people there and the majority of the crowd was black. The game started, it was extremely rough, and the crowd was brutal. The crowd yelled at us. This was the type of stuff we did not get at every game, although I did not think much of it.

The whistle was blown for a foul underneath the basket, and I looked down only to see our center and their center exchanging quick punches. Players began to rush to the fight, but before I took a few steps, I was hit from behind, only to turn around and see the entire crowd rushing the court (around one hundred of them). This was scary because I did not see one other white person besides our families and players. I'm not positive about how long the brawl lasted, but I do know that it ended up with all four of our players on the ground with groups of people kicking us. The police had to get everyone off of us, but when they did about fifty people from the crowd chased two random white kids down the block. The mob turned the corner and we heard a gunshot. No one was really hurt; I had a broken nose, and the others had a few black eyes. We were forced to continue the game, which did not help because every white person at the tournament now migrated to our court and was there in support of us. People we didn't know came up to us and told us to start another fight because now we had more people and would win this one. On one end of the court were all the angry black people, and on the other was a group of angry white people. Policemen stood around the court with their hands on their guns and pepper spray, waiting for another fight to break out. Luckily it never did. I had seen nothing like this ever before.

This event meant a lot to me. Basically every emotion that I had sensed over the years was more real than I had imagined. Here there was a fight between two teams; the crowd that rushed in did not know us at all. All they knew is that we were white. I know this is reverse discrimination, and that such cases are not too frequent, but it just proves the extent of today's racial tensions. It is sad to say that this is symbolic of the underlying feelings in today's society.

Ken was a black student at Howard University. He was called a "nigger" at a soccer game after he scored the winning goal.

During my junior year of high school, my state championship soccer team participated in a tournament in a Southern state. There was a lot of emotion surrounding the tournament because our position as region champs was pending our victory. My teammates were anticipating facing off with our rival team. Because this was such a big game, a lot of our fans decided they would travel with us. Of course our parents were there, cheering us through the matches. The score was tied with thirty-five seconds left. I had a breakaway and scored the winning goal.

After the handshakes on my way back to the locker room, I remembered walking past some of our opponents' fans in the stands and hearing a horrible racial slur, "You *&#@!$* nigger." I felt betrayed to a certain extent, or alienated. Here we were playing as a team, toward one common goal—to win. Yet, I was the only one of my teammates to encounter such a spiteful personal attack. I guess the person who spat out the vulgarity had to let out his frustration on someone, and since I was the "different" one on my team, I was the obvious choice. There was a pounding in my head as I walked on full of anger because I didn't know how to respond. Should I hit that man or be the "bigger person?" I chose to keep walking. However, since that day I cannot help but wonder what compelled that man who barely knew me to label me such a derogatory name.

Denise was a white student attending St. Mary's College. She was given a small insult about playing basketball in the high school cafeteria.

Although this experience isn't one of the worst I've seen, it was confusing and surprising at the time. I played varsity basketball at a high school I had just started attending and I was one of the very few white girls on the team. I had no problem with that but apparently some people did.

I was wearing my jersey because it was a game day and I went to the "other" side of the cafeteria where mostly African American students sat. A young guy who I'd never seen came up to me and asked if I played basketball. I looked down at my jersey thinking the answer was quite obvious and said yes. He said, "Well no wonder the team sucks if they're letting white girls play," and walked away. I wanted to laugh because his comment was so ridiculous, but in truth it was just sad and ignorant.

Abigail is a white student at St. Louis University. Her town was all-white and she describes the fight that occurred when the high school team played an all-African American team.

I am from an extremely small town in rural central Missouri. It is the type of town that you could leave your car running outside of the gas station and no one would touch it. It is a town that is so outdated that my grandpa still calls African Americans the "colored people." This is where I am from. I am proud but yet I feel as though I am missing out on a lot of things. If you live in this town you are either Caucasian or Caucasian.

We only have fifty people in my high school. Since we are all the same race, any interaction with a different race is unheard of. Some of the kids in my high school are too afraid to go to a city where they will see different skin colors. They look for colleges that don't have very many minorities. If they see someone of a different race there is always name calling involved.

During my junior year my school was set to play a rowdy juvenile delinquent basketball team made up of African Americans. Deep down inside I knew that our team was scared to death. This was the only interaction most of these boys had ever had with the opposite race. The whole week people bad-mouthed the boys coming to play us saying things like, "You better beat those niggers," and other unnecessary racial comments. I knew that the night was going to create a lot of heat for both teams.

Sure enough, Friday night rolled around and the boys from the other team walked off their bus and onto our gym floor. They got a lot of stares, bad looks, and name calling. I was so embarrassed. I didn't know why this had to happen. Even on the court our boys would say inappropriate things. By the end of the game, the other team was tired of hearing it. A player from the other team ended up getting in a fight with a player from my school. They were both thrown out of the game. Let's just say in my senior year we didn't play them again and I doubt ever will.

It is sad to say that I don't have many good or bad racial experiences. It is bad that the only experience I have is a ridiculous name-calling fight that never needed to exist. I want to broaden my culture and hope to mix some of other people's cultures with mine while I am at college. Hopefully I will be successful; so far I am.

Karl was a black Hispanic who attended Howard University. He had to learn how to deal with racial slurs while playing hockey.

In high school, I was the only minority on our hockey team in a Midwest state and one of three minorities in the entire league. Because of this, I was the target of many racial slurs. I truly believe that while I played, I heard every derogatory term used for black or Mexican people. In addition, I was almost always the player that the other team wanted to try to take out. Part of this was because I was one of the best players in the league and the other part was because of my skin color.

When I first started playing in elementary school, I did not deal with these racist remarks very well. I would often lash out and want to fight the person who called me one of these names. This was unproductive because I would always end up leaving my team shorthanded by getting a penalty.

The thing that always interested me about it was that these racial slurs began at an early age. I started playing hockey when I was ten. I was amazed that other ten-year-olds knew so many racial slurs. I came to the conclusion that many of them learned this behavior from their parents.

After a while, I learned how to deal with these racial slurs and not let them affect me as much. My mother would always explain to me that by reacting, I was doing exactly what they wanted me to do. I learned to use the hatred of others to help my team and me. When players would go out of their way to hurt me, they would take themselves out of the game. Instead of concentrating on the game, they were thinking of a way to hurt me. Also, I learned to talk back in order to fuel their anger, and in turn, give my team an advantage.

In high school, I had to deal with racism on a greater level than when I was in elementary school. In addition to being discriminated against by players on opposing teams, I now had to deal with fans, coaches, and even referees at times. At the games, fans often yelled racial slurs at me. The parent of a player on my team once had to sit on the opposing team's side of the stands for a game. He told me that he was appalled at the flurry of racial remarks. In addition, upon going to my car after a game, I found the word "nigger" written across my window with shaving cream.

The racial harassment and discrimination was not limited to players and fans. It also included coaches and referees. In one game, the coach of the opposing team and I were engaged in a verbal exchange during a stoppage of play. During this exchange, I distinctly remember him telling me to go back where I came from. Another time, an opposing coach stated, "this isn't basketball."

With referees, I do not recall any of them using a racial slur. However, they often looked the other way when I was the subject of racism. In one game, a player and I were pushing each other until the referee came in to separate us. While the referee was in between us, the player called me a racial slur. In Illinois hockey, a racial slur is supposed to yield immediate ejection from the game and a thirty-day suspension. When the player said this, I told the referee, "I know you just heard that." He looked at me like he did not care. The player did not even receive a penalty.

Dwayne was a black student at Howard University. Initially, he was not allowed to be on the all-star baseball team even though he was one of the best players.

When I was thirteen I played baseball in a small town in California. I was in the youngest age grouping. Even so, I led all four age groups in batting average. I had the highest on-base percentage and the most hits. Yet, I did not make one of the all-star teams. Although the coach for one of the teams told me I was on the team before the season ended, the final roster for the all-star team did not indicate so.

Although I had mild racist encounters before this, I feel this one has made the biggest impact on my life because it made me realize that even being the best isn't good enough for a black male in America.

Three seasons later I played for my district American Legion team. At the end of that season I led the entire state of California with the highest batting average of .590, and I was still not selected to the all-star team until another player came off and I was called on as a replacement. On all of the teams I played on, I was the only black. There were about nine other black players on other teams where I played that were not selected to an all-star team despite having worthy stats.

Dennis was a white student from Villanova. His father was accused of racism because he did not give a black player enough playing time during a basketball game.

I had played on an all-star basketball team at the end of the regular season and was on a team with a majority of black teammates. My dad was the coach of the team and we were expected to win the tournament because we had such great players. I started at point guard and the rest of the starting lineup was my black teammates. It was a great experience and we had a great run in the tournament.

Two years later my dad coached the all-star team for my brother's year and the experience was different. The team was not as talented and also was not as racially diverse. I went to the games where the black parents sat on one side and the white parents on the other side. There was a lot of fighting within the team and ultimately they failed to get very far in the tournament. After the tournament, a parent of one of the black players approached my dad and berated him with racial remarks. He confronted him for only playing the white kids on the team. This was in front of my mother, brother and me. It was the first real taste of race relations that we ever saw.

The following week a letter was sent to the city from the black parent saying that my dad was a racist and should never be allowed to be around children again. I was in tears that someone would think such a thing. The man used race as the reason the team didn't play well. Finally, one of our family friends (who was black) had to approach the man because he was demanding action from the city. Our family friend told the man that my dad was not a racist; that two years earlier he had an all-black lineup, and two years ago he didn't play any of the white kids on the team. The man didn't believe this was true but had no choice.

This was the first time that an issue involving race happened in my life. It was an awful experience made more so because I knew what this man was saying was a complete lie. I was always brought up not to even look at race as being an issue. I went to a very diverse high school and had black friends as well as white friends and never thought of race as something that would affect relationships.

Looking back on it now, the whole incident was ridiculous. We have various friends who are black and have never had any race related problems with any of them. We are a type of family that does not look at race as being an issue; instead we look at people as being just that—human.

Tina was a white student at Villanova. When she was twelve, the coach of the opposing softball team yelled a racial epitaph at her black teammate's parent.

When I was twelve I was a member of a traveling softball team in New Jersey. We had only two nonwhite athletes—Judy was Puerto Rican and Tiffany was black. With only these two minority players, however, our team was the most diverse in the league.

The fact that our team was so racially one-sided, in my opinion, never really affected anyone affiliated with the program. The players and their families were a welcome and integral part of our lineup. Tiffany's father was one of the most active fathers. He was always willing to help out at practice and never missed a game. In addition, Tiffany's mother died from cancer the year before, and I think Tiffany's father saw sports as a healthy diversion and an opportunity to bond with his daughter through their difficult time.

On our last home game, Tiffany was up to bat when the umpire called a ball that probably should have been a strike. It was the seventh inning and a strike out would have ended the game and given our opponent the win. Their coach got off the bench to argue with the umpire's call. The discussion did not go as the coach would have liked and voices were raised, turning the argument into a shouting match. After a few minutes of this ordeal, the spectators on our team's side, including Tiffany's dad, started to join in. This shouting consisted of mostly "boos" and "just let them play" chiming in from the bleachers.

Tiffany's dad was standing up and yelling the generic "let them play," nothing different than the rest, when the opposing manager turned his head, pointed directly to him, and said, "Somebody shut that fucking nigger up." At that, the entire park came to a hush, no one moved and everyone turned to see how Tiffany's dad would react to such a blatant and powerful statement. I still recall the look on his face as if far more than words had just been hurled at him. I had heard that word before that night, but never directed at a person I was so close to, and never with the magnitude and seriousness the coach obviously put behind it.

In addition, I remember Tiffany's reaction. She looked to her father and she began to uncontrollably weep. I think she was more shocked than anything else, although we never really discussed this situation after that night.

The opposing coach was immediately ejected from the game and the park, and the game was stopped. They forfeited the win to our team, but the night would not be remembered as a victory.

I think this memory has stayed fresh in my mind for so long because of both the force and seriousness in that coach's demeanor, and because of how insignificant and menial the situation surrounding the incident had been. If the outcome of a twelve-year-old's softball game could evoke such fervent emotions and hatred in a man, those feelings and emotions had obviously been boiling within in him for years. That day will always stay with me, constantly reminding me of the power of words and that hate may be expressed from anyone with the smallest of provocation.

Adam was a white student at Salisbury State University. When he was playing soccer, he inadvertently called an opposing player a "nigga."

I was in ninth grade, living near Washington D.C. at the time. I was playing goalie and a black player slid into me. I happen to be a white male, and I said something without taking either of these things into account. I said "damn nigga." I said it referring to the uncalled for tackle that almost knocked me off my feet. At this time in my life I was going through a stage where I thought I was a gangster, and for the most part spoke like one. I guess the word "nigga" was used very loosely by both whites and blacks at the time, and I think it was referred to as country grammar.

Upon hearing what I said, the black player started yelling that I had just called him a "nigger," and was telling the referee and his parents on the sidelines. The referee, without hearing what I said, decided a red card was appropriate for the language. The parents on the sidelines were livid and were cheering and yelling things back at me. The parents of the other team happened to be mostly black, but the worst part was, so were most of the parents of my team. Players on the other team were telling me to call my own players a "nigger" too. It was an awful situation that I had gotten myself into and I was embarrassed beyond belief.

After that I made a real conscious effort to stop using the word, nonracially, or otherwise. As I look back on the situation I realize that I was very wrong to think it was not a big deal. It was a terrible thing I said and it has changed the way I still talk today.

Carlos was born in Argentina and was attending the University of California at Santa Barbara. He was often made fun of when he played on the water polo team.

I came to the United States of America when I was ten. Like many migrant families, we came to the United States because it is the land of opportunities.

Unlike many third world countries, if one truly wants to succeed here in America, one truly can. When I started attending school in the United States, I was in elementary school. I was put in all the ESL (English as a Second Language) classes. Eventually I picked up the language rather quickly, like most kids usually do.

In Argentina I used to be in a swim club, so when I got to high school I decided to give the men's water polo team a try. I did not know that water polo is a predominantly white male sport. I was shocked and devastated to hear what some of my peers called me when I walked out to the deck. The most common nickname that I heard everyday till my junior year was "beaner." The seniors started most of the jokes. They used to tell me "Run! Run! Run! La migra is coming! La migra is coming!" "La migra" is the immigration police.

One day we were going to play an away game. We passed a strawberry field and the white kids on the bus saw the Latinos cultivating the land. There was always that asshole that needed to make a loud comment. "Do you want us to stop by and say hi to your parents?"

I also felt racism from the coaches. I remember that my assistant coach played kids that were not as talented as me. He always saw me as the Latino kid who was not going to make it. Well, now I play Division I Water Polo for my university. This goes to show that people can overcome obstacles.

8

Service and Shopping

Many of the initial incidents of the Civil Rights Movement were sparked over unequal access to services. Rosa Park's refusal to give up her seat on the bus to a white passenger led to the Montgomery Bus Boycott. Similarly, the Greensboro sit-in at a Woolworth's lunch counter in 1960 led to sit-ins throughout the South. Eventually, the Civil Rights Act of 1964 would provide that "all persons shall be entitled to the full and equal enjoyment of the goods, services facilities, privileges, advantages, and accommodations of any place of public accommodation."

Although the signs over water fountains that read, "whites only" have disappeared, discrimination in services still occurs. There is research that shows both white and black clerks are often more friendly when dealing with a customer of their own race (McCormick and Kinloch 1986). However, in this chapter discrimination is not just white on black. Daniell, who is black, is passed up by black cab drivers and Kathy, who is black, describes how whites were discriminated against at a restaurant she was in. There are also the more classic examples of racism such as when Daniel and Elroy are given substandard service at a white-run restaurant.

Shopping while black (SWB) is similar to its cousin, driving while black (DWB). The chapter on policing provides a thorough review of the literature on racial profiling in general. Nevertheless, in both cases, blacks are profiled as perpetrators of crime (see Gabbidon 2003). Birzer and Smith-Mahdi (2006) describe how many African Americans often have feelings of anger, frustration, and depression upon being watched constantly while shopping. Shannon describes this experience while shopping at the mall as she was followed around by security and later forced to go to the security office as she states, "I felt so humiliated that they embarrassed me in front of everyone. I was so upset that I started crying." Other researchers suggest many victims of SWB adopt such coping strategies as withdrawal, resigned acceptance, verbal or physical confrontation, and legal action (Williams, Henderson, and Harris 2001).

A survey of African Americans conducted in the mid 1990s showed that 86 percent of African Americans believed they had been treated differently in retail stores because of their race. Many times African Americans may not always be treated as criminals but may receive poor service, denial of a chance to purchase a product, discouragement, or actual verbal and/or physical attacks. However, these experiences are not limited to just African Americans. Carla, a Hispanic student describes her experience as her family received poor service while shopping for a wedding present.

Advocates of profiling argue that it is appropriate to consider past experiences and information about known offenders in order to determine behavioral and demographic factors that can be applied to a population of offenses or offenders (Dabney, Dugan, Topalli, and Hollinger 2006). In fact, Dabney et al. (2006) find that it is often difficult and nearly impossible for observers to resist the implicit cultural stereotypes that shape their views of individuals. As seen in other chapters, Arab Americans, South Asians, Latinos, and Jews are also the victims of racial profiling, often being questioned and detained, since the events of 9/11 (Williams, Henderson, Harris 2001).

In this chapter we have stories of minorities in stores being followed, accused of shoplifting, falsely blamed for making a mess, and stereotyped as being poor. Two of the more interesting essays are from store clerks who were accused by shoppers of being the perpetrators of SWB.

Daniel was a white student at Villanova. He describes how he was discriminated against at a Korean restaurant because his girlfriend was Korean.

I have had many different experiences with discrimination, but one that most recently comes to mind is an experience that I had in Cheltenham, on the outskirts of Philadelphia. I had been dating a Korean woman for some time, and wanted to take her out for her twentieth birthday. Cheltenham, being a very Korean part of the Northeast Philadelphia area, was a prime location to enjoy authentic Korean food. From the moment that my girlfriend and I entered that restaurant, it was immediately evident that the patrons of this restaurant did not appreciate the interracial aspect of our relationship. The people inside the restaurant stared at us in disgust. It was further amplified as the waitress approached us. She assumed that my girlfriend was fluent in Korean and was dumbfounded when my girlfriend did not know the Korean language.

The wait staff was disrespectful. They showed relative disinterest in their service to us, yet the same wait staff paid very close attention to the rest of the patrons. I found this interesting because all the other patrons were speaking fluent Korean and received perfect service. This discrimination and disgust in our treatment by the wait staff was purely based on the color of my skin and my physical attributes. Because I was a white man dating a Korean woman, the patrons of the restaurant and the server staff were very cold to us. I was discriminated against based on assumptions; they thought that I should not be dating a Korean woman and that I had no place in a Korean restaurant.

Daniel was a black student at Howard University. When eating at a restaurant in Indiana, the waitress placed all forty blacks on the same bill, even though they were in many separate parties.

I am from Gary, Indiana, which is in Northwest Indiana. Things are so segregated to the point that the residents cannot even recognize the segregation themselves.

On a particular evening during my senior year of high school, my night at a coronation ball had just ended. My friends and I were hungry, so we made our way to X to eat. X is in Merrillville, just five minutes away. It just so happened that the majority of the people at the coronation ball just happened to be at X. Of course, some of us were acquaintances, so naturally we spoke with one another. The restaurant was populated with approximately forty African Americans eating dinner. We all arrived as separate parties, enjoying our own private time.

As people were preparing to leave, unbeknownst to us, the waiter put every African American in that restaurant on the same bill. They identified us all as the same party, even though "we" were spread out all over the restaurant. Despite us debating with the manager and trying to prove that we were separate, we were forced to all pay on the same bill. We had no choice; they called the police on us all. They threatened to arrest us all if we did not pay. So to avoid arrest, we paid the entire bill—even extra from our own pockets to cover everyone else. To top it off, we got pulled over. To this day I do not understand why that cop had his gun drawn for two teenage boys and a girl.

Danielle was a black student attending the University of Maryland. She was passed up numerous times by minority cab drivers.

Typically, when discussing racism or bad racial experiences, people tend to have this preconceived idea that the situation is white versus black, or more recently, white versus minority. Rarely do people consider the situation to be black versus black or minority versus minority. Having said that, I am a twenty-one-year-old black female. I think I look fairly average, meaning that I do not look intimidating, nor do I look overly innocent. Having said that, my worst racial experience occurred about two years ago. One Saturday or Sunday during the middle of the day I caught the Metro to Georgetown to walk around a little and window shop. By the time I was ready to go home, I had bought more than a few things, it was dark, and I was tired of walking around with all of my bags. Initially, I was going to take the Metro back home, since that is how I got there in the first place, but because I was so tired and had so many bags, I decided to take a cab.

Because I was in Georgetown, I thought it would be easy to hail a cab down there. I stood at the intersection of Wisconsin and M Street for over thirty minutes attempting to hail a cab, but they kept picking up white people. At first I did not notice what was happening to me, especially because most of the cab drivers appeared to be of African or Middle-Eastern descent. It actually took me awhile to realize it. I decided to walk toward the Metro, thinking that I would be able to hail one down on the way. I did not realize I was being discriminated against until I actually reached the Foggy Bottom Metro. I noticed a cab driver that pulled over and was getting out of his car. I walked towards him to ask him if he was on or off duty, and when he noticed me walking toward him he quickly hopped back in his cab and pulled off. I stood there shocked and hurt, watching as he stopped a block later and picked up a group of white people.

What hurt most was that all of the cab drivers who avoided me were minorities. Usually, when talking about discrimination, it is expected of people outside of your own race. What I realized is this: To be a black American is to be trapped in a no-man's land. The battle against racism has not been won. Unfortunately, it has done so much psychological damage to blacks from generation to generation that we subconsciously discriminate against each other.

Elroy was a black student at Howard University. He was told that a restaurant was closed when in fact it was open.

One June day in Michigan I had major back surgery and I was not able to go many places. I asked my brother to take me for a ride. We got hungry and he suggested a restaurant that he wanted to try.

The restaurant looked like a hole in the wall, but knowing that my brother likes to patronize small businesses, I kept my mouth shut. When we pulled in I looked through the door to see if I could see anything but I could not. When we got to the door we saw a closed sign. This sign was not there before. My brother and I checked the hours of operation. The sign said that the restaurant was open from 8:00 a.m. until 9:00 p.m. It was only 3:00 in the afternoon. My brother tried to give them the benefit of the doubt. He told me that maybe I just didn't see the sign when we pulled up. My reply was if they are closed for business then why are there customers inside? As we were pulling out of the parking lot another car pulled in. Inside the car was a white family. We waited to see what would happen. Sure enough, the white family was allowed in! We tried to go back but as we approached the door, both of us saw a white lady look us in the eyes and place the sign back in the door.

This experience really hurt me because I thought that we had put that type of outright racism in our past. I felt like I had stepped back in time to when African Americans had to use separate bathrooms, water fountains, and doors. More than that, I was hurt because my brother was hurt. All he wanted to do was support a small business that looked like it was not doing too well. I never took any action such as alerting the media or calling the Better Business Bureau (which did, along with other courses of possible action, cross my mind), because I did not want my brother to have to keep reliving an experience that made both of us feel humiliated, angry, and discriminated against. The only good thing that came out of this was my brother and me not being blind to the fact that racism still exists. It is not as silent as everyone would like to think.

Kathy was a black student attending Howard University. She offers a different twist on racism in restaurant service.

I, along with my mostly African American debate team and our African American coach, entered a Denny's restaurant in New Jersey. We were traveling with a neighboring high school's debate team, which was mostly Portuguese and white. By the time we had parked our car and entered the restaurant, the other school had already been seated at their table. We sat down right next to the other school and immediately got menus and water glasses from the waitress. After a while, the black owner greeted us and wished us a good meal and a successful tournament. We ordered our meals and received our food immediately.

After a while we noticed that our companion team had not gotten their water or meals since they had sat down. We asked the other coach about the situation and she informed us that the waitress had left to get their water a half-hour ago. She hadn't returned yet. As the other coach motioned for the waitress to come over to their table, it was clear that she was ignoring them. The owner was also greeting every other table with black consumers and ignored the whites. After about ten minutes of waving, the waitress brought glasses of water to the white group without an apology for the wait. When they asked to order their food, she rudely gestured with her hand for them to wait.

We witnessed this blatant disrespect and racism from our table nearby. I sat and listened to the other blacks around us joke about the white group. They spoke of this Denny's as the only black restaurant around that treated whites like "blacks were treated all the time." It took about forty-five minutes for the white team to get their menus for ordering after the waitress brought water glasses.

By this time, the coach for the white team was very upset and preparing to leave. As soon as the other team got up to leave, the waitress came over to take their orders. Because of the late hour and the limited businesses around, the hungry group sat down to eat anyway. By the time the food arrived for the white team, my black team had eaten and sat for about five minutes talking. We discussed the blatant racism that was taking place and how it impacts people worldwide. As we left together, the other coach informed us that their food was very cold when they got it. He also said that their soda glasses seemed smudgy and dirty.

That weekend was the first time I had experienced blacks being openly racist against whites in a place of business. Many times we hear about Denny's giving black patrons a hard time, but the only racism I can speak of occurred on behalf of black professionals against decent people who happened to be white. It felt very awkward being in the majority for the first time, witnessing the oppression of another group of people. The experience did teach me a very important lesson though, about how so many people who did not agree with slavery and the Holocaust did not speak out. I felt strangely comfortable and at ease being with the majority. It would have taken courage to step up. It's easy to say that you would "do this and that" when you are on the outside looking in, but it doesn't always work out that way in reality.

Lynn was a white student attending Villanova. While working as a hostess she had to deny seating to two black men. She feels bad that they might have thought she did it for racial reasons. What do you think she should have done?

I was working as a hostess at a seafood restaurant one particularly busy afternoon. The kitchen was all backed up. We were short on servers and we had lots of reservations. Two African American gentlemen came in and requested a table. I told them that unfortunately, due to major delays in the kitchen, we would not be able to seat them for at least an hour. They jokingly asked if special accommodations could be made for them once they noted several empty tables. I appreciated their good humor and I assured them I could not seat them for some time. (I didn't add the information about being short on servers or having reservations.) They moved off to the side to discuss whether or not to wait, and I attended to the next couple in line. This couple was white, and they had reservations. I felt the eyes of the two men upon me, and so I made a big show of crossing the name of this white couple off of the reservation list. I quickly grabbed some menus and left the hostess stand to seat them, noting the unhappy looks on the faces of the two men.

When I returned to the reservation stand, the gentlemen were still standing there, but they were not talking. They stared at me with disgust and frustration. I didn't know what to do. I had tried to make it as clear as possible that the only reason the other couple was seated was because they had reservations. They continued to stare and I pretended to be busy. Silently, they turned and left.

I felt guilty and upset. I knew the situation at the restaurant, and I know I couldn't seat anyone at that time, regardless of race. My heart knew I had done no wrong. Yet I was unsettled, certain that the two men had walked away with the wrong impression. I thought back to what else I could have done. Should I have said that the other couple was seated because they had reservations? But, weren't they watching when I opened the large, noticeable reservation book? Should I have stared back instead of pretending to be busy? Should I have assured them I wasn't racist? Why would they or should they believe me? They probably thought I was the worst kind of racist— the kind who smiled and acted respectfully in their faces—yet refused to seat them and acted in a racist manner behind their backs. I imagined them telling their families about the incident over the dinner table that evening. I also imagined that this would not be the first such conversation about a racist they encountered. How frustrating it was to think someone would view me as a member of racist society! While I had treated them as I would any other customer, they might have believed otherwise. I don't want to be a part of the problem between the races. I want to be a part of the solution, as idealistic as that sounds. I suppose all I can do is work toward greater equality and understanding, even if that means making mistakes along the way.

Kimberly was a white student attending Villanova. She was accused of being a racist when she asked a black man to leave his backpack at the register when she worked at a record store.

I grew up in the suburbs of St. Louis, Missouri. St. Louis is a highly segregated city and the part of the suburbs where I live is predominantly white and upper middle class. Growing up, I witnessed whites around me express racism through racist jokes and side comments, but nothing was overt. I never experienced racism against me because I am white. However, this changed one summer when I took a job at a local music store during high school. This experience filled me with a lot of emotions ranging from frustration to anger.

Our music store had a problem with theft of CDs. The manager enacted a policy to prevent stealing. He asked all his employees, including me, to ask the customers who entered the store with bags or backpacks to please keep the bags up at the register.

One day it was my turn to stand near the door and take the customer's bags. This particular afternoon two black males that looked like they were in their early twenties or late teens walked into the store and both of them had backpacks. I said to them, "I'm sorry, but I have to keep your backpacks up at the register while you shop. You can pick them up before you leave, but its store policy." One of the men was really nice about it and gave me his bag and walked in ready to shop around. The other started getting really mad and starting yelling and cursing at me. He was saying, "not all black people steal," and that I was a "little blonde-haired girl that had never left her suburban bubble." He went on shouting and cursing at me for a couple of minutes. The manager then came over and asked him to leave the store. I gave his friend his backpack and they both left. After they left I was filled with so many different emotions. I was scared first of all because he was shouting at me and was so rude. It caught me completely off guard and the hostile confrontation made me very nervous. I was also very angry. That man had made me feel like I was being prejudiced against him for doing my job. I was also angry that he thought he could stereotype my whole life by what I looked like and where I worked. He thought he knew enough about me to call me sheltered, racist, and ignorant.

Looking back on it now, a lot or these same emotions come to mind. I still feel frustrated with this man because I felt stereotyped, disrespected, and humiliated. Maybe he has been confronted with situations like this before because he is black. That was not the case when I dealt with him though. Perhaps he took out his anger toward racism on me, but it's still no excuse to assume anything about my intentions.

I also think this experience stirred up the reaction in me that it did because I had never experienced anything like it before. I got a tiny glimpse into what it must be like for a black person to experience racism.

Shannon was a black student at Howard University. She was followed around at a store in a mall and finally forced to go to the security office.

I was born, raised and am currently residing in Washington, D.C., which I consider being a major part of the United States mixing bowl. I have always thought that racial tension will eventually decrease in the United States. However, this is not true for me personally, because I always encounter racial tension while shopping.

The floor salesman, the manager, a cashier, or even a customer often follows me around the store. Sometimes they follow me discreetly but most times they make it apparent what they are doing. I have no idea why anybody would follow me around the store because I have never given anyone a reason to be suspicious. I guess that they choose to stereotype me because of the color of my skin or the way I dress when I go shopping. Maybe it's the stores that I choose to shop in, which are relatively expensive. When I go shopping, I usually wear sweat pants, sneakers, and a t-shirt because I like to be comfortable. The worse shopping experience that still upsets me is when I went shopping at a local mall in the metropolitan area. I was shopping in a store called X. I was not looking for anything in particular; I was just browsing. The second I walked into the store all eyes were on me. The manager came from the back of the store and stood by the door. One of the two females from behind the cash register started to follow me around the store while the other one watched my every move. It upset me even more because she didn't even pretend like she was doing something else like folding clothes. She let it be known that her mission was to follow me around the store. She stood directly behind me, staring at me while I looked at the sizes and prices of each clothing article. I tried not to let it bother me because I wasn't doing anything wrong but I couldn't take it anymore, so I asked her if there was a problem. She said, "No, I'm just doing my job." Then I asked her if her job was to follow me around and she responded, "Oh, that's just the store's policy." When I turned around to look at the price of the white dress behind me, I realized that the cashier was not the only person following me. In amazement, I realized that a customer had been following me as well. I finally got so fed up that I left the store only to walk a short distance before the mall security approached me and told me I had to go with them. When we got to the security room they explained that they were told that I had stolen some merchandise. That was impossible because I was followed around the store the whole time. They searched my bags and checked my receipts and found that everything was paid for. They released me and all they had to say was that they were sorry for the inconvenience. I felt so humiliated that they embarrassed me in front of everyone. I was so upset that I started crying. I sat in my car for an hour and a half before I drove home because I was so upset. Since that day I have never returned to an X store in any mall.

Tyra was a black student at Howard University. She was accused of shoplifting at a store in the mall.

My worst racial experience took place two Christmases ago. I was walking through a mall in Philadelphia with a few of my friends and we decided to go into a clothing store. A white store associate began to follow us. At the time we did not think she was following us; we just thought that she was making her rounds throughout the store.

My friends and I kept looking around, not thinking much of it. All of a sudden the lady walked back to the area where we were with the security guard. She walked over to me and told me to empty out my bag. I asked her why I should empty out my bag and she told me that she saw me put something in it. Now I know that I did not put anything in my bag and my friends knew that I did not steal anything. Even the security guard was looking at the lady with a puzzled face. There were other people in the store that could have been stealing but she was focused on me.

After I argued with her I finally dumped all of my things out of the bag on the floor because I did not want to be bothered. When she saw that nothing was in my bag, she didn't even give an apology for humiliating me in front of the other customers. After I left the store I felt hurt. Throughout my entire life, up until that point, I had never been accused of anything, and to know that I was accused only because of the color of my skin shocked me even more. I knew that racism still exists, but I always assumed that by shopping in a diverse city like Philadelphia, there would be a lack of racism. I guess that you cannot always screen the people that are hired for these companies.

Molly was a white student at New York University. She had to decide how to react when another white woman made a racist comment in a handbag shop.

At a local outlet mall, I stepped into a designer handbag shop. The retail space was small and the number of customers was in the single digits. With so few of us, it was easy to assess each other. I noticed a pair of poised, nicely dressed, and coifed black women. It made me feel self-conscious in my t-shirt and shorts; they were really quite stunning.

As I returned to browsing, a white woman in a pink terry-cloth strapless romper stood beside me. I don't recall if she told me she worked in a convenience store or I somehow decided she did, but she seemed out of place in store with that level of consumer goods.

She then half remarked, half whispered to me that the store clerks should "watch" the black women, insinuating that they might shoplift, despite the fact that they were both toting expensive handbags at the time. I was completely floored. Here was a woman I could only describe as low income suggesting that the well-put-together black women should be viewed with suspicion.

It was the first time I recall being directly confronted with racial prejudice. I looked at her in disbelief and finally stammered that I didn't agree with her. I guess she thought I didn't understand so she reworded her prior statements while gesturing to the women. This time, as the anger welled-up in my throat, I told her that she was way off base and I didn't appreciate her hateful comments.

Rebuffed, she looked at me like I was the one speaking inappropriately, and walked away. At this point my head was reeling with exasperation. I wanted to confront this woman further and criticize her own questionable appearance. Then I thought maybe she was just putting up a smokescreen so that she could steal a bag, which seemed much more likely than the other two women.

My interest in shopping dissipated but I didn't know what to do. I waited until the black women left the shop and then reported the incident to the store manager. It totally ruined my day.

Since that time, there have been a handful of racial incidents I have experienced. Now I do not hesitate to express my disapproval, at which point most people start back-peddling.

Carla was a Hispanic student attending the University of California at Santa Barbara. Her family was treated poorly when they went shopping for a wedding present.

Even though I was born here in California, I am Mexican. I grew up in the Central Valley of California where the majority of the population is Mexican.

When I was about fifteen, my family was invited to attend Heather's wedding. Heather is the daughter of my dad's boss. My dad's boss is very wealthy and his family is accustomed to having the best of the best. In my area, the most expensive store is Gottschalks and that is where Lucrecia registered for her bridal registry. My family never shopped there because we could not afford it, but we had to go in there for Heather's wedding present. My parents decided to go buy Lucrecia's present when my mother was finished working for the day on a Wednesday, which is my dad's day off from work.

On the way to the store, my mom told us to behave at the store and not to touch anything because she did not want any of the store employees mad at us. At the moment my parents, my two sisters, and three brothers walked into the store, we had three pairs of eyes looking at us nonstop till we got to the customer service desk. I felt as if they kept their eyes on us thinking we would steal something. There was no one at the customer service desk so we waited for a sales associate or manager to get there. Then a white sales associate appeared from the back. She made a weird facial expression and said, "Maria I cannot take care of these people. You come and see what they want because I do not understand or speak Spanish." Her expression told me something like, "What are these people doing here? They cannot afford to shop here." Fortunately my mom knows English and responded to the sales associate with these words, "You could take care of me because I can understand, speak, and write in English." The sales associate's jaw just dropped and she was unspeakable. Then, to top it off, they only printed the page with the gifts that were under thirty dollars. When my mom questioned this, they told her that they did not think we would be able to afford anything more expensive. At that point, I was really upset and could not believe what was going on. The sales associate asked if we wanted the rest of the list printed, I told her, "No thank you. I think we will just leave and I will make sure Heather knows the type of treatment we just received. I will ask her to remove her gift registry from here."

As we walked out of the store my mom promised never to step a foot in that store again. The way we were treated was unfair and unjustifiable. Yes, maybe my family and most Mexicans could not afford to shop there. Even if that was the case, every customer should be treated with respect even if that customer will not buy something. That was my worst racial experience and I will never forget it.

Doris was a Hispanic student attending the University of California at Santa Barbara. A white customer harassed her when she used a Spanish phrase. What do you think she should have done?

A few years ago, I used to work at a department store back home in Fresno, California. One customer was an older woman, possibly in her late sixties or early seventies. She couldn't see very well, could barely carry herself, and had an expression of discomfort on her face. She walked over to the jewelry counter. I approached and asked her if she needed help. She asked to see some earrings; I showed them to her. While she was critiquing the high price, a colleague of mine from the shoe department came over. He said something to me in Spanish and I replied with one word, which I cannot remember. The short conversation had absolutely nothing to do with her. She became furious and said: "I don't know why they allow those people to speak that language in this country. This is America! People should speak English." My colleague and I looked at each other, frozen. We said nothing and she walked away.

To this day I cannot come to a conclusion about why I did not reply to her absurd reaction. Those who know me well can confirm that I am an outspoken person and that I am an advocate of human and racial rights. This is why I find it so hard to believe that I said nothing. I was in the workplace and I consider myself a professional employee. I understand that by working for a well-known department store I am representing them and I should do it well. However, as a Mexican American, I understand the hardships my people have been through. I know the history of discrimination that has taken place in this country. So how could I, being such an outspoken person and supporter of rights, not have said anything? I think that question will forever haunt me.

When the customer left, my colleague returned to his department. I thought I was going to break into tears. I felt as if I had let all my people down. I didn't stand up for them when I was supposed to and it hurt. It hurt then and it continues to hurt today. All those years Mexicans were subordinated and most people in those times didn't have enough knowledge of their rights and therefore would not stand up for themselves. But this is the 2000s! I am a Chicana of this era and I know my rights! But why didn't I say anything to her? I used to make myself think it was because she was older and I didn't want to disrespect her. My parents never taught me that. But, she didn't think twice about disrespecting me!

I came to the conclusion that those were all excuses I used to try and justify what I can now diagnose as fear. This was possibly because I didn't know what would happen with my job; I didn't know if I would get fired or written up. Now when I think about it, I know I couldn't have been fired for that. I would not have cared because I didn't need the job; it was just for extra spending money.

I was only sixteen then, and now I have grown and matured substantially. I like to live life without regrets, but I cannot avoid wanting to go back and say all the things I should have—the truth! My parents taught me well but I have taught myself that no matter what the price, I will never let anything like this happen again.

Caitlin attended the University of California at Santa Barbara. She is half-white and half-Mexican. When she was a sales clerk, a black woman accused her of following her.

I once had a very confusing encounter with an African American woman. I have not been able to shake the memory. At the time of the event, I was fifteen years old and working at a Family Fun Center at the harbor. I was working in the gift shop and one of my duties was dusting and cleaning the shelves.

An African American woman and her three sons came in to look around. They had been browsing for some time and out of habit I found myself straightening the shelves and folding the shirts. Focused on my busy work, which had landed me at the back of the gift shop, I glanced up to notice the woman was standing at the register counter waiting for me to ring her items up. I headed to the front of the shop and began totaling up her items as usual when she confronted me. She said that she did not appreciate me following her and her sons around the shop and that she was angry. Shocked that she felt I was profiling her family as ones likely to steal, I found myself hard for words. Playing back my previous actions in my head, I immediately tried to reassure the woman that I was sorry that I offended her. I then proceeded to explain my daily duties to her.

However, even with my apologies she left angry. Immediately afterward, I was confused, and began to ponder two things. First, I felt extremely bad that I had hurt someone unintentionally, but I questioned whether she had overreacted. I couldn't imagine that my behavior could be interpreted in her way. Yet, could I have been watching her family without realizing it? Or even further, did I watch them any more than I would anybody else? I would like to say no.

I am half-Mexican and half-anglo and was brought up in a Mexican household. However, my appearance shows little of my Mexican ethnicity. My background allows me to see racial discrimination taking place from another perspective. If anything, the encounter with the woman educated me and served as a reminder of the reality of racism.

Sarah was a Hispanic student at the University of California at Santa Barbara. A Hispanic cashier accused her of shoplifting.

I am a Salvadorian American. All my life Latinos have surrounded me. I have never experienced racial discrimination until I came to Santa Barbara.

I love to go shopping at thrift stores, and my freshman year I decided to go to State Street. From the moment I went inside the thrift store, the Mexican cashier brought attention to me and asked me to give her my backpack. I did not think anything of it, so I gladly gave her my bag. I then continued with my shopping and I found a turquoise shirt that I thought would look adorable on me. I proceeded to go to the cashier to pay for it. She grabbed the shirt and said, "This shirt doesn't have a price tag, why did you take the tag off? This is delicate clothing, are you trying to get this shirt for a lower price, or steal it?"

When she asked me if I was trying to steal the shirt, at first I felt very confused and I told her, "I didn't know. The shirt was like that when I got it." I started to feel like it was my fault that she had accused me of trying to steal a shirt, but I still wanted that shirt, so I asked her "Is there any way you can find out the price?" She angrily told me "go to the back, they'll tell you how much it is." I was told it was three dollars, and I proceeded to the front and paid for it. When I left the store, I started to analyze what had just happened and I started to feel upset.

I realized that from the moment I stepped into the thrift store and the cashier asked me to give her my backpack, she had already profiled me as a thief. I knew this because she did not ask my friend for her backpack and she was next to me. I am a dark-skinned Latina, and that day I was dressed in second-hand clothing. My friend is Latina as well, but she is very light-skinned and does not have an accent; she could pass for an Anglo person. It made me wonder what, except for the color of my skin and my race, made the cashier ask me for my bag and not my friend.

I was embarrassed and upset that I was accused of stealing a three dollar shirt, but what disturbed me even more was that a Latina woman, the cashier, would accuse me. It shocked me that a woman who might have been discriminated against because of her race would do the same to me.

Mary Jane was a white student who attended the University of California at Santa Barbara. She observed how a fellow clerk at Staples, who was black, was insulted by a customer.

I am a white woman and have lived a sheltered life. I lived in a small town in Ohio where everyone was white. I moved to a small town in Northern California where the two main ethnicities were white and Mexican. I got used to the different colors walking around my school, but nothing prepared me for college. In college, there are different types of people everywhere. They come in all shapes and colors. However, that did not bother me. I treated everyone the same.

I got a job at Staples. I have made friends with everyone I work with. One girl in particular, Porsche, is African American. One day an upset customer called on the phone. Porsche answered the phone and was doing everything to help the customer.

The customer thought he lost his credit card. That can be a very scary thing, so we do our best to look for the card around our registers. We looked in all the drawers and all the imprint machines. After Porsche told him we could not find the card, she asked the man what register he went to. He responded with, "There was a white girl and a black girl working. I went to the white girl because I didn't want to go to the black girl." Porsche simply replied, "I am the black girl." The man was absolutely speechless. He just said thank you and hung up the phone.

Coming from small towns, it is hard for me to understand why someone would act like that. He had no idea who he was talking to. I do not understand how he could be so inconsiderate. Porsche was offended, but she did not let it ruin her day. I, on the other hand, was in absolute shock the rest of the day.

Rosa was a Hispanic student at the University of California at Santa Barbara. She was accused of making a mess at a store when in fact some white children caused it.

I went to visit my cousins and aunt in Nevada. At one point, we went to a shop that had cute souvenirs. As we were looking around and admiring all the different things, I noticed an Anglo mother with her daughter absolutely making a mess of the store. As they walked through the store they literally left a trail of misplaced items. Once they left, the Anglo owner literally pointed me and my sisters out from the small store filled with white folks. He blamed the mess on us. I felt humiliated, vulnerable, and kept on thinking that it was unfair. Had he not seen who had made the mess? We were told to get out of the store. As my sisters and I walked out, we did not know what to say, but you could see on our faces that something wrong had happened.

My mom and cousin soon met us and we told them what happened. All I could remember was having a knot in my throat and forcing back tears. My cousin responded sympathetically, yet in a way that shocked me, with an attitude that suggested, "It happens, I know." My mom was embarrassed for us but said not to tell my father because he probably would have gone back to the store and beat up the owner. Aside from a hug and kiss from my mother, the situation was left with an unsatisfactory closure.

9

Discrimination

Long-held racist stereotypes are one of the many reasons minorities have been limited in terms of educational opportunities, economic opportunities, and living the "American Dream." While most Americans have endorsed the principles of racial equality and egalitarianism, there has been less support for racial policies targeting minorities in an effort to fulfill the goals of these principles (Krysan 2000). In this chapter white students such as Nolan write of the unfairness of policies perceived as more advantageous to minorities in university admission and scholarships.

While old-fashioned overt racist actions may be less frequent than in the past, the stereotypes associated with African Americans still have a massive effect in employment and housing. Frazer and Wiersma (2001) found in an experimental study on decision making in employment interviews, interviewers later recalled that the answers that blacks gave to interview questions were significantly less intelligent despite the fact that the interview conditions were identical. Candidates for employment who have distinct African American names are less likely to be called back for an interview (Bertrand and Mullainathan 2003) and there have been a variety of experimental studies using paired testers that document discrimination in mortgages, rental housing, and housing insurance (e.g., Turner et al. 2002). Contemporary forms of discrimination are more subtle and therefore, more challenging to detect and combat (Dovidio and Gaertner 1986). While overt forms of discrimination have declined, it has been difficult to determine the extent of covert discrimination and how it affects the lives of individuals. Likewise, measuring discrimination is equally challenging and documenting discrimination, both real and perceived, often eludes traditional survey based measures (Smith 2002). For example, numerous questionnaire studies demonstrate a positive change in whites' racial attitudes. However, experimental results show a different picture (Wittenbrink, Judd, and Park 1997). Other researchers have found that racist attitudes toward blacks are actually more prevalent than what has been revealed in survey data (Pettigrew and Meertens 1995). Discrimination is often discussed and researched as institutional discrimination against a group. For example, such discriminatory institutional practices may include zoning laws, mortgage criteria, school funding, bail, college admissions, and legal systems (Tuch and Taylor 1986; Bond and Williams 2007; Hodge, Dawkins, and Reeves 2007). In fact, as there has been a decline in overt racial prejudice it has been more difficult to detect how institutions contribute to racial inequality.

Nevertheless, while institutional discrimination is a powerful explanatory factor for socioeconomic disparities, personal or individual discrimination often has an immediate psychological effect. Individual discrimination is most strongly related to several stressors including psychological (e.g., depression), emotional, and physical stress, all of which are relevant to mental health (Taylor and Turner 2002). Michelle describes the stress her family endured after her parents were discriminated against in the workplace stating, "We had no income in the household for quite some time and it was very stressful."

Accordingly, in this chapter we see examples of minorities being discriminated against in employment at law firms, restaurants, and offices. Feagin (1991) finds that discrimination continues to be a significant problem for black professionals and indeed Caroline describes how a young, Ivy League educated, African American attorney was treated in a southern law firm stating, "The partners treated Daniel as an anomaly within their elite white corporate environment." Clay-Warner (2001) describe the discrimination experienced by African Americans is often "subtle" such as poor restaurant service. However, such forms may be more detectable than we think as indicated by the essays in the service chapter.

How does racial discrimination affect students' lives? The essays within this chapter provide a snapshot of the lasting impact of discrimination and racism and more importantly, how students cope with discrimination and racism. Wong, Eccles, and Sameroff (2003) found that a strong connection with one's racial/ethnic identity often serves to buffer the deleterious impact of discrimination. Interestingly, Phinney and Chivera (1995) find African American parents in particular are more likely than other minority parents to use a form of racial socialization to emphasize the importance of achievement and countering problems with racism. Fein and Spencer (1997) find that individuals may engage in prejudice and acts of discrimination as a way to affirm the self.

The literature clearly shows that prejudice and discrimination reveal themselves in implicit and explicit ways. Throughout these essays we learn how individuals cope with prejudice and discrimination in their lives, how it impacts them, and most importantly how it changes them.

Caroline was a white student attending Tennessee State University. In this essay she describes how her coworkers treated an African American attorney employed by the law firm where she worked.

For the past twenty years, I have worked as a legal secretary and paralegal in the largest and most prestigious law firm in Alabama and Tennessee. The recruiting process for lawyers is highly competitive and candidates who have Ivy League educations and graduate at the top of their class are favored.

Several years ago, I worked for a law firm that hired an African American associate I will call Daniel for the purpose of this paper. Daniel attended an Ivy League institution and graduated summa cum laude from college and law school with a promising future. However, this firm hired Daniel as their first, only, and "token" African American attorney. The firm did employ African Americans; however, they worked as secretarial and support staff. Southern law firms maintain strict class structures. Most lawyers I encountered view their employees as lower class citizens. While Daniel had all of the necessary qualifications as a lawyer, he did not fit into the elite social hierarchy.

The partners treated Daniel as an anomaly within their elite white corporate environment. They took Daniel to lunch and introduced him to their colleagues; yet, the manner in which they treated him and white associates was different. They offered real friendship and camaraderie only to white associates. Daniel surely felt the contradiction.

It was not just the partners who displayed this distance when working with the token black attorney. Normally, one secretary serves two attorneys. In this case, two new associates, one white and one African American, were paired with a new white secretary. Her feelings toward Daniel were obvious. The majority of the time, she seized any opportunity to refuse finishing his work. There are times in every lawyer's career, especially when sharing a secretary, that he has to search for a volunteer to do his work. In this case, Daniel had to rely on a mostly white secretarial force to help him. The whispers in the break room were deafening and brutal. Daniel was not the only attorney requesting help; he just happened to be the only African American attorney. The lack of respect was obvious. The secretarial pool accused Daniel of expecting special treatment because he was African American. He was acutely aware of these attitudes and in turn, became defensive and abrasive.

When he responded in this fashion, it was a double-edged sword. Secretaries complained, and Daniel was reprimanded by the partners. He was in a hopeless situation.

The partners assigned Daniel all of the drudge work. He was passed over for the important cases, regardless of his qualifications. I overheard conversations concerning this practice, and the reasoning was simply prejudice. Daniel was a highly qualified attorney doing the work of a paralegal purely because of the color of his skin.

I watched this phenomenon and was amazed at the blatant prejudiced opinions from my peers in the secretarial force. Conversely, the underhanded bigotry dealt to him by his peers and colleagues was much worse. He worked extremely hard, graduated summa cum laude from an Ivy League college and law school, and never received a real chance to prove himself in the workplace. The law firm used Daniel as their trophy African American to show to the world, yet within the walls of the firm, these "intelligent" men could not see past his skin color. To this young attorney's credit, he handled the racism with patience and aplomb. If his frustration boiled over, it never occurred inside the office walls. On the contrary, he seemed determined to prove his worth in an unbalanced system.

The law firm that employed both Daniel and me was a prestigious Southern firm that worked with clients and firms from New York, Boston, Atlanta, and Los Angeles. When outside firms visited our offices, their African American associates accompanied them. However, Daniel was never taken anywhere to represent our firm. The fact that there were over two hundred lawyers and only one of these lawyers was African American told the story more eloquently than I ever could.

Although I witnessed most of this treatment from the sidelines, working in this environment appalled me. Lawyers are stereotypically known for egotistical behavior, and at times that behavior enhances their job performance. In Daniel's situation, I was horrified that the ego stemmed from their racial identity and not their accomplishments. Daniel's intelligence had been proven, yet he was treated with condescension because of his race. I found it difficult to comprehend that this attitude prevailed so unashamedly in the 1990s. Despite the strides made by the Civil Rights Movement, racism and prejudice are still alive and well in the corporate business world today.

Shelly was an African American student who attended Howard University. She was denied employment at a restaurant by a black owner who said they already had too many black waitresses.

One day I applied for a job as a waitress in a trendy restaurant in downtown Washington, D.C. The head waitress seemed very pleased as she looked over my resume! She told me to come back the very next day to meet with the owner of the restaurant, who ultimately had the final say. The next day I returned to the restaurant, and the head waitress escorted me to the office of the owner.

The owner looked over my resume, and told me that I had a lot of experience and would be a good asset to any restaurant. My smile quickly turned upside down when he politely said, "I would love to hire you but right now I already have enough black girls." I couldn't believe what I just heard. I was shocked! How could anyone still be stuck in time, thinking such primitive thoughts at this day and age? How could someone allow that to pass through his lips being an African American himself? I got myself together and asked him, "Are you serious?" He replied, "Yes I'm sorry, but I already have enough black waitresses on my staff, but I wish you luck on your endeavors." I promptly left the premises after I collected my belongings.

Two months later I am still in shock over my experience! Racism is clearly plaguing society and it must stop!

Jeff was a white student attending St. Louis University. While he was in prison, he was discriminated against because he was white.

For the first sixteen years of my life I had a diverse group of friends. Although I went to a predominantly white boy's school, I thought I was an open-minded individual who judged people for who they were. I didn't judge people because of their skin color. Two years ago I made some mistakes and found myself behind bars for a short period of time.

In the movie *American History X*, there is a line that I find to be remarkably true. It is at a point in the movie where the white supremacist finds himself in jail with a black inmate. "Just remember, in here, you're the nigger." I can assure you that after being behind bars, a phrase like that cannot be any more correct.

Many of the correctional officers I interacted with were black. Honest to God, I have nothing against someone because of their skin color, but I can safely say they were prejudiced because I was white. I was looked over and passed up for many opportunities. I was not given the same privileges as others. This included simple things like an extra meal plate or five more minutes on the phone. It came down to the fact that I wasn't like them and because of this, I was turned down.

Later I realized it was because of my race that I wasn't as lucky as the prisoners of color. I was the minority and it made me so angry that I couldn't do anything about how I was being treated. In a way I guess I could say it gave me a glance of how it is in the real world outside the correctional system.

Stacy was a black student at Howard University. She was not allowed to work in the front office at her job.

I worked at a resort office in San Diego, California. It wasn't a very prestigious job, but it paid the bills. It also exposed me to one of the worst racial experiences I have had.

After working there for a few months booking timeshare appointments, I wanted to be a front desk receptionist and clerical worker. I noticed that *all* of the frontline faces for the office were white women. I inquired about a front desk position. The powers that be kept brushing me off. The office manager, Chris, kept making promises he had no intention of keeping. It seemed that there was a new white face working the front desk and front line of the office every day. What pushed me over the line was when a white woman was given the front desk receptionist position when they had just informed me, a few breaths ago, that there was no opening for the position. According to the powers that be, there were no openings for *any* front desk or clerical position.

I didn't accept this new hire too lightly. I went to see an EEOC investigator. He happened to be African American. He gave me a brief lesson in California Labor Law. Although he felt my pain, he also told me that California is an "at-will" state. Pretty much, an employer can do what they want "at-will" unless there is an employment contract. He also stated that hiring a white female also covers hiring a minority under federal law. I learned a harsh lesson in reality under the law. Just because it seems morally wrong, it's not legally wrong.

April was a black student attending Howard University. White and black employees were treated very differently at the amusement park where she worked.

This past summer I worked in an amusement park in Virginia. The workplace was a segregated atmosphere. Despite equally auditioning and equally performing their best, all of the black employees were placed in one section of the department and all of the white employees were placed in the other section. The black employees had poor working conditions and more difficult work relations with all the white employers, managers, and supervisors. Over in the "white part of town," there were better working conditions and the managers and supervisors were more cooperative, friendly, and helpful to the white employees. The black employees worked as hard if not harder than the white employees and they deserved equal and fair treatment at the job.

My job reminded me of the "separate but equal" clause. This was when predominantly black neighborhoods, schools and businesses were usually ignored and were not provided the vital necessities required to maintain a sense of decency. While this was going on, white neighborhoods, schools, and businesses were able to thrive with more than enough facilities, resources and funding.

Anne was a black student at Howard University. She believes she lost her job because of racism. Do you think there are other reasons why she might have lost her job?

I grew up in the South, and my family has experienced a number of textbook racist incidents. My mother was one of six black students to integrate her high school in her school.

When I was seventeen, I got a summer job at the Better Business Bureau. I was the youngest employee in the office by about twelve years, and one of three black employees in an office of twenty-one. The person who had the job before I did was a white young lady who had been at the Bureau for about a year. She was leaving because she had received an offer from a firm that included college assistance tuition. I acclimated quickly to the job. The office was about fifty years behind in terms of technology, and I was the only person in the office who knew that the computer was capable of more than word processing. I always seemed to finish my work a great deal faster than normal. This seemed to bother my supervisor, who always took an aggravated and angry tone when speaking to me. She called my work into question several times during my tenure there. Each time, she was wrong, but she never offered anything in the way of an apology for her accusations.

Finally, about three-quarters of the way through my scheduled time of employment, she came to me and informed me that there was no longer sufficient money in the budget to continue paying me, and perhaps I should seek other employment. If I chose to stay, my hours would be severely cut back, but it was my decision. Not really having much else to do, I chose to stay with the nearly empty schedule.

One day, the young lady who used to have my job called the Bureau and asked to speak with my supervisor. From the end of the conversation that I could hear, she was crying, saying how much she hated her new job and how much she wished that she had never left. My supervisor offered her her job back (the job that was currently mine). I was a bit puzzled about why there was suddenly room in the running-in-the-red budget for the job that there was no room for two days ago. I thought about it and spoke with my mother, the two other black employees, and a couple of the white employees as well. It was the first job that I had lost, and the first time that I experienced such blatant racism in a professional setting.

Jimmy was a white student attending the University of South Florida. He could not borrow enough money from the bank to afford the asking price of a home he liked in a black area because the lower valuation of the property. Was this something other than a market question of location?

By living in a racially divided community for most of my life, it's been impossible not to encounter racism of some form or other on just about a daily basis. I'm a product of my environment, which is white, non-Hispanic, American, Southern male.

It was not until about a year later that my eyes were opened to the disturbing fact that race may play a major role in the selling price of real estate. I found a cute house listed for $54K—not a bad price for a two bedroom, one bath, with an attached garage and spacious living room that had a vaulted ceiling, and screened porches in the front and back of the house. The place was nice. Even the appliances were in good shape. There were beautiful oaks in the yard, it was four or five blocks from Tampa Bay, and it had a fenced-in backyard, newer roof and carpet. The general condition of the neighborhood and surrounding houses were comparable to mine. So I called my broker and said I think I found a deal. He looked into it and what he came back with shocked me.

There is a list of comparable home sales in every area called the MLS. It tells you what homes are going for in the area that you are looking to buy. It also tells banks how much to lend and in this case how much not to lend. My house, in a predominantly white neighborhood, listed for $85K. The house I was looking to buy, in the black neighborhood, was worth about $34K according to MLS.

"$34,000?!" I said. That's all the bank will give, he said. "Why?" I asked. He said, "It's the area. It's black!"

Joseph was a white student attending Villanova University. He watched a heating technician grossly overcharge an African American customer.

Several years ago, I was with somebody who happens to be a technician, and he received an emergency call. I agreed to go with him as an observer. An African American customer had a heating problem, even though she bought and installed a brand new heater that was a little over one year old. Unfortunately, she had a warranty for only one year and it expired. The problem was minor, that is, the defective part was under $5, yet she was charged almost $1,000 because she was an African American. The technician also made a racial slur.

My reaction at first was shock and I was somewhat embarrassed. I was in a dilemma. In fact, I was scared and almost in a frozen position because I did not know how to act or what to say. I feared that I might say or act in a wrong manner, revealing the truth. Yet, at that time, and as I am trying today, I wanted to be a good Christian, that is, following the gospel of the Lord Jesus Christ's teachings. I was in a dilemma. I remember this situation somewhat vividly, and I would appreciate if you would not mention my name concerning this particular unjust incident.

Nolan was a white student at Salisbury State University. He was denied admission to a university while his black friend was admitted.

During my senior year in high school, one of my black friends and I both applied to the University of Delaware. It was the number one university on my list of three or four, as well as his. Since he was a good friend of mine I knew his grade point average, his SAT scores, and his extracurricular activities. We were very similar in our scores. He was accepted and I was put on the waiting list, and eventually denied acceptance. When we returned for the winter break and started catching up on each other's lives at college, he said his grades were not very good and he did not think he belonged there. He said he thought the only reason he was accepted was because of his background. It then hit me why he may have been accepted over me.

Affirmative action programs make universities fill a quota of races at their school so that they are a diverse university. To this day I still do not understand why that is. If a college wants to hold high academic standards, why is it that they let students who are less qualified in over others? This does not make any sense to me at all. In these days of equal rights for everyone, why is it necessary to have affirmative action programs to advance people who are not as smart as others?

I was always raised to believe that the best and smartest people succeed in life and you earn what you're worth. Nothing is ever given to you. Affirmative action, however, does not follow those basic principles in life. It rewards less qualified people based on their ethnic background instead of their worth to society.

Denise was a white student attending the University of California at Santa Barbara. She took a part-time job at a doctor's office and was mistreated by two Hispanic coworkers.

Being brought up in a very liberal city in northern California, race was not a pressing issue in my life as a child. I had friends of other races and never experienced any form of racial prejudice or stereotyping as a kid.

I worked as a medical assistant in a doctor's office as a part-time job while I attended college. The two women I worked with were of Mexican American descent. At first they were very friendly and personable, helping to show me the ropes of the office, but through my first day I noticed that they were speaking a lot of Spanish to each other and not including me in any of their conversations. I really had no problem with this; I understood that they had been working together for a while and Spanish was their native language. I really did not what to interrupt their working relationship.

As the weeks wore on my coworkers kept speaking Spanish to each other, often responding to me in Spanish when they knew I didn't speak a word of it. Out of all the patients that went to the office, there were only about a handful that spoke Spanish themselves so I knew that the Spanish was not needed in a professional sense.

It wasn't until one day when a Spanish-speaking patient came in that a situation arose that I was really embarrassed and humiliated about. When the man came up to the desk he spoke a few words of Spanish. I went back to get my coworker who would be able to speak Spanish to him. She acted as if she was annoyed and bothered that I had interrupted her. Knowing that I couldn't just ignore the situation I apologized that I had interrupted her and said that because I didn't speak Spanish fluently, I thought she was more suited to deal with the patient. In response she rudely yelled something back in Spanish and she and my other coworker just started laughing. In English she then responded with the fact that she understood, that I was just this lazy rich white girl who had taken a job from one of her friends that I really didn't need. She asked why I would bother working here when I didn't speak Spanish or didn't need the job. I was in shock and did not know how to respond. It was the first time I felt I was being judged and stereotyped based on my race.

After the situation occurred I was really exposed to a world I never knew. Never in my life had I experienced this kind of judgment. I had always heard of situations and stories when people were racially judged and humiliated but I had personally never experienced it. At first I was very shocked when the situation occurred.

I understood that on some level they were angry with more than just me. Unfortunately, things were never the same with my coworkers and the isolation I felt just became worse. I was able to learn something from the situation and take some important lessons from it.

Michelle was a Hispanic student attending the University of California at Santa Barbara. Her parents were fired from their real estate office when minorities complained about discrimination.

About three years ago, my mother and father worked for a real estate office that shall remain unnamed. Both of my parents were born in Mexico and gained little formal education. However, after enduring much hardship and struggle, they both managed to become successful real estate agents in a predominantly Caucasian community. They became highly experienced in this field throughout the years and become top producers in this particular real estate office.

Despite this, the manager of the office treated my parents like part-time workers. They were provided with only one desk, one phone, and one cubicle. They worked long hours and took their work very seriously. Even as a child, I knew that their working conditions were not suitable for the amount of time they spent in the office.

My mother would often approach the manager, a Caucasian woman, about the unacceptable conditions that she and my father were forced to work in. She would ask for another cubicle but the manager would always give her a pathetic excuse or blow her off. At an office meeting led by the manager, my mother complained about discrimination. She observed that the manager provided her Caucasian friends, all whom were either part-time workers or inactive agents, with the large private offices in the building. Once my mother had initiated this topic, other agents who were ethnic minorities supported her by openly agreeing that they too felt they were being discriminated against. Each one provided one example or another of having been a victim of racism in the workplace. Even some Caucasian workers displayed support by clapping or uttering remarks whenever my mother or the other women spoke their opinions.

Shortly after, my mother and father, along with the others who had spoken out at the office meeting, were given letters of termination from the office. Outraged, my mother and the three other women decided to take this matter to court. We had no income in the household for quite some time and it was very stressful.

Unfortunately, my mother did not win the case. Naturally, the manager was able to get a better lawyer than my mother and the other temporarily unemployed women could find. This was a sad time for the family. I could only imagine the amount of humiliation my parents felt during this time.

My parents were able to recover from this temporary setback. It only made them stronger. My mother is working in a different branch of this same company and is currently the top producer in the office. My father is working for a mortgage company and is also doing well. I suppose it can go without saying that they each have their own desks now.

Brenda was a white student who attended the University of California at Santa Barbara (UCSB). She grew up among Hispanics and felt discriminated against because she could not get a scholarship reserved for Hispanics. On the other hand, she does not identify with the whites on campus.

Growing up in south San Diego, only a few miles from the Mexican border, I definitely feel that by being white with blond hair and blue eyes, I was a "minority." I grew up in bilingual elementary school classes and almost all of my friends through high school were Latino. In addition, my grandfather remarried a woman from Mexico when my father was a teenager, making half of my close family Mexican. So from a very young age, the social construction of race for me was a very blurred line. I now realize that

I was blessed enough to grow up color blind, almost completely oblivious to the fact that I was not like everyone else. I looked different, I spoke differently, and I was of a different culture while still being submersed in the Chicano culture. While there are many benefits to growing up in diversity, it is an inevitable fact that today's society has only perpetuated the racial norms and standards, and at some point, we all will experience discrimination in one form or another.

My worst racial experience came at the end of high school. I attended a private Catholic high school, which was approximately 90 percent Latino. I had a perfect 4.0 GPA. I was president of the student council, on several sports teams, and a member of several leadership clubs. I felt that I had worked extremely hard in high school, and the confirmation of this arrived with my acceptance letter to UCSB. However, tuition was an issue, since I did not qualify for very much financial aid since I had two working parents. They consequently could not afford an entire tuition because I have other siblings that would be attending college as well. The exciting thing was that my school offered a $4,000 scholarship based on academics, school involvement, and leadership qualities, BUT, the recipient must be Latino. Several of my close friends, with similar transcripts and resumes who were much better off financially, did receive this scholarship, and I, obviously, did not. Although I understand the purpose and intention of such scholarships, I could not help but feel hurt and confused that there was not an "all white" scholarship, or rather a scholarship which was granted to well-performing students regardless of their race, social class, gender, and so on.

I felt that my family and I had grown up always being the minority in our community and schools, specifically in the context of our racial backgrounds. However, the Chicano community was where I felt most comfortable and where I felt the most like myself. It was my life, my home, and my family. It was not until I arrived at UCSB that I felt the real confusion of racial identities. There was an abundance of whites with whom I found nothing in common because we had not come from similar backgrounds. All of the Chicanos that I knew banned together and made me feel that I did not belong with them either because I obviously was not the same. But somehow, since this is where I felt most comfortable, I felt most like them. More and more I struggled with the idea of what race even is because for me it was not about the color of your skin, but it was about the culture and group of people you best identified yourself with.

So was the scholarship I failed to receive rewarded on behalf of one's skin color, or on behalf of who they really were inside, and the struggles that they faced because of this? It is a question not easily answered, but definitely worth pondering for the sake of our country's struggle for equality and human rights.

10

Stereotyped

Stereotypes are one of the essential elements of racism (Levine, Carmines, and Sniderman 1999). Much of the relevant scholarship research on stereotypes pertains to whites' stereotypes of African Americans. However, with an increasingly diverse society, racial and ethnic stereotypes beyond whites' perceptions of African Americans warrant greater attention. The essays within this chapter show that not only are African Americans negatively stereotyped, it also extends to whites and other minorities.

Based on their looks or the color of their skin, people are judged as being violent, less intelligent, not interested in academic interests, dishonest, great at sports, bad at sports, having a lack of empathy and being racist. Stereotypes exist as cognitive structures that contain the "perceiver's knowledge, beliefs, and expectations about human groups" (Hamilton and Trolier 1986). In fact, stereotypes often underlie our explanations for cultural and racial differences. Delia describes how while attending a mock government conference "the girls kept commenting about the difference between my hair and the other black girl's hair. They were perplexed that I had what they called 'silky hair.'" Stereotypes are based on our experience or lack of experience with different social groups. Dixon and Rosebaum (2004) find that increased contact with other groups can help overcome stereotypes. However, despite the diversity in our nation, the only interaction many people have with a different racial or ethnic group is through television and the media. Henderson and Baldasty (2003) describe racial diversity on prime-time television programs as often in the form of secondary and guest characters and "white culture remains central to television production." The lack of diversity on television programs and advertisements conveys greater attention and favorable images of whites but limited and marginal images of minorities. Racial bias has also been seen with regard to news reporting and is perhaps no more evident than the media coverage since 9/11 as stereotypical images of Arab nations often pervaded news accounts (Verma 2005).

Some research has indicated that whites often perceive African Americans as being less motivated or lazy and that this is a reason for racial inequality (McDonald 2001). African Americans are most often stereotypically associated with poverty and crime, even within social science research, as discussion regarding the disproportionate number of African Americans in poverty often provides context for discussion (Gilens, 1996; Jones and Luo 1999). However, both positive and negative racial stereotypes of African Americans exist. Racial stereotypes within the workplace exist as barriers to African American advancement. Marshall (2001) describes the phenomenon of "working while black" where African Americans are often stereotyped as being part of the cleaning staff, deemed incompetent, or angry employees. In a study of ethnic images, Smith (1990) found that despite the increase in ethnic tolerance and attitudes, most Americans see minority groups in negative light, which subsequently impact attitudes regarding civil rights, integration, and other policy issues. We have all of these elements in the essays in this chapter. Hispanics have endured similar stereotypes to African Americans, however it has been argued they have been incorporated into white society to a greater extent and in some cases labeled as white since the U.S. Census labels Hispanics as an ethnic group of any race, while African American is a distinct racial group (Dixon and Rosenbaum 2004).

As previously mentioned, essays throughout this chapter document where white students feel they have been stereotyped. Interestingly, there is little academic literature on how minorities may stereotype whites. One reason for this is that most stereotypes based on African Americans, Hispanics, and others, are *racial/ethnic* based, rooted in assumptions about these racial/ethnic groups. However, the research on white racial identity, what it means to be white, and perceptions of *whiteness* is limited. Croll (2007) finds that personal characteristics such as age, gender, education, in addition to beliefs about prejudice and views on diversity, affect the racial identity of whites. Thus, stereotypes pertaining to whites may indeed be perceptions of whites on these dimensions as well. For example, Tony describes that "The unfair stereotypes ascribed to white people in this class eventually brought down the credibility of the curriculum in my eyes." Another student, Karen ponders what it means to be "white" and asks, "So why is it that all pale-skinned people can all be classified as white? I am Italian. I am British. I am Irish, I am German. All of these 'race' identities come together to create who I am; I am not limited by the 'white' title."

Marilyn was a black student at Howard University. While on the Metro, a white passenger started to talk to her in stereotyped black slang.

As I began to think of instances in which I have experienced prejudice or hate on the basis of race, I came to the conclusion that no one experience is more astonishing than any others, because each experience feels as though it is the first. They all hurt the same and evoke the same emotions. The first instance in which I can remember being confronted with this issue was when I was in middle school. A few of my friends and I were on the Metro when a group of white teenage males got on the train and approached where we were sitting. They began to snicker and make comments under their breaths that I was unable to make out. Finally, one of the teens tried to engage in conversation with us. It became blatantly clear that he was more interested in showcasing his ability to relate to African Americans than with really talking to us. This was evident through his use of slang terminology (which he used incorrectly). After a while, we realized that he was being sarcastic and was basically just trying to get a reaction from us.

I will never forget the question he asked, "Why do you people feel the need to talk like that?" At this point, I was livid. How dare he stereotype every African American in such a way? But, the most offensive part of the whole ordeal was that he referred to us as *you people*. When he exited the train, he shouted "A'ight, homeys." I felt a mixture of emotions. I was shocked at the fact that he felt the need to speak to us like that. I was also angry because he didn't know a thing about us, yet he managed to categorize us with a small entity of the black population. I was embarrassed because his loud and inappropriate behavior had gained the attention of the other passengers. I was also furious at myself for not setting him straight. Now that I look back at this incident, I am relieved that I didn't stoop to his level of immaturity and ignorance. My responses out of anger would have just perpetuated his already jaded views of African Americans. I have come to the conclusion that the whole incident can be summed up with one word: ignorance. This gentleman was so eager to please his companions that he felt the need to humiliate others in the process. How can anyone living in today's society still hold such ridiculous stereotypes about others in our diverse world? With age, I have come to believe that this type of behavior is learned. Until society makes it abundantly clear that these types of actions will not be tolerated, then I think that this type of behavior will continue. If the passengers on the train and I would have spoken up; then maybe the young man would have learned this valuable lesson that day. My only hope is that he has come to learn this.

Marco was a Filipino student at Villanova University. He discusses how he has been stereotyped since elementary school. Do you believe he is overreacting?

Being a Filipino American, I can safely say that I have had many bad racial experiences. Ever since I was a little seven-year-old boy, moving with my family from the Philippines to Manhasset, New York (a predominantly rich, white town), and up until this very moment, there has always been a constant focus on my nationality and how I am different. I would have to say that this is the worst racial experience of my life—the continuous con-centration on how I am atypical.

On the very first day of elementary school, several kids said I was prob-ably smart like the Japanese kid in our class. Two kids commented on my rather "weird" lunch. The other kids had their ham sandwiches or lunch from the school. The two kids seemed so amazed at the fact that I was eating rice for lunch. One of them asked me, "Is that good?" I nodded, im-plying that it was good. The other kid said, "I don't think he understands English." I found it amusing that my teacher later commented about how my grammar was better than most of the students in her class.

However, no one ever treated me badly because I was "different." Once I got to fourth grade, a young kid saw me in the bathroom. For some rea-son, he pulled at the corner of his eyes, making them "squinty" and started making "Chinese" sounds. "Wang, ching, chung," he said. I asked him what he was doing. He told me, "You're Chinese, right? Ching, chang, choo." A little bit puzzled, I just shook my head and left. I thought to myself, "Why would he think that I was Chinese? I'm very different than Chinese people." It bothered me that he thought that I was something different from what I really am. It was very ignorant and rude of that kid to do that.

However, now, at twenty years old, I still experience that very same thing. Just a couple of months ago, I was playing pool with a few of my friends, two of whom also happened to be Filipino. Two young kids were there as well. They started making those very same "Chinese sounds," directing it toward my friends and me. I was a little offended, but what can I do about it?

There is nothing I can really do other than try to ignore it. On the other hand, there are just some things that I cannot let go. When I said that my worst racial experience *is* the constant concentration on how I am atypical, I did not just mean other people focusing at the fact that I am different. Sometimes, I catch myself thinking, "Wow, I'm the only nonwhite person here," and other things like that. I know and truly believe that there is nothing wrong with that, but sometimes, for no apparent reason, I just get uncomfortable. It is like two warring worlds in my head—I know there is nothing wrong with being Asian, but there is always that constant question in the back of my mind—do they look at me and think things because I am different?

I have been dating my girlfriend for three years. She is 75 percent Irish and 25 percent Italian. When we started dating, I never thought about the differences in our culture. I just always saw it as two people who really cared about each other, and nothing more. Attending Villanova University, one will notice that there is constant focus on race here because it is a "very white school." Earlier this school year, my girlfriend and I took part in an interview done by two seniors researching interracial couples. I was glad to do it, but I thought to myself, "Why is there even a need for that? Is it that strange that a white girl and an Asian guy are dating?"

Even though I try not to let the "race issue" bother me, I have spent many moments of my life wondering. I wonder if I belong. I wonder if people look at me differently just because of how I look or act or talk. I wonder if people see me and think about the many Asian stereotypes. I also wonder why people look at other people differently, strictly based on skin color and cultural background. I am proud to be Filipino. I am proud of where I came from and what I have become. I am a unique individual, just like everyone else, so, why look at me in a different manner? Everyone is different.

Janet was a black student at the University of Maryland. Many white students believe she received admission and scholarship because she is black, and not because of her abilities.

I am fortunate enough to not have experienced a gross example of racism but I have received many misguided comments that have collectively lead to my worst racial experience. The situation began when I started to apply to colleges and continues to this day.

Let me give you a little background on myself. I am a junior physiology/ neurobiology and psychology double major at the University of Maryland, College Park. I am a member of the Honors and Gemstone Program and have a cumulative GPA of 4.0. In high school I was also an excellent student. I graduated with a weighted 4.38 GPA and earned a 1420 on the SAT. In addition to academic achievement, I made varsity in two sports and participated in two others. I was also in a variety of clubs and organizations including Ecology Club, a local environmental awareness group, and Young Life, a Christian outreach organization. You might say I was a bit of an overachiever.

I do not say this to brag. The point is, based on the color of my skin, my peers and teachers assumed certain things about me. The number one phrase I heard while discussing my college application process was "you don't have to worry about getting into college; you're black." It became almost a mantra as I talked to other people who explained their college choices. This infuriated me; these were the same students that I have had class with for four years, the same students who had participated in sports and other activities with me, as well as students who were mere acquaintances. Many of these people knew my work ethic and still said these words to me.

This idea traveled with me when I decided to attend this university. When some students learned that I am here on a scholarship they repeated, "Oh, well you probably got the scholarship because you're black." Again, relative strangers deemed it appropriate to immediately infer that my scholarship was the result of the color of my skin and not my credentials.

All of the above statements were made to me by whites. This should not come as a surprise, since research has shown that white and black Americans often differ in their perceptions of reality. Obviously there is a disconnect between the reality of affirmative action and people's perceptions of its effects. I got into all the colleges to which I applied (University of Pennsylvania, Duke University, and Johns Hopkins University to name a few). I truly believe I gained acceptance into these competitive colleges based on my merit, not race, and I that I am just as worthy and capable as any other college student. This idea is hard to maintain at times, not because I doubt my ability, but because I sometimes wonder whether other similarly worthy candidates were denied admission because of me. But, I don't let this stop me from achieving my goals. Regardless of whether other students had the credentials to gain admissions but did not, the fact remains that I deserve to be here and will not let other people's opinions deter me from achieving my goals. It is crucial that all students, both black and white, realize their own worth and not allow anyone's opinion to damper their aspirations.

Kevin was a black student attending the University of Maryland. Another black student called him white because he did not want to play basketball.

During the summer before my eighth-grade year my parents enrolled me in a summer enrichment program called F.A.M.E. The program was for minorities who were interested in engineering. It was the first time in several years that I had sat in a classroom where most of the students were black. I discovered that almost all the kids in the program came from middle-class backgrounds like I did so I never felt any difference between me and the other students. One day during our free time period a kid came up to me and asked me if I wanted to play basketball. Even though I liked playing basketball I was engrossed in a book I was reading at the time, and said something like, "Not really, I want to finish reading this book." The kid, who was black, gave me a dirty look and said, "Man, why you act like a white boy?"

I will never forget how deeply wounded I felt when he said that to me. I remember mumbling something to him and walking away. For the rest of the summer program I was referred to as "the white boy." I was deeply hurt because I felt that my own people had rejected me and stripped me of my blackness. The whole issue of "acting white" is harmful to the black community because it is dangerous for us to stereotype ourselves. It causes us to fill the roles of the stereotypes instead of just being who we are. There is an interesting aspect of the "acting white" issue and the kid who accused me of "acting white" is a perfect example of this. I would later find out that his father was a prominent judge in the city of X. I remember my parents telling me that his family had much more money than we did and they lived in an upper-class *white* neighborhood. Yet, because I would rather read a book instead of playing basketball, this kid feels he has the right to call me a white boy? This is because the black community has stereotyped itself. Through the different forms of the media, blacks have defined "acting black" as engaging in activities like having lots of sex, having fancy cars, and buying lots of diamond jewelry. Tragically we have classified activities like reading as "acting white." That is why that kid, who had a judge for a father, feels that reading is an activity that white people do. How sad is it that by the age of twelve that kid had learned reading was not for black people. Instead of this kid behaving like an upper-middle class kid from his neighborhood, he is trying to act like his favorite rapper. Black people need to be whom they truly are instead of trying to fill the role of some stereotype.

Kimberly was a white student who attended the University of Maryland. She was told her opinion did not count in an African American literature class.

I am a white English major with a concentration in literature of the African Diaspora. I believe that I have very different experiences from other white people because of this fact. My classes have a majority of black students, are taught by black professors, and deal with books about blackness by black authors. My worst racial experience recently occurred in one of these classes.

In one of my African American literature classes, the class was discussing two works by Jamaica Kincaid. During the class discussion one girl said that I would never understand the books because I am white. I wonder how it is that my opinion is somehow invalid because I am white. If I can't understand black literature, black art, or black people then how can they understand me?

It is this burning question that tears me apart. I will never know what it is like to be physically black, but then how is my whiteness so easily understood, so simple?

I sat in class and I brooded. What right does she have to tell me I don't understand because my skin is pale? The girl was from an affluent suburb in Montgomery County, not Antigua; she had a maid in her house and she was never a slave. I hate slavery, I hate colonialism, and I hate oppression in whatever form it takes.

So, maybe this wasn't the worst experience after all. Perhaps this was the best one, as it forced me to really do some soul searching.

Cary was a black student at Howard University. While she was attending a summer science program in Colorado, she had to deal with the stereotypes of the white students.

My worst racial experience took place during the summer before my senior year in high school. I was selected to attend an eight-week program called Frontiers of Science at the University of Northern Colorado. The program was intended for high school students from all over the state of Colorado, who proved to have a high interest in science. During the stay, each student was to conduct and present a scientific experiment of their choice with the help of a few college professors and graduate students. Of the thirty-five students selected, I was the only African American and the only person from Denver.

I remember the first day I arrived at the dorm and saw everyone else. My heart just fell to my stomach. I was so worried about what they would think and how they would react to me. I thought I was going to be sick the whole eight weeks.

I was very uncomfortable for the first few weeks and I stayed to myself because I felt like I was constantly on display. The other students had never really known a black person and they believed many of the stereotypes about black people. They were always asking questions like, "How do you guys get your hair to do that?" or "Do you ever get sun burn?", or "Do you guys really fight all the time?" I could tell that some of them were afraid of me based on the fact that I was black. Anytime I would speak to them or ask them a question, they would try to cater to me. They were even afraid to have a civil debate with me.

Eventually, I got tired of being the display, so I decided to call a meeting with everyone in which I told them that I didn't appreciate the way that most of them reacted to me just because I'm black. I didn't mean that they had to be afraid of me or treat me any differently. I let them know that even though I grew up differently then they had, I was still a person who obviously had something in common with them or I would not have been selected for the program. They all apologized for their actions and told me that they did not mean to make me feel uncomfortable but they were curious. I could understand that and I told them that we were all mature and if they had a question or wanted to know something, they should ask me in a respectable manner. From then on, things got better and I was able to be more involved with group activities. However, I could tell that they were still a little shocked at the greatness of my experiment presentation on the Further Characterization of Morphine-60-D Glucuronide (M6G), but I still try not to fault them for that. I know that we all hold certain views of different races and it is not always our own fault. I still keep in contact with most of them through e-mail.

Wanda was a white student at Steven Austin University. She lives in Jasper County, Texas where a recent notorious racially motivated murder occurred. She is stereotyped because she comes from that county.

On June 7, 1998 at 9:00 a.m. the body of a black male, minus the head and right arm, was discovered on Huff Creek Road in Jasper County.

A black man, James Byrd, Jr., was walking down Martin Luther King Drive in Jasper, Texas one evening and a pickup truck stopped and offered him a ride. Three white males occupied the truck. The fact that the driver offered a black man a ride upset Bill King, one of the white passengers. King eventually took control of the vehicle and drove to Huff Creek Road, which is a dirt road in the middle of nowhere. When King was asked what he was doing, he replied, "Fixin' to scare the shit out of this nigger." King then stopped along the dirt road, and began beating the black male until he was unconscious. They then chained him by his ankles to the pickup and drug him to pieces along three miles of road. The remainder of his body was left in front of a predominantly black church. The day of June 7, 1998 marked the beginning of a racial hate crime that would tear the community of Jasper apart forever.

Several weeks after the crime was committed, the Ku Klux Klan and Black Panthers held rallies on the front lawn of the courthouse. These two gangs tried to divide whites and blacks in the community. Jasper schools and businesses were closed in order to help prevent racial problems from arising.

The Jasper community stuck together, did not attend the rallies, and did not allow these gangs to influence their lives. As time passed, the KKK and Black Panthers finally left Jasper and the town was left to reconstruct and heal on its own.

As a Jasper citizen, I experienced the racial crime and the hatred two gangs brought to one small community. This crime not only caused problems between races, but it gave Jasper a reputation of being racist. Anytime someone asks where I am from and I tell them Jasper, they always come back with a remark such as "that's where they drag blacks" or "nigger killer." Just because it happened in Jasper, doesn't mean that everyone is racist toward blacks. People shouldn't be judged based on other people's actions or their race.

Delia was a black student at Howard University. She was stereotyped when she attended a mock-government conference in California.

The time I had my "worst racial experience" may seem surprising to most people.

It was not a moment of outright humiliation or degradation, but it summoned emotions that were perhaps worse than these things; pity and disgust. I was left feeling offended by the oblivious ignorance of my perpetrators. When it came down to it, their assault was unintentional, but all the same hurtful. To be hurt as a result of subtlety or mere implication is something that can cut deeper than a knife.

I had been the chosen delegate from my high school to attend the 2000 "California Girls' State" sponsored by the American Legion Women's Auxiliary. The event was an opportunity for sixteen-year-old girls to experience the life of government and politics for five busy, fun-filled days. You have the opportunity to run for offices and vote. It was an honor for me to be chosen. I noticed one thing right away: Out of the five hundred delegates, I was one of very few black girls present.

My city was called the city of Hart and out of twenty girls, only two of us were black and one was Hispanic. Coming from a neighborhood where white people were a minority, it was definitely something I noticed. Nevertheless, I did not look at them differently or skeptically. For one thing, I was raised without prejudice, and for two, I had never put that much emphasis on race, but rather, on character.

So, with that said, you can imagine my astonishment when I found the other girls in my city paid an inordinate amount of attention to the fact that the other girl and I are black. They exhausted us with questions about our neighborhoods, our clothes, our terminology, and perhaps most upsettingly, our hair. For example, the girls kept commenting about the difference between my hair and the other black girl's hair. They were perplexed that I had what they called "silky hair." Another aspect of my person that caught their attention repeatedly was that I am so light-skinned. They insisted that I was "mixed."

I think what hurt the most was that these girls didn't realize how insulting they were being in their dissection of us. It was as if we were a different species and they were fascinated by us. Why couldn't they just look at us as fellow human beings? Why was it important that we were black? Why did they distinguish us as being so different? What did that have to do with our purpose for being there? I found myself wishing that I was around people of my own race so I wouldn't be subject to such an underlying presence of racism. That is probably a key reason I am here at Howard University today.

In retrospect, I wish I would have told those girls that black people come in myriad different shades too numerous to count. I wish I had told them that black is not synonymous with "kinky hair" but that our textures range from the tightest curls to the straightest, silkiest locks you can imagine. I wish I had told them that we have our own terminology because we are intelligent enough to switch it up from "street" to "corporate" whenever need be. I would say that I wish they could understand that we are more than the "gangsters" and "hoodlums" and "criminals" that are so often portrayed by the media. But, I think they figured that out when I won the state election and became California Girls' State Superintendent of Public Instruction.

Myranda was a black student attending Howard University. She has been stereotyped as a "nonentity" in a variety of situations.

I have never gone through a bad racial experience. I have never been called a nigger, never been spit on, never been stopped by the police, and I have never had a cross burned on my front lawn. Many people say that racism of that sort is only still alive in the south, and the type of racism in the north is more undercover. My experiences with race in my home state of New Jersey have consisted of simply being ignored and underestimated.

When on a train, for instance, if a white man accidentally bumps into me, he usually does so without taking the time to say he is sorry. If that same man drops his wallet, and I return it to him, he does not say thank you. The man simply takes it and walks away. I once asked someone why this is, and he told me that in the eyes of a professional white male, I am neither a threat to his well-being nor am I someone that would affect his life in the future, so I am ignored.

In school, if I were to get a B- in a class, I would be praised. However, if a white student got the same B-, she would be reprimanded for not getting an A. It was as if I was not supposed to get the same grade as my white counterpart, because a black girl could not possibly be as smart as a white girl. Therefore, throughout high school, I found myself not working as much as I could, and not getting as good of a grade that I knew I was capable of. I would do average work because I was made to believe that I was only an average student.

My experiences with race caused me, in my early teens, to believe that I could never be as valued or as intelligent as a white person. However, I now understand that I am just as intelligent and as important as anyone whether he or she is white or black. I could never force that white man to say, "excuse me" or "thank you" on the train. My white teachers in school probably still congratulate black students for getting Cs on their grade reports. It is my responsibility to rise above them and show them that I am at least worth a polite gesture or an A paper.

Torrie was a black student at Howard University. In her freshman year of high school she had a bad sexual encounter with a white student at a school dance.

The high school I attended was a private Lutheran high school in Wisconsin. It had approximately eight hundred students, of which 90 percent were Caucasian.

At one of the dances during homecoming season, a white sophomore that I barely knew approached me and asked me to dance. I danced with him and was enjoying myself when he began to touch me inappropriately. I told him to stop and he refused. I walked out of the dance and he followed me. He asked me what the problem was. He thought black girls were fast and wanted to be touched like that. I was appalled. When I told him that he was incorrect for believing that, he said it didn't matter anymore because the only reason he wanted to talk to me was because he wanted to kiss a black girl and find out if we tasted like chocolate or just different from white girls in general. I immediately left the area for fear I would physically harm this young man. I warned my friends about his actions so he wouldn't try to experiment with anyone else. A month after the incident, the young man was kicked out of school on drug charges and I have not seen him since.

Tony was a white student attending the University of California at Santa Barbara. He feels that he and other whites have been stereotyped in the class for which he wrote this extra-credit essay.

My worst racial experience was at times both humiliating and uncomfortable. It concerned my being in this class. This paper in fact is an extra credit assignment for the class. The Chicana studies class consisted of nearly 90 percent Chicano/Chicana students. I felt singled out and horribly incorrectly portrayed. It was not as if the professor would point me out in class, but I took her lecture personally. Movies shown in the class would project white men as sex-hungry pigs with small penises that have no respect for women. At one point the professor gave a description of what white society believes to be beautiful. Before giving the description, she told of how this image was hurtful to Chicanas and was the cause for eating disorders and low self-esteem. She also portrayed white people as only being concerned with outer beauty rather than inner beauty. The description that was given was an exact picture of my friend—a thin white female with blonde hair and fair skin. The professor went as far as to give the perfect size of a dress, which matched my friend as well. The unfair stereotypes ascribed to white people in this class eventually brought down the creditability of the curriculum in my eyes.

Fellow white students would joke about the stereotypes. There was nothing else that we could do. It was either believe that I am the sole cause of problems for people of other ethnic backgrounds, or laugh off the accusations. I felt class only provided one side of the story.

Nothing was ever said that applied to me and the setbacks that I encounter. For example, at my job I have a Chicana and a Chicano boss who have all the power. Hispanic employees that I work along side automatically make over one dollar more an hour than I do because they speak both English and Spanish. Every example given in class showed the limits and boundaries for Chicanos/as. There was nothing said that showed the advantages and benefits of being Chicano/a. The teaching just pointed the finger at other people and said, "That's the problem."

However, I am actually glad that I decided to take this class. Even though I am skeptical of the concepts taught, I feel as though I have learned much and I can now relate to people of color that I encounter.

Keri was a student at the University of California at Santa Barbara. She was often mistakenly identified as Chicana and treated accordingly.

My brown skin, dark eyes, round face, and curvy figure automatically qualified me as a Chicana to my peers and my counselor. The majority of students at my school had similar physical features because they were Chicana. In fact, I am part Filipino, Hawaiian, and Caucasian. My Caucasian heritage is undetectable since my skin is dark but with a closer look, one can find the subtle slants of my eyes which finally distinguish me as having, "some type of Asian background," as many of my high school peers declared.

Actions speak louder than words. Stereotyping does not necessarily have to occur verbally. My high school counselor dealt with numerous students who found it difficult to obtain their high school diploma. Unfortunately, she took one look at my Chicana features and assumed I was just another probable high school dropout, when in fact I was an aspiring UC student-athlete. At the first orientation of my high school career, my counselor insisted on the lowest level classes offered, along with the minimal amount of credits. She knew best for the students who did not plan on going to college. My counselor's carelessness and stereotyping proved to greatly affect my college career. With the low expectations she set for me and the lack of preparation, I find myself at a disadvantage in college.

The curriculum offered at my school could have been sufficient in preparing me for college. The majority of honor students were wealthy and white, and I definitely did not fit that description. Looking back at my unfortunate high school experience helps me recognize how easily people stereotype and how devastating such actions can be to someone's life.

Alberto was a Hispanic student who attended the University of California at Santa Barbara. He was stereotyped as a "good" Mexican by whites.

It was not until high school that I started noticing all the comments that people made regarding race. I cannot say how many times somebody has spoken about their dislike of Mexicans in front of me, but I have always just brushed it off because in a way, I felt that they were not talking about me. I would always hear people say that "Mexicans are dirty," yet their comment was always followed by, "but not you Alberto, you're a clean Mexican." To some extent, their racial comments never really offended me. Looking back now, I believe that a primary reason for my ignorance of racism might be the fact that I grew up in a completely white neighborhood. Through my elementary and middle school education, I was the ONLY Mexican in my class. Therefore, people never really expressed their racial experiences to me and I never noticed the racism behind such comments. In was not until high school that I was placed in classes with other Mexicans and students of other racial backgrounds. It was not until high school that I heard people complain of their own racial encounters. This helped me reflect on my own racial experiences and I finally realized the racism behind people's comments. Ironically, through being Mexican and growing up in a white neighborhood, I was "accepted" by my peers because to them I was the "exception" to their perception of "dirty Mexicans."

I never really thought that I experienced racial encounters, but in reality, I had been experiencing racism all my life. By people saying that I was the "exception" and that I was a Mexican that was not "dirty," they were talking about my family and friends. Looking back now, I do not think that there could be anything worse than when people call me the "exception" for their misconceived perception of Mexicans. Growing up, I never thought of being a target or a victim of racism, but I think it was my innocent way of thinking that blinded me from seeing the true racism in people.

Karen was a white student who attended the University of California at Santa Barbara. She discusses what is wrong with racial labeling.

"What race are you?" Julia asked with little interest. It was meant as more of a joke. My race should appear to be obvious as I am the typical blonde-haired, blue-eyed, pale-skinned "white girl." I replied with "Well I am half Italian and a mix of British, Irish, and German." The response I received was "Oh. So you are not white?" I just laughed.

What does "white" mean exactly? Most classify white as Anglo-Saxon, but now the "white" classification has extended to include all Europeans and even Middle Easterners. My close friend Julia, whose parents are from El Salvador, is commonly mistaken as being Mexican. She finds it extremely offensive that most people assume all Latinas are Mexican. So why is it that all pale-skinned people can all be classified as white? I am Italian. I am British. I am Irish, I am German. All of these "race" identities come together to create who I am; I am not limited by the "white" title.

Moreover, I am American. I grew up in Sunnyvale, California, more commonly known as the south part of the Bay Area. From elementary school until high school, I have always been the minority. I am not the stereotypical "white" girl who grew up in suburbia, in a house with a white picket fence, spending all of my time shopping and dreaming about boys. That stereotype doesn't exist. I grew up in a single family home, being raised by my mother, along side my two brothers. My friends come from all different backgrounds and races and my boyfriend identifies as first generation Mexican American.

I enjoy being who I am and not allowing any labels to define me. I can be a "white" girl who loves to eat tamales while listening to Jazz music. I am content with my life, and I will not allow any race labels to affect me. Racism does exist for everyone but we need to rise above that, first by getting rid of stereotypes and labels and just seeing people for who they are. Hopefully in the years to come, we may all be color-blind.

11

Racial Slurs

Racial slurs represent a very common experience for many of the students' essays. In this chapter students describe their feelings and experiences when they were called a racial slur or heard a friend, family member, or someone they knew use a racial epithet. In fact, one poignant essay describes how a young woman felt when *she* used a racial epithet during an argument with a classmate.

Recently there has been great discussion on the resurrection of racial epithets and racial harassment. Celebrities such as Michael Richards and Mel Gibson have been in the news for their rants and use of racial slurs. Likewise recent reports of nooses being used around the country to intimidate and frighten African Americans serve as reminders of the painful history and power behind these acts and symbols. The essays in these chapters serve as testament that racial slurs and racial harassment are still common and painful experiences for many people.

Racial jokes and slurs are expressions of prejudice that serve to demean or psychologically injure the individual or the group of which the individual is a member (Aboud and Fenwick 2002). Some students describe how they felt when they were called "nigger" for the first time, a theme discussed on racial experiences during childhood. There are many instances when students were called a racial epithet in school. However, this often occurs in unsupervised school settings (Aboud and Fenwick 2002). Many teachers often fail to recognize the pain that racial slurs cause children and adolescents (Sherman 1990). And when teachers have observed incidents they rarely intervene on behalf of the victim. Carla describes how she was changed after hearing a hall-mate use a racial epithet toward her and other African American hall-mates; "I now took on a new outlook, abandoning my naiveté about the realities of this world." Andy describes when he was called a racial epithet at a Mardi Gras parade, his family treated the incident like a rite of passage. In another essay, Rick describes his thoughts immediately following the incident stating, "This is actually the first time I have told anyone of the incident. I thought about it a lot that day. I thought about why he had called me a nigger. I thought about what would have happened if I would have said something, or even hit him."

Several essays in this chapter describe how students felt when they heard a friend, family member, or an acquaintance use a racial slur or racial epithet. Some describe how even those who were not victims of a racial epithet or racial harassment were profoundly changed by the experience of hearing such words come from people they thought they knew. Aboud and Fenwick (2002) describe how "bystanders" to racial prejudice can play an important role in influencing others' racial attitudes and behavior. Research on *bystander intervention* indicates that most people are reluctant to intervene as they do not feel personally responsible for stopping the offensive behavior, they perceive the behavior as not harmful, or they worry about putting themselves in jeopardy (Aboud and Fenwick 2002, p. 778). Pricilla wonders why she didn't speak up upon hearing a hospital patient say disparaging remarks about African Americans. She states, "I knew I could not be disrespectful to him since he was a patient at the hospital, but I know I could have said something." Other individuals may feel social pressure to join the behavior. Paul describe how he was pressured to use the word "nigga" when talking with his friends as he states, "After awhile they asked me why I was not calling them niggas. They made fun of me for not saying it. It was really awkward." Other essays describe the disappointment felt upon hearing family, friends, or acquaintances. Derek describes his profound disappointment when he learns of the racist sentiments of men he admired while he was a caddy at a golf club: "I just really felt foolish and disillusioned for putting these men on a pedestal and for living in my own little world where I thought racism did not exist." Olivia is perhaps one of very few essays where she describes her feelings when *she* used a racial epithet. Olivia provides a glimpse of how family affects our racial beliefs and how she came to use the word; "because my parents were prejudiced, they didn't encourage me to look at everyone equally. Somewhere along the way I formed my own thoughts and values towards others."

Throughout this chapter the essays show how victims, innocent bystanders, and perpetrators are affected by racism, particularly the use of racial epithets and racial harassment. As we are most accustomed to hearing the viewpoints of those who are the victims of racism, the essays in this chapter provide additional perspectives for thinking about how racism affects everyone.

Kenya is an African American student at Howard University. She describes when a woman referred to her as a "nigger" at a Taco Bell. Kenya was ten years old at the time.

Growing up in Tulsa, Oklahoma, I dealt with a lot of racism. One incident I remember in particular happened when I was about ten years old. My mother, cousin, and I were shopping and decided to get some lunch. My cousin and I wanted tacos so we decided to go to Taco Bell. The part of town we were in was called Sand Springs, which is an area settled mainly by whites. We ordered our food, got our trays, and sat at a booth near a trashcan. We were enjoying our meal and conversation until an incident, which I vividly remember, took place.

A girl about my age and her mother (white, of course) were finished eating and were leaving. The mother carried her tray and walked past us without looking. Her daughter was behind her carrying her tray. While passing our table the daughter dropped her tray and sent her trash flying all over my mother. The daughter looked really scared and began picking up the pieces of trash without saying a word to my mother or any of us at the table. When the girl's mother noticed the girl was no longer behind her she turned to see where the girl was. I remember her face to this day; it had turned red in a matter of seconds. She yelled, "Rachel, what on earth are you doing?" The girl was scared and replied, "I dropped my tray and my trash fell on her (pointing to my mother)." I could tell that my mother became upset at the young girl referring to her as "her," but she kept her cool. The girl's mother walked over to her, grabbed her hand while looking at my mother, and said, "There's no need to pick up the trash, she's only a nigger." I had always been told that this word "nigger" was bad but I had never actually heard someone use the word.

At hearing this word, my mother calmly stood up and looked the woman straight into the eyes. I then heard my mother ask, "Excuse me, what did you call me?" The woman answered with no hesitation, "nigger." My mother looked at my cousin and I and calmly said, "Kids, this is what you call an ignorant person. She knows not right from wrong because she was not raised properly. This is who you don't want to be like when you grow up. Let's go." The woman stood there with her mouth wide open but no words coming out. My cousin and I slid out the booth and took my mother's hands. My mother looked down on the little girl, and said, "I'm sorry that you have this woman as your mother." We then walked out of the Taco Bell with the mother yelling all kinds of profanity.

This experience hurt me because I could see that it hurt my mother. This experience taught me that racism is an unfortunate mindset that is passed down from generation to generation. I believe that racism will always exist, but more people need to speak out about it so that even if children are learning it at home, they will know that it is not acceptable in society.

Caroline was a white student at Middle Tennessee State University. She describes how awkward it was when a white acquaintance inadvertently used a racist remark in front of some black men in her apartment complex.

My worst racial experience made me very uncomfortable. It occurred last summer while I was suntanning with my best friend at a pool. The pool is at a local apartment complex by our campus, so everyone there were college students. There were about fifteen of us in the hot tub; two black guys that had been at the pool for about an hour were nearby. Most of the guys in the pool are what you would call "very country-like" and very loud. All of us in the pool/hot tub were white, so when the two black guys got into the hot tub everyone noticed. It had an awkward feeling for a moment because everyone stopped what they were doing to look at the guys, but after a few seconds everyone continued and it was nothing unusual. One of the guys in the hot tub has a very loud and obnoxious personality and he was having a conversation with a few of the other guys sitting next to him when out of the blue he said, "Quit acting like a nigger." He was directing it to one of his friends, but as soon as it came out of his mouth we were all looking at him, at the two black guys, and at each other in disbelief. All of us in the hot tub were totally silenced. As soon as my friend fully realized what he had said he apologized to the black guys and said that he didn't mean to use that word. The black guys just sat there looking stunned, and then one of them said that it wasn't cool of him to use that word. I was so embarrassed and felt so sorry for the two black guys. I didn't want them to associate me with this "friend of mine," because I am not a racist and never have used the word nigger in any sentence or in my thoughts. The black guys accepted my friend's apology after saying choice words first. After staying another five minutes, the black guys then got up and left. As soon as they left, we were all yelling at our friend. Not one person in the hot tub agreed with what he jokingly had said and we were all embarrassed and angry. I know that this isn't a very bad racial experience, but to me it was horrible and mortifying just to be present and a witness to the incident. By simply association, I felt so ashamed for what that one shallow friend had so unthinkingly thought and than unthinkingly blurted out.

Derek was a white student from Villanova University. While working at a country club as a golf caddy for a group of people, he was offended when they exhibited racist behavior toward his fellow caddy.

I caddied at the country club near my house. I did it on a fairly regular basis, got to know many of the members, and because I enjoyed golf so much, the job was pretty enjoyable for me. All this led me to become a fairly decent caddy. As a result, I quickly received the loops with the best golfers who usually paid the best money. They were very courteous and considerate to me, took my opinion on different matters into consideration, and most importantly to me, paid me well. All the men were successful in their occupations, well respected around the community, and very good at golf, so in many ways I looked up to them.

I don't want to sound too dramatic, but all of this changed one morning when I was paired with a new caddie on the other two bags. He was black and while there were fewer black caddies, they were not uncommon at the club. For the first few holes everything seemed normal, but it seemed as though Brandon was doing more work than I was. I guess because I was young and stupid I assumed that Brandon was doing more because he was new and these guys knew me. I thought it was a seniority thing.

On the eighth hole of that round, one of the men hit a ball way to the right into a hazard. Brandon and I stomped around the hazard with the other men, attempting to find the ball until two of the men told me to give up and take their bags up to their own balls. As the three of us walked to the balls, one man said to me "You are working pretty hard today, relax and let the nigger do the work," and the other man responded with, "Yeah, his ancestors are used to doing the work for us." The men chuckled about the joke, with smiles that were so condescending and superior.

Those words hit me like someone had kicked out the back of my legs. I had in many ways idealized these men and may have painted them in a light they could never fulfill. However, for me as a fourteen-year-old, the shock was that I had always seen racists portrayed in a negative way—as coming from a poor background, having little education, and living in trailer parks. These men did not fit any of these stereotypes. I just really felt foolish and disillusioned for putting these men on a pedestal and for living in my own little world where I thought racism did not exist. After this I began to change the groups for which I would caddy. While I did caddy for this group occasionally, I did not do it nearly as much nor did I enjoy it as much as I did in the past.

Paul was a white student at Villanova University who was criticized in sixth grade for not calling his friends "nigga."

I remember when I just started sixth grade and I was walking down the road with two of my friends drinking Slurpees. My friend told me to try his Coke-flavored Slurpee because it was "the best" and I should have gotten it. I did and I liked it so I took another slurp. He yelled at me to stop and said "Don't be a nigga." My other friend yelled and called me a nigga too. I did not say anything to this. After awhile they asked me why I was not calling them niggas. They made fun of me for not saying it. It was really awkward.

It made me feel awkward because despite having had more intense racial experiences since then, that one was my first experience where I felt the hatred and ignorance that causes the racial divide.

I have lived my life with little conscious experience of blacks. My worst racial experience is only having one racial experience. As I walked down that road with my friends I found out that I was not a "nigga."

Pam was a black student at Howard University. She was riding her bike with her father when a group of high school students started taunting them.

As a youngster I loved to ride my bike. My father use to take me to the high school in my town and watch me ride for hours. Riding a bike was something that my father and I shared. My father taught and I learned. On one bright summer day I was riding my bike at the local high school. A group of white teenagers was also there. For a while they were fine just sitting there enjoying the day. As it grew later in the evening one of the kids said to me and my dad, ".Why don't you niggers leave and go back to Africa where you belong?" My dad was livid. I did not understand exactly what was happening but I knew this child had made my dad very angry. My dad, as a man alone with a little kid, just said something nasty to them as he grabbed me and stormed away. As we were leaving, the kids taunted us chanting "niggers, niggers." That night I had my first lesson in the history of that horrid word. My mother explained to me where that word originated and why it was not a nice word. To this day riding a bike still reminds me of that experience. At the time the whole incident did not really hurt me because I was too young to understand, but as I grew older I did.

Carla was a black student who attended the University of Maryland. During a study session, a white roommate referred to the four black girls as coming from Monkeyville.

I never had to worry about race before this stage of my life. I grew up in Prince George's County, which predominantly consists of middle-class African Americans. Racism was only heard of. I started anew at the University of Maryland and things were drastically different. Brown faces were replaced by a variety of colored faces and more than any other color, white faces.

It was spring semester of my freshman year. My communications exam was Wednesday morning, and my friends and I planned a study session for

Tuesday night. We all gathered our lecture notes and past quizzes and met in Lauren's room, which was at the end of the hall. She was the sweetest girl you would ever want to meet. It never occurred to anyone that the friction between Lauren and her roommate Lindsay was because of their races, because after all, "one of Lindsay's best friends was black."

The study session convened and things were going well, until Lindsay loudly flung the door open and interrupted us. She immediately called a friend and commenced to laughing and carrying on in a rather boisterous manner. When we couldn't take the interruptions any longer, an Ethiopian classmate, politely asked her, "Could you please turn it down a notch? We're trying to study." Lindsay completely ignored her request and continued on the phone. She said to her friend, "Guess I'm back in Monkeyville, yep, Monkeyville. There's about four of 'em here in my room!" and continued to laugh. The four of us studying on the floor all froze. I could feel my entire body heat up. I couldn't sit still. We were simply stunned, grossly offended, and furious. I yelled for her to "man-up" and call us niggers if that's what she wanted to do, and in turn she would get a fist, and maybe a foot, or elbow, in her mouth. Lindsay got flustered as she realized what she had just done. She left and went for the resident assistant because I had "threatened her."

To make a long story short, my friends and I took the mature, intelligent route in dealing with this incident. We reported the incident by writing to the resident director and also by individually meeting with her to discuss how Lindsay's comment made each of us feel. The resident director then contacted the proper authorities and Lindsay was expelled from University of Maryland housing.

This experience enlightened me about the types of injustices blacks have faced, and will continue to, for a long time in this country. I had heard of racism, but had never seen it for myself. I now took on a new outlook, abandoning my naiveté about the realities of this world. I learned that there are always going to be people who will try to bring me down, tempt me into violence, or who will judge me based on the color of my skin. It is easy to assume that Lindsay simply hates African Americans, and that she will always be a racist. However, racism is not innate or biological. It is learned or taught, and many times comes from misconceptions and misunderstandings.

Andy was a student at Howard University. He was called a "nigger" at a Mardi Gras parade in Alabama. His family treated in like a rite of passage.

The worst racial experience to ever happen in my life took place at a Mardi Gras parade in Mobile, Alabama. I was nine and my aunt had taken my cousins as well as my sister to the parade. As one float came by, many people were bunching together and I accidentally bumped into a white girl who appeared to be approximately fifteen. Before I could utter an apology, the girl angrily looked at me and said words that would never slip my memory: "Nigger!" I was so shocked that I couldn't think of anything to say. My body wouldn't allow me to move. Never in my life had I felt so low and dirty. This young girl threw words that hurt like rocks to me.

I told my aunt and went home to tell my mother, but instead of being able to console me, they spoke to me as if the incident was some sort of rite of passage. Both my mother and my aunt went to the high school during the era of bussing in Alabama. They were accustomed to hearing that word shouted at them, so the little incident I went through was nothing compared to what they faced regularly in high school. Although this incident was the worst racial incident I ever faced, I know it could have been a lot worse.

Rhoda was a white student attending the University of St. Louis. An acquaintance clapped when hearing of a black man who drowned. Since then, she has had many "heart-to-heart" discussions with the acquaintance.

I have encountered many incidents. After all, I was born in Texas and have two adopted African American brothers. What was most shocking to me is an incident the summer I moved to Saint Louis.

I must have lived a sheltered life because I had never heard the "n" word used until that summer. Having two African American brothers of my own, I am always extremely defensive and let it be known that I will not tolerate that kind of language around me.

This particular night, I was watching the news with my boyfriend and some of his friends, one of whom is extremely racist. A story came on about an African American man drowning in a flood near the Saint Louis area. The guy I was sitting with began to clap.

Never before had I witnessed such hatred and disregard for someone just because of their race. I was extremely upset and ended up leaving the room. As I sat outside, I realized that I was not only sad about the incident, but I was sad for the guy inside; it must be a sad world one lives in when their heart is consumed by such hatred.

It is funny how the world works though. It has been a year and a half since the incident, and now, this young man has become my friend. We have many heart-to-heart discussions, and I make it clear when he is out of line. With time, I noticed his new behavior around me, and an open-mindedness to take a walk on the other side.

Amy was a black student at Howard University. She was with her father when her father was called a "nigger" during a parking altercation.

I was around twelve years old and I was riding in a car with my whole family in Baltimore. We were looking forward to a wonderful day of perusing the toy store and catching an afternoon matinee. My father pulled up to a parking space and was preparing to parallel park. As soon as my father put the car in reverse, a car came out of nowhere and started honking their horn uncontrollably. My father stopped to see what was going on, and immediately a white man said "Hey jerk, that's my spot." My father replied as calmly as he could and said, "Sorry Sir, but we were here first." What happened next would leave an imprint in my mind for the rest of my days. The man pulled up to my fathers side of the car and said, "You are ignorant! That's why they call you people niggers!" He went on to spit on my father's car and sped off. Needless to say, our whole day was ruined and even today I am very wary of parking situations.

Darlene was a black student at Howard University. When she was at the beach, a man said to his friend that he didn't know that "niggers" needed to get tans.

This past Fourth of July, my friends and I decided to celebrate the beautiful day by going to the beach located near our homes. We prepared picnic baskets, towels, and put on our swimsuits to enjoy the day of independence. My friends and I, about ten of us in all, located a spot between sunbathers and children playing in the sand to spend our fun and relaxing afternoon. Although we did not notice, it was later brought to our attention that we were the only people on the beach of African American and Latin American descent.

I never paid much attention to the uneven race distribution in Los Angeles, because I was raised not to look at race. Unfortunately, that day brought my first bout with the cruelty and evils of racism. I noticed that after we had been on the beach for a while a nearby Caucasian couple kept eyeing our area. It was very apparent that we were the topic of their discussion, but I tried to ignore the unwanted attention we were receiving. About a half an hour later, the couple gathered their towels and belongings. Though we were out of their way, they walked past my circle of friends, and the man sarcastically remarked to the woman that he didn't know "niggers and Mexicans needed to get tans" and that "there was no need for them to be on the beach." The mood immediately went from light-heartedness to anger. We were in fact more hurt than angry, but when people are hurt they usually mask it.

Rick was a black student attending Howard University. He was called a "nigger" by a student in fifth grade. The student immediately apologized.

My family's house was located in an area of Illinois where the majority of the population were white and the majority of my friends, classmates, and teachers were too. However, with the success, education, and liberal atmosphere of the Upper Midwest and this area in general, I was taught and treated like I was no different from anyone else.

As I was walking up the staircase at school one day, I was having a conversation with one of my friends. At the top of the staircase stood a sixth grader. I recognized him as living in my neighborhood, although I didn't know or talk to him. As my foot hit the second to last top step our eyes met as he leaned over the top banister looked straight at me and said, "You nigger!" I was shocked to say the least but I have always been a person who contains my emotions. It seemed like time stood a little still at that moment. I didn't do or say anything. I turned my head, and it fell toward my chest a little. The next thing that happened was also surprising. He put his hand out as to stop me and immediately upon seeing my reaction said how sorry he was for saying it. I knew he was sincere because of the way he said it. I said ok and went on my way.

This is the first time I have told anyone of the incident. I thought about it a lot that day. I thought about why he had called me a nigger. I thought about what would have happened if I had said something, or even hit him. I wonder what made him immediately apologize to me. It was such an ugly word and it was the first time I heard it in reference to me. I believe it was the first incident where I felt that no matter how much money my parents had, or how big our house was, or how well I spoke the King's English, or how much I thought I fit in, I would always question what someone really felt about me.

Pricilla was a white student attending Florida State University. She discusses how other whites voice bigoted opinions.

I have been fortunate because I have not had any terrible racial experiences. The only racism that I have been exposed to has come from white people. I am constantly amazed that even today I hear derogatory remarks from white people about blacks, Hispanics, Jews, etc. I find it interesting that white people will assume that because they are in the company of other white folks, that they have the right, and it is acceptable, to make racist comments.

One particular instance stands out in my mind, partially because the man with whom I was interacting was a complete stranger to me, yet he felt comfortable spewing his racist remarks.

I was working as a patient advocate in a large hospital. The job entailed getting insurance information and payments from patients before they received services. I was helping an elderly man when the stranger started making racial slurs about some of the African Americans employed at the hospital. He went on and on about how lazy and stupid they were and how they should not be working in the hospital. I was very angry and uncomfortable, but I didn't say anything. This incident occurred about twenty years ago but I still think of it often and wonder why I didn't say anything. I knew I could not be disrespectful to him since he was a patient at the hospital, but I know I could have said something. At one point I thought I would tell him that I didn't appreciate his comment, especially considering my husband was black. (He wasn't, but I thought if I said he was, it might give the man something to think about.) For whatever reason, I still chose to remain quiet. I think I will always regret not speaking up.

Voicing my opinion is something that I have done with family members that are racially prejudiced. It has not, however, changed their way of thinking and has only resulted in huge arguments. I have learned that when it comes to the subject of ethnic groups, I am better off keeping my mouth shut.

Denise was a white student attending the University of South Florida. She had an argument with her boyfriend's father about his use of racial epitaphs.

I was pretty close to the father of a man I was dating and we had many intellectual conversations on a regular basis. One conversation, that turned out to be our last conversation, all started when we were discussing football at my boyfriend's apartment. My boyfriend's father, who we will call Frank, made a racial comment about how "there are too many niggers in football." I was shocked. I automatically asked him to apologize and not to say such things in my presence. He did not like this. He called me a "nigger lover" in retaliation and went on with his game. I was so upset that I started to get a bit heated and began yelling at him. Apparently he enjoyed my reaction and it was all downhill from there.

The argument turned into an all out scream fest between the two of us. I told him he was ignorant for thinking this way and he just spouted off every racial remark he could think of. I was so upset that I asked him to leave. I didn't have my car at the time so I couldn't leave and he refused as well, stating that he "had more of a right to be there then some nigger-loving bitch." To my astonishment, my boyfriend said nothing. Frank continued to make racist jokes and remarks, ignoring anything I had to say in retaliation. Then I said the one thing all racists hate to hear—I called him white trash.

Frank actually was hurt by this remark. I found this a bit amusing, considering all of the horrible things he had been calling me. He, of course, said he was only joking (even though he had me in tears). I never talked to Frank again and I broke up with my boyfriend for not standing up for me. I can only imagine what they say about me now.

Olivia was a forty-two year old white student who attended South Florida University. She called a black classmate a "nigger." The essay highlights both the effect of family and what happens to people in the "heat of the moment." It is one of the few essays where a white person talked about using the "n" word.

My worst racial experience happened when I was in the sixth grade. We lived in a small town in upstate New York. There were few blacks living in the area. Both my parents worked so I had to ride the bus to and from school.

I had a black classmate whose name was Ricky. Ricky came from a nice family. I didn't think twice about him being black. The whole incident started one day when my friends on the playground said that Ricky wanted me to go out with him. I liked Ricky as a friend, but I didn't want to date him nor would I have been allowed to do so by my parents. I had a friend tell him that I wouldn't go out with him. Ricky was mad and felt that I wouldn't date him because he was black. We must have exchanged words because what happened next was my worst racial experience. I called him a nigger. I think I called him this in front of others. I knew it was wrong to call him that, but I had the type of personality that told you like it was. I either liked you or I didn't. There was no pretending.

It was the next day and I had arrived at school and had been waiting outside until the bell rang. Ricky walked up to me and swung a 2 × 4 hitting me in the leg. I did not suffer any permanent physical damage. He said this was for calling him a nigger. I was stunned but I didn't tell on him. There were no teachers that saw him hit me. I knew I shouldn't have called him that name. I don't think I even told my parents.

Ricky and I remained friends throughout high school. We never talked about that day and I'm not sure why it remains in my memory. It was probably the shock factor. I couldn't believe he brought the board to school and actually hit me with it. Despite my upbringing, I was not prejudiced. I had black girlfriends throughout high school and college. When I got to college, I was surprised that there were wealthy black people. I figured that they were all poor because back home the areas where most of them lived were poor. I think about that today and I realize that is how stereotypes are formed. Because my parents were prejudiced, they didn't encourage me to look at everyone equally. Somewhere along the way I formed my own thoughts and values toward others. I believe that we all have choices and it's those choices that give or take away equal opportunities to get what we want out of life.

Anica was a Hispanic student at the University of California at Santa Barbara. She told a white student that she was offended by his racist jokes.

All my life I attended very diverse schools. I have learned to get along with my Latino classmates as well as the white classmates.

It was the spring of my senior year in high school and I was in my auto cad class. As always, we were talking and joking around as we did our work on our computers. One of my white classmates looked over to another white student and said, "Hey I just heard this joke. What do you call a pregnant Mexican?" The other student looked back at him and said he didn't know. At this time one of my Mexican classmates joins the discussion and says he to wants to know the answer. By this time the jokester has the attention of most of the class and the response—"a bean bag." Most of the class began to laugh. The joke itself was not the worst part. As stated above, all my life I have gone to very diverse schools. Jokes like this are common and most likely just seen as that—jokes.

However, this joke did not just end with the answer to the joke. He went on with several other such jokes. I was sitting at my desk, just hearing their conversation and quite honestly getting offended. At this time, the girls that I was helping out stopped doing their work and began to listen to the three boys "joke around." Some of the students were laughing and others just sat around looking at them. By this time they had everyone's attention. The jokester turned around, looked at me, and said, "This is some funny stuff isn't it?"

That is when I stood up and pointed out that what they are saying was wrong and offensive. They looked at me as if they did not care and quite honestly they didn't. I continued on by telling them that joking about other ethnicities was not right and in fact they would not appreciate it if I started to make fun of them. I keep talking and since I was upset I could not quite remember everything. At first I saw that they were not listening to me, but as I continued to talk more of the people that were offended began to speak up.

By the end of the discussion I could tell that all three jokesters and the people who had laughed along with their jokes realized that what they had done was wrong. Unlike many racial experiences, my experience had a good ending in a way. Not only did I stand up and speak up to my offenders, but most importantly they listened to me. However, the most important part was the respect I gained that day. The main jokester stopped his ways. In a way I felt that he finally respected me as the person I am. My bad racial experience turned out to be good for me because I saw what really happens when one stands up. Too bad that this is not the case in every bad racial experience.

Denise was a Hispanic student at the University of California at Santa Barbara. She has heard several anti-Mexican comments since attending college.

Growing up in East Los Angeles allowed me to identify with people of different cultures and races. My high school was composed mainly of Hispanic, Asian, and black people. Once I left East Los Angeles to attend college in Santa Barbara, I was anxious and nervous about the individuals I would encounter. I was looking forward to interacting with people from all over the world, and learn about the diversity that exists amongst individuals. However, I quickly realized that oftentimes I was left out of certain events or social gatherings because I could not relate to the white culture. Nobody really approached me or seemed eager to get to know me or my culture. Sadly, what I encountered at UCSB was something that I had never experienced growing up in East Los Angeles. What I encountered was racism.

Racism plays a large part in my unhappiness here at UCSB. I oftentimes feel secluded and alienated amongst white people who tend to stick to their own kind. There have been numerous times when racism was directed towards me or other Chicano/a students. My freshman year here was extremely difficult for me simply because I was not making friends as quickly as the other girls in my dorm. I was one of three Mexicans that lived in my hall of forty kids.

I remember one incident in particular that really hurt. One of the girls that lived on the same hallway came into my room to speak with my roommate. I had just woken up from a nap, but I remained still in my bed. The girl that came to visit told my roommate, "Oh my sister is coming to visit me this weekend!" However, she made a look of disgust and my roommate asked, "Why do you make that face? Do you not get along with your sister?" She replied, "No its not that, it is just that she is coming with her fiancé and well . . . he is Mexican . . . and I don't like Mexicans." I was shocked to hear her say that because she had always pretended to like me. However, I soon realized that she really disliked me and people of my race simply because we are Mexican.

Another experience that I witnessed during freshman year was during one my hallmate's birthday parties. One of her friends came down from San Luis Obispo to celebrate her birthday. We were all gathered around in my friend's house, and we were all having a good time until the guy from San Luis Obispo made a racial comment about his belt. He asked all of us, "Hey girls! Do you all like my belt buckle?" to which the girls replied, "yeah! It is really cool." Then he said, "I don't know I was thinking of changing it, my dad says I should get a new belt buckle because he thinks this one looks like one of them 'beaner' belts, and we don't want to be associated with them kind of people." All of the girls in the room started laughing, but I was completely offended and I felt uncomfortable. One of my good friends that was present at the party immediately turned to look at me. She is half-Mexican and half-Caucasian, and although she completely looks white, she was not laughing either. We both made eye contact and looked at each other, and knew exactly what we were thinking. I could not believe that the guy had made that comment in my presence or the presence of any of the other girls. I stood up and left the room. As I was leaving the girls asked me "Where are you going?" and I told them, "I'm leaving. I am not feeling this conversation and I do not appreciate the comments that your friend is making." The girls looked at me with confused looks on their faces, but I realized that a lot of them did not realize what I was feeling inside.

Kelly was a white student attending the University of California at Santa Barbara. She was called a rich white kid the first day of junior high school.

I had just come from a quite smaller elementary school, where I had spent my childhood very protected, very safe, and very comfortable in my little bubble of a world where everyone knew everyone, and we all came from similar circumstances. So going to this big junior high school was, to say the least, a big adjustment for me, and quite a scary one at that. A military air base station was close to my school, and all the kids of the military families attended my same junior high school. The majority of these kids were Chicanos and African Americans.

I was sitting in my math classroom, and we had to get to know the people at our table by introducing ourselves and telling each other a little bit about who we were. After I had introduced myself, one of the kids who lived on the military base asked me where I lived. I replied, "Turtle Rock." What he said next was something that introduced a completely new issue into my life. "Oh, you're one of those little, rich, white girls," he said, in a very insulting tone. I was stunned. No one had ever said anything to me like that before. The thought that my race and my social class might be the object of someone's criticism of me had literally never crossed my mind.

My initial reaction was that of utter embarrassment. I was literally humiliated that this is what someone's first impression of me was, and also that he had announced it in front of my other peers in such a devaluing way! I panicked, and just shyly giggled and shrugged my shoulders. Inside though, I was absolutely mortified. I just couldn't understand why someone would label me in such a way.

Looking back on it now, I can understand why I had been so embarrassed that day because it was basically the first time I was confronted with the reality of racial tension. Nowadays I see this as a really good learning experience for me. Beforehand, I had never been faced with any real world problems, and this was definitely a wake-up call.

Geraldo was a Hispanic student at the University of California at Santa Barbara. He was called a "wetback" by an older man when he was in second grade.

I was a carefree child in the second grade, when the incident happened. My mother took me to buy school clothes and she gave me one hour to find what I needed. I was to meet her at a certain time, being late meant being spanked. Therefore, time was a major concern. I found what I liked and wanted to go to the toy store next door, so I asked an elderly man "excuse me sir, do you know what time it is?" All I remember was his response, "Time for you to get a watch you little *wetback!*"

I stood there shocked at what I heard him say to me. The rest of his words have escaped me since. I know he said much more than that, but I never was able to process anything else. I could not understand why he was so mad at me. I asked nicely as I was told to do. Did I offend him? Was I rude? What did I say wrong? All these questions ran through my head as I stood there listening to the mean words of the old man. After a couple of minutes he walked away laughing and I just cried. No one had ever made me feel like that and I did not like it.

After crying for what seemed like forever, my mother came looking for me and spanked me for not meeting her on time. I did not cry out of physical pain but out of the pain that the old man's words caused me. Soon after that, I developed a strong resentment against white people. I refused to do the flag salute or take part in the Thanksgiving celebrations at school. I do not know how, but I knew I was not an American, nor would I ever be accepted as one. My teachers kicked me out of class and gave me detention, but I never participated again. For many years, I held this hatred against white people for what they have done to colored people throughout time.

Recognizing that my hatred was counterproductive, I reevaluated what I felt was important and productive towards aiding my people. Hatred was not one of the traits I chose to keep, but rather, simply the knowledge of the incident. I am grateful for the incident now. No matter how hurtful those words were, they ignited the fire in me to assert my Chicano identity and for that I thank the old man.

12

Skin Color

The literature review pertaining to self-image, identity, and stereotypes describe the many issues and dilemmas of students struggling to fit into their respective minority group and be accepted. This acceptance often comes in the form of fitting in *physically* as well as *culturally*. As previously mentioned, one of the primary ways people distinguish their respective "ingroup" from an "outgroup" is through skin color. The essays in this chapter describe how many students experience racial bias because they lack Eurocentric phenotypic characters (e.g., lighter skin and eye color, straight hair) and are therefore considered unattractive, or because they are of lighter tone and do not fit into their respective minority group.

"Colorism" in the United States is rooted in slavery and racial oppression (Hill 2000). The perception that "whiteness" is identified with being civilized, virtuous, and beautiful continues to exist today as seen in the media and such industries as modeling and entertainment. In fact, as of this writing, the cosmetics company L'oreal is under fire for its advertisement featuring a much lighter and blonder Beyonce, an African American female entertainer. However, colorism has greater policy implications; significant skin color bias is seen in our criminal justice system, employment hiring, and economic advantages. Colorism is closely related to racial prejudice as "individuals will perceive or behave toward members of a racial category based on the lightness or darkness of their skin tone" (Maddox and Gray 2002). Darker-skinned African Americans often receive longer prison sentences, are less likely to receive professional promotion, and are more likely to live in segregated communities (Hochschild and Weaver 2007). Within the United States racial minorities with darker skin, particularly African Americans, have faced more disadvantage, greater discrimination, and been stigmatized more than those with lighter skin (Maddox 2002; Keith and Herring 1991). Hochschild and Weaver (2007) as well as others have found a strong relationship between skin color and socioeconomic status with lighter-skinned African Americans having higher economic status than darker-skinned African Americans (Seltzer and Smith 1991; Hill 2000). While colorism is most often discussed within the context of African Americans, this is also true across other races as well. Massey and Denton (1992) have found that racial barriers to residential integration are significantly greater for Mexicans of mixed European/Indian ancestry than for white Mexicans. Furthermore, Hispanics of African heritage often face greater racial inequality than non-black Hispanics.

Many scholars contend there is a cohort affect in terms of skin tone variation and equality. Gullickson (2005) has found that beginning with cohorts born in the 1940s, there are significant declines in colorism as it pertains to education and employment. However, color preferences continue to exist in terms of spousal preference with African Americans preferring lighter-skinned spouses. Indeed, many of the essays within this chapter show the experiences of students who indicate it is people within their own race who exhibit color bias or *intraracial discrimination*. Tammy and Ken describe their experiences of being ridiculed and not accepted by other African Americans because their skin was "too dark." Tammy was dismissed by her "crush" because she was dark skinned. Interestingly, Tammy admits to her own color bias stating, "Like him, I still won't acknowledge darker skinned men as potential mates in my life because of their skin color. Because of this, I am not any less racist than the next person." Ken describes how he was the butt of numerous jokes growing up due to the color of his skin, all coming from people of his own race. He states, "White people have never discriminated against me; it has been black people that I have had to worry about." Jabari a black student from Nigeria states, "The black students saw me as dirty and they weren't interested in me at all." Lighter skin is most often associated with physical attractiveness and greater physical attractiveness is associated with being more likable, more desirable, and more intelligent (Hill 2002). Hunter (2002) has found that lighter skin is almost a form of social capital for women of color as a study of Mexican American women and African American women show lighter skin predicts higher educational attainment, greater personal earnings, and spousal status.

Other essays describe struggling against stereotypes and being accused of "acting white." Many Hispanic students in this chapter often face this accusation by their peers if they do not speak Spanish. For example, Belinda describes how she is often confronted with, *"How can you call yourself Mexican, when you don't even speak the language?"* This was and still is a question I have been faced with from Mexican, native-Spanish speakers." Caroline describes how she was accused of acting black and asks, "Who were they to say who was black and who was not?" Tyson, Darity, and Castellino (2005) describe the notion of "acting white" as used in reference to blacks who use language or ways of speaking that are considered to be more in line with white cultural norms.

The essays within this chapter show the diversity of experiences across races as "colorism" enters the lives of these students. These students exhibit a range of feelings dealing with issues such as anger, pride, and confusion, particularly when dealing with intraracial discrimination.

Tammy was a black student at Howard University. A lighter student would not date her because she was dark-skinned.

As a dark-skinned African American woman, I have had many racial experiences, even though I am only twenty years old. Out of all the experiences I have ever had, the one that remains within my thoughts is an incident that took place with someone of the same race. When I first came to Howard University, I thought everyone believed that being black is a beautiful thing, no matter what your skin tone was.

Wow! I sure was surprised one day when a young man on campus confronted me about my boundaries as a dark-skinned woman! The young man just happens to be someone I was "crushing" on or interested in at that particular moment of my life. I hadn't known him very well, but I had seen him around campus quite often. During Valentine's Day weekend, I decided to enter a contest in which he happened to be a participant. I won the contest and received the prize, which was a date with him. Unfortunately, he didn't fulfill his part of the deal because he never showed up for our "date."

When I saw him the following Monday on campus, he came over to me. At first, I thought he was coming to apologize, but when he opened his mouth the first thing he said was, "Why did you pick me?" Of course, I looked at him surprised but also intrigued, thinking that he was flattered by my enthusiasm. After a few minutes, which seemed like hours of pleading with him to explain his reasoning for acting this way, he gave in to my begging. His voice began to become louder and deeper and more serious, and he started making assumptions about me. Without any further hesitation, he blurted out his true feelings by saying that because I am dark-skinned, he didn't like me nor could he possibly ever like someone like me. Before he could even finish his last words, I walked away. Although I felt angry, upset, and confused, I didn't release those emotions to him. I decided that just walking away from the situation would bring me more dignity and respect. The incident didn't make me feel resentful or bitter toward those who have a lighter complexion than me. However, it made me aware of some light-skinned black people's views or feelings toward darker-skinned black people.

Now when I look back at the incident, I recognize that in many ways I am/was just as ignorant as that young man. After all, there have been times when I wouldn't even glance at a man because he was my complexion or darker. Even though I have never lashed out at anyone like the young man, this doesn't leave me without fault. Like him, I still won't acknowledge darker-skinned men as potential mates in my life because of their skin color. Because of this, I am not any less racist than the next person.

Dina was a black student at Howard University. She is from the West Indies and discusses how other black students did not feel she was black enough.

In middle school I learned how black Americans feel toward blacks from the West Indies. I have found that even though I am a black woman, my nationality means more than my color.

I attended a traditionally white middle school where whites outnumbered blacks by far. I knew almost all the kids in the school since third grade, but it wasn't until I reached middle school that racial problems began between black and white students. The biggest problem was when black guys were dating white girls, and somewhere down the line, these black guys were getting in trouble by the police and the school because the girl told a lie. The school wanted to unite the blacks and try to find a solution before the problem escalated. White students were scared because black students began starting fights and calling their houses, forewarning them about getting beat up. The school organized an all-black group for these students to sit down and talk about their issues. I was in this group because I was seen as a well-respected student who had outstanding grades and got along with all kinds of students. I was beating the odds and was not the school's regular black student.

One day in the group the topic of discussion was how the white school viewed and treated its black students. The students were telling the teachers and principal that they felt like the school was unfair to all black students and that the teachers were racist and hated their black students. I had a different view. I didn't feel that all the teachers or this community was at all racist. I simply told them that they were not proving the school or the community wrong in their way of thinking. Next thing I knew, everyone was getting mad. One of my closest friends in school spoke and said the most unthinkable thing. She replied to me by saying, "Dina you are a not black. You wouldn't know anything about me, anybody else in the room, how we feel, and what we go through on a daily basis." Then she went on to say that I fit into the white world, and kissed up to all the white teachers and that was the reason why I had good grades. She finally said that she thought I had no right to be in the group because I am Jamaican and Jamaicans are not black, but West Indian. The part that hurt me was that everybody, including some of the white teachers, agreed with her.

My heart was so hurt that all I could do was cry and call my older sister to come pick me up from school. I was so angry with my friend and everyone else in the group that I didn't go to school for the rest of the week. I got sick and mom knew why so she just let me learn how to get over it. My mother taught me and my two older sisters, who were having the same problem at the time, that as black West Indian women we will never please anyone. So, we needed to concentrate on just pleasing ourselves.

We all became friends again later in high school, but those words have always stayed in my heart and mind. As a child, those words and actions were a sign that I really didn't fit into the black American society. I had to learn how to still be proud of my nationality, while at the same time, beat all the odds white Americans have against blacks and the stereotypes about people from Jamaica.

Not only do I have to prove myself as a black woman, but I also have to do my part in the correction of typical Jamaican stereotypes. Because of nationality, skin tone, religion, and other factors, the world will always oppress blacks because blacks oppress themselves.

Jabari was a black student from Nigeria who attended the University of Maryland. He was treated better by the white students than the black students.

My "worst racial experience" involved African Americans discriminating against me, an African from Africa. Shortly after I arrived in the United States of America, I attended a middle school where the black students didn't want to have anything to do with me. They saw me as strange and different because I didn't talk like they did, and I didn't act, behave, walk, or dress like they did. The black students saw me as a foreigner. They couldn't identify with me in any way except that we both had the same black skin color. The black students saw me as dirty and they weren't interested in me at all.

When I got to high school, the black students seemed interested in me a little bit more. But, there were cases where the black students made fun of me because I was from Africa and I had an accent. Sometimes, they made fun of my name. The black students at both my middle school and my high school made jokes about Africa. They thought all of Africa consisted of tribes of black, dirty, strange people.

However, the white students and the other nonblack students associated and interacted with me more than the black students did. They didn't make fun of my name as the black students did. The white and other nonblack students seemed interested in learning how to say my name. They sat with me in the cafeteria during lunch and they seemed interested in me and my culture.

One reason I believed that the white and other nonblack students might be interested in me and my culture was because they saw that I was different from the blacks they knew. The white and other nonblack students saw that I talked, walked, behaved, acted, and dressed differently from the African Americans they knew. They saw that I was hardworking, behaved properly, was respectful, and I didn't rap or listen to rap music. I believed that some of the white and other nonblack students might be curious about my behavior, tolerance, and diligence, so they wanted to know why I was different. Sometimes, I felt more comfortable around some whites and nonblacks than I felt around some blacks.

When I got to college, the black students in college seemed very open and tolerant. The black college students didn't make fun of my name or my accent, nor did they make fun of me in any other way. The black college students seemed more mature than my fellow middle school and high school students.

In conclusion, as a foreigner, I received better treatment from whites and nonblacks than I did from my fellow black people.

Chantelle was a black student attending the University of Maryland. She was not treated well by her preschool classmates because she was light-skinned.

Growing up as an only child in a predominantly white neighborhood, I lived a very sheltered life. The white children in my neighborhood did not play with me, but I am unsure whether that was because I am black or because of a crime my father committed. The one thing I am sure of is that I was treated differently in elementary school. I attended an all-black Christian school with black instructors. However, I experienced a not-so-Christian welcome when I went to the school. There were factors that made me think I was different—the main factor was my appearance. People assumed I was arrogant or selfish based on my appearance.

I am a black woman of Irish and Sioux heritage, but I look like the average "Joe." The things that set me apart from the crowd are my hair, which some people would categorize as "good" hair, and my eyes. I have light hazel eyes that are a blend of green, gray, brown, yellow, and blue. Although those two features made me appear different from another black child (who would typically have brown eyes and "regular" hair) I did not feel any different from them.

When I entered pre-kindergarten my class consisted of about twenty-four students. There was a mix of dark-skinned children, medium-complexioned children, and light-skinned children. The light-skinned girls did not like me because I was too brown and the dark-skinned and brown-skinned girls did not like me because I had "pretty" eyes. Before they had a chance to know me, they passed judgment on who I was, based on what I looked like.

It took me a while to figure out how kids could be so mean, especially when we were in the same battle. Thinking back to slavery, when the owner separated the slaves, he picked the lighter slaves to work in the house and the darker slaves to work in the field. In my opinion this act divided a community that would never be whole again.

When I first entered pre-K, I felt that maybe if I acted in a different way the other children would like me more. I thought that maybe if I brought candy to school they would be my friend. Then I realized no matter what I did they still rejected my friendship. One day I went home crying to my grandmother, and she reassured me that as long as I loved myself and knew that I was special, things would work out in time. She also advised me, "Instead of trying to get the whole class to be your friend, start with one person." That one person became a lifelong friend.

In conclusion, my experience did not make me dislike other black people or hate my classmates. It made me strong and able to look for deeper qualities in a person—not just the color of their skin.

Antoinette was a black student at Howard University. She discusses how different people react to her skin tone.

In high school in Colorado I was the pretty black girl; just about the only black girl. The white boys always told me I looked nice, and complimented me often, but I never seemed good enough to date even though I wasn't interested in dating at the time. I also thought that I was dark-skinned. It took at least my freshman year to get over my own color complex and be happy being beautifully brown. I recall coming back from a family vacation in Jamaica where I got very dark and one of the boys in my class was like, "Wow Antoinette, you got really dark; you look like burnt toast!" Now I don't think he meant to be offensive, but when comparing what I finally thought was beautiful brown skin to burnt toast, I wanted to cry.

When I eventually got here to Howard University, I was once again struck with a color complex. Howard and blacks in general have taken a liking to those who are on my lighter end of the black color spectrum. While I am confident that I am a beautiful black woman, I don't want men to be attracted to me for the wrong reasons. One gentleman, who ironically is dark-skinned, told me I was his ideal woman because I was lighter-skinned and had "good hair." It seemed to me that he looked past the other fine qualities that I possess, almost as if to say that women who need a perm to maintain their hair and could not pass the brown paper bag test could not meet his ridiculously high standards. In response, I said, "So you must not think your mom is beautiful." He became rather quiet.

Currently I am dating a nice guy, who is light-skinned, intelligent, a hard worker, and positive in all aspects, but has a racial wall in his life. He is light-skinned and prefers his woman to be the same. When I came back from vacation in Jamaica, I had cut my hair and was significantly darker. When he picked me up at the airport, he had a look of disgust on his face. His response was one that offended me almost as if to say that my newly tanned skin and corn rowed hair weren't good enough for him. Eventually he did say, "You're not going to leave those things in your hair are you?" Is it just a coincidence that the men I date or that are attracted to me all think in this narrow-minded fashion? Or, has society conditioned black people to feel that lighter is better, straighter is better, and the two together seem to be perfection?

Jan was a black student at Howard University. She is Creole and African American and because of that she received negative treatment from her schoolmates and her extended family.

As I've grown up, I haven't experienced the typical amount of racism that other African Americans seem to typically experience from white America. There's been an occasional extra long stare from an Asian store-owner. I was even followed once by a white security guard in a store that was about the size of my kitchen. I would say I've experienced racism the most as a child from the people of my own nationality. Having an African American father and a Creole mother caused me to experience racism from both my African American and my Creole counterparts. I attended a predominately African American school in Oakland, California. From kindergarten through eighth grade, I experienced racism that was almost unbearable at times. My African American peers treated me as if I was an outsider because I was so light in color. In elementary school they thought I was white, and from looking at my mother, I thought that maybe I was at least half-white. My mother never gave me a good explanation about what it really meant to be Creole so when being called "white girl" every day at school, I didn't know how to prove them wrong. I would dread my mother coming to school on back-to-school nights or coming in the classroom to check on me periodically throughout the school year. Seeing her with pale white skin and fine hair assured them that I had to be white. It was clear to me that I was black because although my father did not play a consistent role in my life, I knew without question that his dark skin and kinky hair were signs that I was part African American. With a part time father, there was never a time to show my critics that they were dead wrong about their conclusions about my race. There was nothing I could say or do to prove them wrong. My skin color, mother, and use of proper English were clean indicators to my peers that I was white. I think that by being so young and growing up in a minority community, my peers only saw black and white.

On the other side of things, I experienced racism from my own family. My mother was born and raised in a small town right outside of New Orleans. Growing up in the South during the 1950s and 1960s with strict Creole parents caused my mother and her siblings to have very racist views. At the time, my mother growing up as a Creole was something of which to be proud. Although Creole is part African American, it set them apart from other African Americans. Being able to pass for white was something that made things easy for Creoles during the times when African Americans were being lynched and terrorized day-in and day-out. Although we live in a time where things are a lot calmer and more liberal than they used to be, I can still sense that my family still has many of the same racist ideals as they had growing up. I am one of the darker family members with thick kinky hair, and a broad nose, while my family has fine hair, and even lighter complexion and small noses. Although no racist comments have ever been directed to me personally, the way blacks are talked about and ridiculed has been an indirect way of showing rejection of who I am. "Nigger" is still used frequently in my family. Dating African Americans isn't necessarily looked down upon but it isn't glorified either.

By having a strong sense of self, I turn my cheek to their ignorance. I am unwilling to fight a battle I know I will not win.

Ken was a black student at Howard University. Other blacks made fun of him because he is so dark.

I grew up in a predominately black neighborhood. I did not attend school with a white person until middle school and did not see a large Asian population until high school. Despite the absence of white people, there was still a color pyramid, and it has existed in our society from the times of slavery until today. In this pyramid, those who are light-skinned are at the top and those who are dark-skinned are at the bottom.

Growing up as a dark-skinned male, I was often the butt of many jokes and the destination of many names that peers threw in my direction. People would call me "blackie," "charcoal bliss," and during seventh grade I became a new mock superhero, "Nightman." My pearly white teeth did not help my disposition any and it would emphasize the dark complexion of my skin. Instead of being subjected to *interracism*, I discovered *intraracism*—or what I like to call colorism—the racism that is within. White people have never discriminated against me; it has been black people that I have had to worry about.

Racism began with whites and blacks have kept it alive. I never understood why black people would talk about me for being a dark person. I never understood why it was better to be lighter. The understanding of black self-hatred did not hit me until I arrived at Howard and I learned how the lighter slaves were given preferential treatment over the darker slaves. Usually the lighter slaves were the children of the slave master himself. It is sad that the effect of this is still being felt today.

Caroline was a black student at Howard University. She was tired of not being "black enough" to her peers.

I was very tired of hearing her mouth. Keisha went on to say that I was not black because I did not sound like a black person, I do not listen to "black music," nor did I dress black. "You need to stop faking and trying to be white. What's the matter with you? Did you go to a school with white people, or is your momma white?"

I was not interested in giving her a reply, but this torment had gone on since I'd arrived at the university. I rationalized that if I shut her up once and for all, she and her ignorant cronies would leave me alone for good. "Just because I do not say 'ain't,' 'fitting,' and 'fixing,' I'm not black. I'm not black because I like Smashing Pumpkins and not Luke. I wear Birkenstocks, not high heel sneakers, and because of this I'm not black." I raved.

I was sick and tired of these people, my "peers," picking on me. Who were they to say who was black and who was not? In retaliation, I started asking them "black questions." Who was the first person to reach the North Pole? Who invented the mop, comb, light bulb filament, or stop light? How is Angela Y. Davis important to the Black Panther Party? All of my questions were met by dumbfounded stares. None of these "black" students had a clue what I was talking about.

If I was so busy trying to be white, why did I have natural hair, and not a perm? Why did I wear clear and not blue or green color contact lenses? I guess my natural reddish brown hair color was not the typical blond that real black people have. I had never been so upset in my life. These people had the nerve to stand in my face and say I wasn't black, yet they could not answer a simple question regarding African American history or tell me why they were running off to get yet another perm kit for their hair.

All I could do to keep from screaming was to slam my room door. I felt good for a minute to have shown Keisha how "black" I was, but that feeling did not last. Why did I have to prove myself to other people? I really wanted to think that African Americans did not belittle their own people, and as students, we would all stick together. You'd have thought that was the case. Why did I have to spend many a night alone in my room, or crying on the phone to my mother, because my own people had rejected me; because I was not "black enough?"

I eventually left that university, not because of Keisha and her friends. I would not give them the satisfaction. I try not to look back on the mean-spirited people I met there, but it is hard not to look back. Now I try to use their hate for good, and make myself a better person because of them. I try to be tolerant of people with different views and ways of life. I guess I never want another person to have the same bad experiences that I did.

Karen was a Hispanic student attending the University of California at Santa Barbara. She has been accused of not being Hispanic enough.

My race has always been a personal identity struggle, especially because I am always asked, "What are you?" I always thought I was an American, but I later realized what that question actually meant. My background is Guatemalan and Spanish, so I grew up with two different cultures and languages. My family lived in the wealthy Jewish area of West Los Angeles and my friends, neighbors, and schools were primarily white. Growing up I began taking on this identity as well. I never grew up with Spanish music or traditional Hispanic cooking. I even lost my Spanish language. I thought of myself as "American." However, that changed completely when I entered high school.

My high school was located in a very diverse area of West Los Angeles; it was 50 percent Latino and 50 percent black. I was very scared at first because I felt I was not going to fit in with either group. The very few white people that were there were my friends. I remember the day I had an altercation with this one Latina girl. I was coming out of the bathroom stall and she and her friends were there hanging out and ditching class. I was washing my hands and she approached me asking me for a mirror, but said it in Spanish. My response was to ask her in English what she meant. She turned around and laughed; her response was "you're a disgrace to your people, you white-washed bitch." I believe that was the point in my life where I questioned who I really was. I began to embrace both cultures and began to see what my culture was about. I began to take part in cultural settings and events and became aware of the meaning of being Latina.

I moved away from Los Angeles to Santa Barbara for college, and a culture clash struck me. I finally felt I could be myself here; everyone was white and I lived with all white girls. I finally felt like the other half of my identity was complete. It was in my Chicano studies class where I was speaking Spanish to my friend that this girl approached me after class and asked me, "What are you?" My reply was "I am Latina." She then said, "I thought you were white and that's why I didn't want to talk to you. Now that I know you're Latina I can talk to you."

I later realized that racism and stereotypes not only occur between two different races, but within races as well. In the Latina community, if your skin is white they assume you are white. I never thought I would experience this racism here in college. I listen to Spanish rock, I speak Spanish, and my Spanish culture is within me, so why do I have to be like everyone else? A lot of Latina girls still do not like me, and to me it's ok now, because I know who I am. I know my identity. I'm bicultural and I love having both my Latina side and white side.

Amir was a student attending the University of California at Santa Barbara. African American students made fun of him because he is from Nigeria.

When I was a student in high school, I experienced a great deal of racism. The African Americans did not dislike me, but at the same time they disliked the fact that I mainly associated with Asians, whites, and Latinos.

Once after football practice we all went on a water break. There was a group of eight or nine African Americans who were socializing. One African American spoke, claiming that "this is Kunta Kinte." Kunta Kinte is a story about one man's "roots" and the African slave trade. The rest of the boys in the group laughed and giggled. Another student claimed that, "That's my homie. We go way back to the days of the jungle." Another person said, "Hey Kunta you might need to stay out of the sun. You are getting darker now."

The worst of the comments I heard was when one of the African American boys asked about the type of food we eat. I told him out of anger that it was none of his concern. He exclaimed by saying, "If I gave you this candy bar, I bet you that it would feed your country." My response to his comments was passive but I was also angry.

I get offended when somebody attacks my place of origin. On the other hand, I also view it as a misunderstanding by my former colleagues. This is because people of African American descent in America have deplorable views about the Motherland. I believe that many African Americans have dehumanized views about Africa. I also believe that all other Americans think the same way. The difference is that African Americans can say it to someone similar to them and get away with those comments as opposed to someone who is not as dark. They can't talk about a white person the same way because that would be racism. The fact that I come from a black background makes them feel ok to bash me.

Belinda was a Hispanic student who attended the University of California at Santa Barbara. She has often been accused of not being Mexican because she does not speak Spanish.

"How can you call yourself Mexican, when you don't even speak the language?" This was and still is a question I have been faced with from

Mexican, native-Spanish speakers. The first time this happened was some time between second and third grade. Someone asked if I was Mexican, and I replied, "yes." The next question was, "Do you speak Spanish?" When I said no, they would laugh and shake their heads and tell me that I was not Mexican if I didn't speak Spanish. It did not bother me at the time, since I was usually the smartest one in the class. I figured the other children didn't know what they were talking about. It was not until high school that I became bothered by this, and truly realized the effect of this statement.

My parents and grandparents were born in California. Just because I did not know Spanish and was more Americanized than most, did not mean that I was any less Mexican. One day I was having a conversation with a couple of girls in a class. One of the girls named Claudia asked, "What are you?" At first, I was caught off guard not fully understanding the question, but then realized she was asking about my ethnicity. I looked at her confused, as if she couldn't tell that I was Mexican, with my dark brown hair, mocha colored skin, and almond shaped brown eyes. Did I need a sign on my forehead that said, "I am Mexican?" I replied to her (thinking she was crazy), "I'm Mexican, what else would I be?" All the girls looked surprised, and said in a manner where all their voices were in sync with each other, "You are? But you don't even speak Spanish!" I was shocked. I began to wonder how many other people did not know I was Mexican.

I went home that day feeling a bit confused and also hurt. I always assumed everyone knew I was Mexican. I was never Americanized enough to be on the same level as Americans, which was not a bad thing because it made me culturally different.

As time passed, I began to get angry. I eventually realized that there was not one person on this planet that could tell me what my ethnicity was. If I was Mexican, then that was that. I may not have spoken Spanish but I was just as much Mexican as anyone else. I experienced the same hardships as most—broken homes, financial dilemmas, and fighting to have a voice. I valued my family and loved ones very much, just as most Mexicans do. We had family get-togethers every weekend, and we ate some of the best tasting food. We had tamales for Christmas, menudo for New Years and enchiladas for birthday parties. My family and I had just as many Mexican values as any other family. I came to the conclusion that I was a Mexican in my own way, and nobody could take that away.

13

Language

It is difficult to separate out language and racial discrimination. Goto, Gee and Takeuchi (2002) found that 18 percent of Los Angeles Chinese residents faced discrimination at some point in their lives because of race and 13 percent because of language. Surprisingly, those who lived in the United States longer were more likely to say they had faced discrimination. The authors hypothesize that longer-term residents are more attentive to racial cues and more likely to have contact with those who discriminate.

According to the American Community Survey, of the 279 million over the age of five people living in the United States in 2006, 20 percent are not exclusively English-speaking. Five percent of households are labeled by the U.S. Census Bureau as "linguistically isolated." This includes 28 percent of household where Spanish is spoken and 27 percent of households where an Asian or Pacific-Islander language is spoken.

Arriagada (2005) reports that language retention among Latinos is often retained beyond the first generation. She references the National Survey of Latinos and notes that 47 percent of the second generation of Latinos is bilingual as well as 22 percent of later generations. Using statistical modeling she concludes that Spanish proficiency is more likely in intact households where co-resident kin are present and in neighborhoods where Spanish is likely to be spoken.

Nevertheless, like most immigrants, English is learned by most Hispanics. Miller (2007) has fifty-five successful Latinos tell the tale of how they learned to speak English. Some contributors to Miller's book tell of facing discrimination in the process while discrimination was a non-issue for others.

Lindemann (2005) argues that evaluations of nonnative English language speakers more often examine the group rather than the language, and these evaluations are usually negative. However, Lippe-Green (1997) contends that not all foreign accents are evaluated negatively, only those linked to skin that "isn't white."

Many examples throughout this chapter show how respondents, family members, and friends were affected by language discrimination. Interestingly, all of the respondents in this chapter are Hispanic or Latino. Indeed, as Lippe-Green (1997) finds, there are many examples of the interaction of language and racial discrimination and some degree of confusion when respondents felt like they were treated as if they were inferior. For example, Delores, a Puerto Rican asks, "I didn't understand why people treated us like we were stupid."

In this chapter, we have tales of how respondents, family members, and friends were affected by language discrimination. In many of these essays, we see the interaction of language and racial discrimination.

Delores was a Puerto Rican student attending South Florida University. Her mother was treated badly because of her accent and this had a tremendous effect on Delores.

My first encounter with racism left me confused and angry. It made me vow to myself that I would never let someone treat me the way they treated my mother. I was six years old and my mother had picked me up from elementary school in Newport News, Virginia. We were hungry, so we stopped at McDonalds. My mother began to order our lunch. Her English was very broken. The restaurant worker, a short and stocky blond woman in her late twenties, looked at my mom strangely. More people started to walk into the restaurant and a line started forming behind us. The cashier told my mom she couldn't understand what she was staying. My mother, looking a little embarrassed, repeated our order. This time a little more slowly. The employee then started to make a big deal about not understanding my mother and proceeded to call the store manager to the front of the store to help us.

I could hear the snickers behind us. One man told a construction worker next to him in line that people shouldn't be allowed to come to this country unless they spoke English. Another woman chimed in saying that she was tired of having to give Hispanics special treatment and attention.

My mother couldn't understand what these people were saying but I could. As a child I had picked up on the foreign language quickly. When the manager walked to the front of the store, I clasped my mother's hand and began to order lunch for us. I was embarrassed but so angry at the same time. I didn't understand why people treated us like we were stupid.

I didn't understand why something as simple as ordering lunch was turned into such a big deal.

I saw the way people were looking at my mother. They were looking at her with disgust. They were annoyed. When I got home that day, I remember going into the bathroom and watching myself speak. I had an accent.

My parents were both native Puerto Ricans and I knew that I would have an accent similar to theirs if I didn't do anything. That's when it all started. Almost every day after that incident, I spent time in front of the bathroom mirror watching myself speak. I would watch the shape of my mouth as I said certain words. I also over-enunciated words. I did this in hopes of erasing any trace of an accent. I didn't want people to treat me and to look at me like they looked at my mother. I verbally tried to erase any clue that would hint about what my heritage or language was. I didn't want people to see me as this "Spanish girl" but as a "regular girl."

When I think about the incident today, I can't help but wonder how my mother felt that day. We've never talked about it but it's so hard to forget the look on my mother's face as she was humiliated in front of her child.

I still see how it affects her. In public she rarely speaks English in front of us, and if we're at a store and she wants something, she'll ask me or one of my other siblings to ask for her.

I believe that the situation only helped me in the long run. It made me work hard. It made me want to succeed because success was the only way I could prove people wrong. It is the only way that I could show them that someone of Hispanic heritage could grow up to be educated and help make a difference in their community.

Raul was a Hispanic student at the University of California at Santa Barbara. A Hispanic student he was with got dissed by an African American because she did not speak English.

When I was in high school I met a girl who was from Central America. She looked so scared. I asked her "Hi, how are you?" She said, "No English.' I decided to talk to her in Spanish so she could feel more comfortable and confident about herself. She told me how she immigrated to United States and how hard it was to be in an unknown country. We have become good friends.

Then, one morning we were going to the cafeteria to have breakfast together. While she was getting her meal, a male African American asked her what time it was; she did not understand anything so she stayed quiet. The young man got mad because he thought that she was ignoring him. In a soft voice she said, "No English." He said, "Oh my God how can this be possible? You are Mexican. You do not speak English. What are you doing here? America does not need people like you, go back to your country." All the students in the cafeteria were laughing at her. She started crying and ran out to the restroom.

I felt so miserable because I think that they did not have any right to discriminate against her. Since this day I am more able to understand immigrant people who come to this country hoping to find new opportunities. They face unfair racial treatment because they do not speak English, or because their accent or appearance makes them perfect targets for racism.

Also since that day, we became more attached to each other. We are both in college and she has really improved her English. I really admire her for what she does for others. She is currently serving as an English tutor at a local middle school back in Los Angeles, our hometown.

Isabella was a Hispanic student attending the University of California at Santa Barbara. In first grade recess she was told to stop speaking Spanish by the parent of another child.

I was born and raised in Santa Maria, California. I grew up with Spanish as my first language. I attended a Catholic school from first through eighth grade. My mostly Caucasian school had very few working-class children.

It was recess time in first grade and all the children were outside playing. During recess we always had mothers of other children watching the kids as part of their volunteering. I always played with another girl who was also Mexican. We played with each other because we felt more comfortable with each other than we did with the other little Caucasian children. As we played we would speak to each other in Spanish. One day we were on the swing sets playing, laughing, and just being children. All of a sudden, one of these mothers came up to us and told us that we had to stop speaking in "that language" and that they were going to have to talk to our parents.

I was so confused by this remark. I thought that everyone understood the language. Scared of getting in trouble by the school and my parents, I stopped talking. My participation went down and my involvement with other students declined. I didn't want them to think that I was a bad student so until I learned how to speak English without having an accent, I wouldn't speak up.

This incident played an important role in my life. I am very self-conscious about my public speaking skills. I would prefer to write things than say them. I don't like to participate in class and prefer to get the lower grade then give my opinion on a matter. I think it is because I am scared of being wrong and looked down upon.

Sonia was a Hispanic student who attended the University of California at Santa Barbara. She was made fun of by other Latinos because of her Spanish accent.

I was born in Guadalajara, Mexico and came to the United States when I was ten. When my parents decided to move here, I did not understand why we were moving to the United States. We were doing well in Mexico. We were finishing our house and my parents both had a good job. I didn't want to move. It was the middle of the year, I had my friends, and I just did not want to move.

Luckily I made a couple of friends on my first day of school, which made things easier. One of them was Marlene. She was the only one who helped me understand how to do classwork and homework. Learning English was very difficult, especially coming from a non-English-speaking household. I remember how much I struggled not to let my classmates' comments bother me, but they always got to me—to the point that I didn't want to go to school anymore. When my mother asked me why I didn't want to go to school, I told her because my classmates made fun of me by asking me how I crossed the border.

I told her that they said if I swam here then I was a "wetback," and if I crossed the border with a "coyote" then I was a "border hopper." They used to make fun of the way I spoke English. If I did not pronounce a word well, they used to laugh and point and tell me I was stupid. What made this situation even worse was that my classmates were Latinos just like me. I could not understand why they were making fun of me; they were once in the same situation that I was in. When they called me "wetback," I knew that I was not illegal, but that word gives a negative connotation to those whose only crime is their desire to come to "America, the land of opportunities," and to have a better life than the one in their native land.

Today, I'm a student at the UCSB and I do not let ignorant people make me feel inferior to them because I am a minority. I control my feelings, not them. I do not get embarrassed when I mispronounce a word because of my accent, because that's who I am. I'm a Mexican young woman living in the United States who loves her accent, her skin color, Spanish features with indigenous complexion, her ethnicity, her race, and most importantly, being bilingual.

Paloma was a Hispanic student attending the University of California at Santa Barbara. Her mother was mistreated at a hospital because she did not speak English.

My mom doesn't speak English. For as long as I can remember, whenever she would receive a letter in English, I would be the one who translated it for her. At times, it was hard to translate the letter because I was too small to understand the meaning of some words, but I still did my best. I remember one time she received a letter from the hospital. The letter was actually a bill asking her to pay a large sum for something the insurance company had already paid for. My mother immediately called the hospital to inform them about their mistake. When the hospital staff picked up, they had her on hold for a really long time trying to find someone who spoke Spanish. After about thirty minutes they came back on the line and told her she had to call back some other day because no one was available to speak to her in Spanish. Upset, my mother hung up the phone and then asked me to go with her to the hospital to speak to them.

When we arrived, my mom tried to get help but no one would help. Finally, I asked a Caucasian employee who was sitting down to help us. My mom then had me tell her why we were there. The white lady then said that she was very sorry but she couldn't discuss those matters with a child. I told my mom what the lady told me and she asked me to tell her that it was fine for her to do so because I was her daughter. The lady then said that she wasn't going to talk about those things with me and that if my mom wanted to get that fixed she suggested that she learn English. Then she walked away. As soon as I heard those words I felt as if a knife was slowly cutting trough my veins. I didn't know how to tell that to my mother. When I finally translated it to her, my mother's eyes were rapidly filled with tears. She tried pretending everything was fine and we walked out of the hospital. We went home and until this day she hasn't mentioned one word about the incident.

Even though I was only a child and my mother didn't say anything about that incident, I understood the pain that came from it. I was aware of what had occurred. I knew that we had been discriminated against not because I was a child trying to resolve "adult" business, but because my mother didn't speak English. My mother didn't have to tell me how much it hurt her because I saw her pain and I felt it too. Ever since that day, I've regretted not saying anything back to the white lady. I regret not defending our rights as people. Moreover, I regret not defending my mother. I felt that because I spoke English, I had the power to defend our rights and voice my opinion. I felt I could have said what my mother would have liked to. I don't know if it was due to fear or shock, but for some unexplained reason, I didn't.

14

Other Ethnic

Prejudice is not only targeted at people who fit into America's traditional racial classifications. In this chapter, we encounter experiences from people whose ancestries were Jewish, Muslim, and German. While research on anti-Muslim sentiment is a relatively new enterprise in the United States since 9/11, research on prejudice against other ethnic groups has a long history. However, since ethnic groups such as Italians, Jews, and other white ethnic groups have assimilated into American culture, researchers have focused on groups with more identifiable *racial* differences such as African Americans, Asians, and Hispanics. Readers who wish to read more on anti-Semitism in America should see Dinnerstein (1995); on anti-Muslim sentiment readers should see Panagopolous (2006).

However, despite the focus on racial minority groups there are many individuals from ethnic minority groups that have suffered from discrimination as indicated in these essays. In fact, Alba (1999) describes how "nonwhite" immigrant groups such as Irish, Italians, and eastern European Jews became white by distinguishing themselves from African Americans. Additionally, once mass European immigration ended in the 1920s white ethnic groups became incorporated into the economic strata and labor market thus facilitating their incorporation into American society.

Many scholars contend that because white ethnic groups were not subjected to the same legal discrimination suffered by African Americans this is evidence that these groups were never viewed in the same way as African Americans and did not face the same injustices. Therefore, the kind of discrimination faced by these groups was different then and is different today, but that doesn't mean it hurts any less as evidenced in these essays. Sarah describes the fear she felt when hearing boys in her class make anti-Semitic remarks.

Other students describe their experiences of being mistaken for another race. Maya describes getting involved in a verbal altercation over what box to check when applying for a new social security card. Maya's experience supports what many researchers have said, such as Harris and Sim (2002), "Rarely are multiple observations of an individual's race obtained, and the basis and perspective of racial classifications are rarely made explicit"; therefore, resulting in an oversimplification of racial identity. Other students such as Anwar describe being harassed after 9/11.

The range of experiences in this chapter show yet again, that no one is immune from feeling the affects of a racist experience regardless of your racial, ethnic, or religious background.

Jerry was a white student at Middle Tennessee State University. He was assaulted when he was mistaken for being a Muslim.

I am a white male from an affluent family, so I pretty much have gotten things in life handed to me. I have been pretty sheltered my whole life by being sent to Catholic school for my education. There was discrimination, but none of it was due to race. I have, however, been a victim of discrimination because I was mistaken for another race.

I was walking home from work two weeks after September 11. I was new on the job so I had just been given my uniform shirt. I also had my rain jacket on because it had been raining that day. It was one of those September days when it's still hot, so it was really humid from the rain. I didn't feel like wearing my jacket because it had quit raining and I was hot. It had been a long day of work so the thought of carrying all these articles of clothing was not very appealing. So I did what any normal person would do in my predicament—I wrapped all the clothes around the top of my head.

Halfway on my trip home, I heard one of those dueled-out compensation trucks with the loud exhaust coming up behind me. I didn't think much of it until I heard someone from the truck yell at me. He called me a "Muslim motherfucker." Before I had time to figure out what the hell he was talking about, something struck me in the back of the head, knocking me to the ground. My first reaction was to grab the back of my head. Apparently, a beer bottle is what had done the damage. After grabbing the back of my head, I came to two conclusions: (1) the articles of clothing atop my head had limited the damage and (2) the articles atop my head were the reason why they threw the bottle at me. I immediately stood up and yelled at the truck, "I'm white you assholes." I then started to laugh because I thought this would make a good story and it does.

When I finally got home I realized what had really happened. It wasn't funny. Yeah it's funny because it happened to me, but post-9/11, I'm sure many Muslim Americans had experienced what I had gone through and worse. Just because they thought I was a Muslim, they threw a beer bottle at me. What kind of ignorance is that? The thing I learned from this experience is to respect Muslims. Yeah Muslims committed those attacks, but ninteen people shouldn't give a bad name to a billion people.

Adinah attended the University of St. Louis. She is of Egyptian ancestry and was born in the United States. She discusses comments made by people in school.

Fortunately, I am lucky that tolerant and intelligent people surround me. Besides a few instances in high school, I haven't had anyone say or do something to me that, in my opinion, was worth mentioning. The only thing I have had to deal with, besides the occasional look when I am with my family, which I brush off anyway, was a few high school instances.

I was late to class one day because it was a religious holiday. My dad had called the school ahead of time to tell them I would be in for only half a day. When I went to the attendance office to sign in, I told the lady that my dad called earlier and she said she didn't remember receiving a call. She checked to make sure while I signed in and asked why I was absent half the day. I told her that it was a religious holiday and she replied, "Oh you're one of those people." I didn't really think anything of it at the time and, even though it was a prejudiced remark, I still don't see it as that big of a deal.

When I was in junior high, I had a few classes with some boys who just loved to cause me trouble. In my English class they picked on all the girls but another girl and I were the only ones who would talk back so we were picked on the most. They would call me "camel jockey girl" and ask me questions like "Do you ride a camel to school?" and "Do you live in a hut in the sand?" The teacher would never comment on anything they said. In fact, I got the impression that she didn't like me because I talked back to them. I think she thought that I caused just as much of a disturbance as they did.

I learned to save my breath and just ignore them. I guess nothing they said really bothered me. I didn't really talk back because they upset me; I just did because I liked to argue. Plus, I figured that they weren't going to last at school very long anyway. I was right. They all dropped out of school the next year and turned to drugs. Since they were just ignorant teenagers who couldn't make it past the ninth grade, I didn't take anything they said seriously anyway.

The thing that affects me most is when I hear that intelligent friends I had in high school have turned incredibly racist. I think that perhaps they were racist in high school too but were just too scared to say anything to me. It seemed as though they had respect for me and I'm assuming they just thought I was "different from the others." One old friend of mine said that minorities do not contribute to society. Another said that her reason for going to war is that an Iraqi's life is not as valuable as her own or any American's life for that matter. Ironically, this girl was in my eighth grade English class and defended me against those boys.

This may not be a good example but to me the worst thing I have to deal with is watching the news. It may not be a "racist experience" but media bias definitely paves the way for it. That, to me, is worth mentioning. When the news causes you to be ashamed of your own racial identity, which it has done to me on many occasions, it is just as bad as any direct racist experience.

Rexhep was an Albanian student attending Florida State University. When he came from Albania, people treated him badly because he was different.

When I first came to the United States at the age of thirteen, I worried a lot about my language barrier and different style of clothes. Having to deal with all the bullies in and outside of school made my first couple of months in the United States miserable. I wanted to go back to my country, where I had all my friends. Most of the kids at my school did not know where my country, Albania, is located, so they thought that I wasn't white. They would call me names, but I did not know what they were saying because I did not understand English at the time. I didn't understand how people could be so unfriendly. All I was trying to do was fit into the new society.

There were days when I would try and act like I was sick, just to skip school. I couldn't handle another day of humiliation and embarrassment. In my country I was a popular kid. Now, being the kid that is always the last one to get out of the class is very uncomfortable. It takes a lot of strength to get through a situation like this. My style of clothing was a major part of all the humiliation. Being from Europe, we are used to wearing tight jeans and tight shirts, but here it was different. I had to change my style because I couldn't stand it anymore. I was actually thinking of dropping out of school, but my family encouraged me to stay. After a couple of months, I made some friends and picked up the language very quickly. After all the things that I went through, when a new person would come to my school, I would be the first one to talk to them and make them feel welcome. I couldn't just sit and watch them go through a horrible time like I did. This experience really changed my life.

Nora attended the University of South Florida and is of German descent. A friend of hers started blasting all Germans, not realizing that Nora was German.

I am a young white female of German descent. My family and I moved to the United States in 1970. It was not until I became a young adult that I first realized others around me have prejudiced ideas against me because of my heritage. In fact, I did not truly understand race until I had first-hand experiences. Sure, I have heard the Nazi jokes and have seen the Hitler sign on many occasions, but the following event had a more overwhelming effect on me because it came from a good friend of mine.

Over time I have developed a wonderful friendship with someone who is from Norway. One evening many of us were out celebrating. While sitting at the table, this friend expressed profoundly how much she dislikes Germans. She must have used every negative word there is in the dictionary and rambled on for what seemed like an eternity. I, and many others, were in shock at her words and stared at her like a deer in the headlights. I believe we all were wondering when she was going to realize that I am one of the very persons she was speaking of and that she should cease this conversation. She essentially said, "Germans are white trash, disrespectful, filthy, and should never leave their country. They smell and are mean-spirited." After a few seconds of silence and the aftershock of what I had just heard, I let her in on the apparent secret that I am German and she had truly insulted me as well as my family. Apparently feeling bad about what she had done, she actually suggested that I was lying about my heritage and asked me to stop it. I became even more appalled and distressed. She said, "You are not German, Nora. You are too nice and love everyone. You are the opposite of Germans and could never be one."

Once she realized I was sincere, she wholeheartily apologized and was looking for forgiveness. Of course, after discussing what had taken place and how disrespectful she was, I excused her actions. We continued to be good friends, of course with a new understanding of keeping your opinion to yourself if you have nothing good to say. It is easy to spread our negative opinions about others without recognizing who really is in our party and not understanding the ramifications that may follow. But the truth is do we really know everything there is to know about someone? So what if one is German, black, Jewish or Catholic? The bottom line is we are all, in essence, one and the same. One passage I like to pursue is the words from our reliable source, the Bible—"*Love thy Neighbors.*" What a better place we would live in if we were not out to make ourselves look better by putting down others.

Marty was a Jewish student at the University of South Florida. His temple was trashed when he was younger.

My family has been members of the same temple, Temple Beth-El, for the past eighteen years. I've learned to appreciate other religions, but was raised Jewish. When I attended Sunday school, one of the things I learned about was the scope of hatred in the world including racism, bigotry, and anti-Semitism.

I will never forget the day that I walked into my temple youth group lounge and found that the walls were covered with swastikas and other derogatory comments. This was my first encounter with such hatred toward my religion. As I opened the door to the lounge I was in shock; I didn't understand why someone would do such a horrible thing. I was so naive to think that someone couldn't hate you because of your religion. I thought anti-Semitism stopped a long time ago. I found out in one split second that I was wrong.

These people didn't even know us and judged us on our beliefs and religious affiliation. They ruined everything—the walls, the furniture, the soda machine, etc. I was angry, but I was more hurt at the fact that they broke in and ruined the property. I just have one question—when is it going to stop?

Maya was an Egyptian student attending Salisbury State University. When she was replacing her social security card she got into a verbal fight over what race to mark on the questionnaire.

I lost my social security card and I went to file for another one at a local office. The women sitting behind the glass was a blond-haired, blue-eyed, middle-aged woman. At the bottom of the card there was a race question with little boxes to check off for race. The choices were as follows: white, black, Hispanic, Asian, or Pacific Islander. Well if you looked at me, you would think I was just an average white person but in fact my parents are both Egyptian and I was born in Egypt. The best choice that matches my background out of all the boxes would obviously be the box marked "white." She crossed out my answer and checked off Asian or Pacific Islander. I asked her, "How is Egypt in Asia or the Pacific Islands?" I refused to have that box checked off for my race. I told her I clearly didn't look Asian and I was far from being a Pacific Islander. The blond woman sat coldly behind the glass and was very distraught over this situation. After I fixed the application, she took it with a very negative attitude. She must have thought I was trying to tell her how to do her job, and she probably thought I was incompetent in filling out a form with my race on it because I am a foreigner.

George was a white student who attended the University of California at Santa Barbara. On 9/11 he saw a student from the Mideast get hit by members of the football team.

My high school was in New York State. My teammates and I hopped out of the showers and were having breakfast at the snack bar in the commons. Another friend walked up to us and said, "Planes are falling out of the sky!" We remained glued to the television for the entire class. During lunch, word was spreading of a relatively unknown Osama bin Laden masterminding the attacks on the World Trade Center.

Our high school is primarily composed of white, upper-middle-class students, with a few minorities mixed in. A student was leaning up against the wall with a half dozen of his friends. His hair was wrapped up in a red turban and his beard drooped down to his shoulders. As he stood there, a group of football players rounded the corner of the ticket office. They quickly walked up and the lead guy lunged into the unsuspecting kid's chest. He fell down onto his side while one of the guys shouted "Arab!" His friends slowly helped him up.

I curiously watched the kid walk across the quad. People were staring at him and shaking their heads in disgust. Everyone in the whole school seemed like they despised the kid. I felt sorry for him but I couldn't comfort and support him because all my friends would desert me and my reputation would be ruined. Not until he reached his classroom at the end of the quad did he escape the torment that he underwent in his endless trek across the quad.

Just because he was Middle Eastern and looked like what we thought terrorists looked like, he was suddenly the most hated kid in school. I didn't understand, and still don't understand why these students would treat him so horribly, when he didn't do anything. I guess since we were so sheltered from the rest of the world in our community, we didn't know any better. We had to blame somebody, and he was our scapegoat. At the school, we immediately thought that being Arabic was bad. I was amazed with this more than three years ago and I am still amazed now.

Sarah was a Jewish student who attended the University of California at Santa Barbara. In high school some boys made a variety of anti-Semitic comments.

I grew up in Newport Beach, not exactly the diversity capital of the world. The average income is fairly high.

I am Jewish and was never afraid to hide that until my freshman year in high school. In elementary school, I always felt that the other kids thought that me being Jewish was cool. My mom would come into class once a year during Hanukkah to throw a Hanukkah party. It was the social event of the year, and everyone always looked forward to it. When I started high school, this comfort zone of everyone knowing me was suddenly gone. In my world history class we were studying the Holocaust. Because I have ancestors who were kept in internment camps, this topic is very close to my heart. I sat in front of a few boys who were in the "cool group." That day I found out that the supposed "cool group" was based on putting others down.

As our teacher was talking about the Holocaust and the horrible things that normal people were put through just because of their religion, I could hear the guys who were sitting behind me begin to quietly laugh. I turned around to find them drawing swastikas on their desks. This was my first year going to school with either of these boys. They had never attended one of my Hanukkah parties and they did not know that I was Jewish. Not only were they drawing swastikas, but they also were talking about how Hitler was right and making anti-Semitic jokes. I just sat there quietly not saying anything, but I was crying inside. Truthfully I was scared that they would physically hurt me if I defended my religion and told them that what they were saying was offending me.

I must have cried for a week after this incident. I never experienced something so awful. Before high school I had always felt accepted and never felt as though I had to pretend to be something that I wasn't or hide who I really was. I told my mom what happened and she proceeded to have a meeting with my teacher. Although my teacher was sympathetic, I do not believe she ever punished either of the boys. My seat was moved so that I did not have to sit next to them anymore but I do not believe that any disciplinary action was taken.

Looking back on this experience, I do not know what I would have done differently. I would like to say that I would have said something and stood up for myself but at the same time it was a very scary experience. It is hard to tell when someone is making serious threats versus empty threats.

Anwar was a student of Egyptian descent at the University of California at Santa Barbara. He and his grandfather were harassed after 9/11.

The infamous attack on September 11, 2001 sparked many racial attacks on innocent Middle Eastern Americans in the United States. Although a lot of people were committing these racial attacks because they were confused and wanted someone to blame, they still caused a lot of distress to the people on the receiving end.

My grandfather and I were taking a walk around our neighborhood one day. He was dressed in his native land's clothing, the long Arabic type of clothing that extended to the feet. He also had an Arabic hat on, and maintained a beard for the sake of his religious beliefs. He lived a very humble life, never being violent or encouraging violence amongst family, friends, or anyone else.

That day we were innocently walking when a group of yelling and screaming teenagers came driving in their convertible car. When they spotted my grandfather's obviously unorthodox clothing, they screeched back, starting cursing at us, and eventually threw soda bottles at my grandfather. I became incredibly angry and cursed back at them, threatening them as they threatened us. They simply harassed us because we looked similar to the suspects who committed the atrocious acts on 9/11. But they failed to realize that we were just harmless people, such as them, trying to go about our lives in a peaceful manner and restrain ourselves from any potential violent situation. They proceeded to mock us and call us "terrorists" and other names. I yelled to them that their ignorance was making them blind, but they ignored me and kept on verbally harassing us. During this event, my grandfather tried to comfort me in our native tongue (Arabic) that these kids were merely confused and needed someone to blame. So, we kept on walking, and eventually they became weary of their own childish games and hastily left in their car. This will forever be embedded into my memory, because I actually felt scared and harassed because of my racial heritage. This particular event changed my perspective on people's nature of being harmless; instead, I developed feelings of abhorrence towards society and their innuendo of ridicule toward a particular race of people.

Sarah was a Jewish student at St. Mary's College. She was told by her best friend that she was going to hell because she was Jewish.

My worst racial experience occurred in middle school. I was walking with my then-best friend, who was a staunch Christian. Out of the blue, she turned to me and said, "Look, I'm saying this because you're my friend, but I'm really worried about you. You *do* know you're going to hell because you're a Jew, right?"

This type of statement has been an issue in my life a few times. People I didn't know had called me "kike," but never a friend. It was extremely unnerving to see that she really didn't accept me and that being a good person was enough to make it okay to be friends with me.

15

Self-Image

In this chapter students describe their own personal struggles of coming to terms with who they are and accepting who they are despite the negative messages they may have received from family, friends, acquaintances, and the media. The identities individuals express may not find validation in their family and school environments. Thus, the belief of how one may be perceived by others may influence how individuals construct and express their racial identities (Brunsma 2006). Indeed, Rockquemore and Brunsma (2002) find that the social networks such as family, neighbors, and peers influence the shaping and defining of one's identity.

The increase in diversity in schools, colleges, and universities has certainly led to greater tolerance of racial and ethnic subgroups. However, ethnic and racial differences are now more visible and have complicated the task of forming one's racial and ethnic identity (Wakefield and Hudley 2007). Members of minority groups must determine how they will retain their ethnic/racial identity, how they will identify with other minority groups, and how will they be perceived by the dominant group (whites). Adolescents often pass through three stages as their race/ethnicity becomes part of their personal identity: unexamined ethnic identity, ethnic identity search, and achieved ethnic identity search. Often it is an encounter with racism, prejudice, or discrimination that initiates the move through these different stages (Phinney 1996).

Dutton, Singer, and Devlin (1998) find that many of the social problems that impact minority children such as low self-esteem, delinquency, and misbehavior can be attributed to experiences with racism. Likewise, family and the school environment have a strong affect on the development of racial identity and self-concept. Dutton, Singer, and Devlin (1998) found that children attending less integrated schools were more likely to dislike other races when compared to children attending more integrated schools. The implications are such that children exposed to racism are deprived of the ability to function at their full potential as children and adults (Comer 1989). Zirkel (2004) examines integrated schools and finds that racial stigma continues to exist in a study of minority students within an integrated setting. Minority students were found to be more isolated at school and as a result less interested in academic work. Nevertheless, a positive ethnic identity provides adolescents with the coping skills to face adversity. Wakefield and Hudley (2007) found that a strong ethnic identity had an impact on how students might respond to racial discrimination depending on the context or situation. However, in general African American males with a strong ethnic identity were less likely to endorse a passive response to discrimination.

One of the common subthemes in this chapter is feelings of isolation because they are a minority. Karen describes how she felt she couldn't be truthful about her experience as a young black woman for fear of being judged or not accepted by her roommate's parents. Karen later feels that her fears were unfounded and it was her own discomfort that altered her perception.

Other students describe their experiences of accepting who they are. For example, Colon describes how he felt inferior because he was Hispanic as he states, "I felt extremely uncomfortable. I felt and still continue feeling uncomfortable when I walk amongst masses of white crowds. I feel that I don't belong in such a crowd. I felt minor, puny, unimportant, dirty, and savage." Similarly, Kai was affected by several incidents that caused her to feel ashamed of her Chinese ethnicity as she states, "Many of these little incidents have made me ashamed of my background. For a while I tried not to tell people that I was foreign born. I used to hide my Chinese magazines when my white friends came over."

Interestingly, the literature regarding Asian and Hispanic minorities and self-esteem is somewhat limited. In fact, most of the literature focuses on how the individual feels about his or her group identity with a focus on acculturation and assimilation and how structural forces such as colonialism, ethnic competition, and labor market incorporation from the "group image component of self-concept" (Porter and Washington 1993). These paradigms have been criticized because they fail to link personal identity to culture and social structure as demonstrated by the essays mentioned above. These paradigms are in contrast to those used to understand African Americans where the vast majority of the paradigms are rooted in frameworks from psychology such as relative deprivation theory and socialization into a changing subculture (Porter and Washington 1993).

Campbell and Troyer (2007) found that individuals who identify with one racial group but are often mistaken for being a member of another racial group often experience stress and negative outcomes. Specifically, individuals with an ambiguous racial appearance often experience conflict between their own racial self-identification and ways others classify them. Maddox (2004) asserts that the focus on racial categories limits our understanding of racial categorization and identity among racially ambiguous social targets. The increasing level of racial integration and multiracial children presents a number of complexities regarding perceived identity and personal/individual identity (Maddox 2004). Some students in these essays describe how they were often mistaken for another race or ethnic group and this impacted how they viewed themselves. Delores describes how" classmates always mistook me for Hindu because of the dark color of my skin. . . . I was ashamed of my heritage and blamed my color on my father." Research finds that in general, Mexican American children have lower personal self-esteem than whites and African Americans while Korean and Japanese Americans often have a poor body image when compared to African Americans and whites (Porter and Washington 1989).

The essays in this chapter demonstrate how these students struggled against the many stereotypes of their racial and ethnic background as they came to learn who they were and accept themselves. Interestingly, all of the essays are written by minority students who describe how they struggled against cultural stereotypes and in many instances how it has taken years to accept who they are.

Sarah was a black student at Howard University. She is from Trinidad and describes how she was made fun of at school by other blacks because of her skin color and accent.

Being born into an environment where people aren't really divided by race, the concepts of "black" and "white" were not defined to me until I came to America. Upon coming to America, I was taught that African Americans could be capable of the worst type of racism against their own kind.

After being enrolled in the fourth grade at a predominately African American elementary school, I was taught that I was black. From the beginning of fourth grade to the end of fifth, my classmates would continuously call me "darkie." Being a darker shade when compared to my lighter classmates, the term slowly became my unwanted nickname. I became so accustomed to the name that I made myself believe that it was a term of endearment, specially designed for me. Along with the color of my skin, my accent became another dividing factor in my childhood. Having spent my earliest years in Trinidad, I was unaware of my accent until classmates began to mimic my tones. Besides finding fault in my accent and complexion, my "natural" hair was never viewed as anything more than "naps." Being of such a young age, my mother felt that I was not old enough to have my hair straightened, so every morning before school she would adorn my cornrows with bows and hair clips. Yet, no matter how many times I had her fashion my hair in new and creative designs, at school I was viewed as nothing more than a nappy-headed foreigner.

Granted, my experience at that school was not one of enjoyment, the actual hurtful experience was when I began to hate myself. The names, the "accidental" nudges while in class and in hallways, eventually subdued and became so natural to me that upon being placed in advanced class I was oblivious to the fact that I was no longer being picked on. My earlier experience that led to my dislike of school had evolved into a dislike of myself. While saying my prayers at night, I began to beg God to make me lighter. I began to feel as though I was lower than those around me because of my skin. To avoid the stares when I spoke, I learned to drop my accent. It became so natural to me that I recently discovered that around my family and others from the Caribbean, my accent is more defined when compared to an American set. While speaking with my American friends, I find myself dropping my accent and, as my mother would say, beginning to speak "more American."

Karen was a black student attending Howard University. When she attended the University of Buffalo, she felt very uncomfortable hanging out with her roommate's parents. Do you think she was justified in her feelings?

To be the only minority can sometimes be tough. Growing up in a single parent household, my mother always encouraged my sister and me to love everyone and acknowledge that people are just people. On the other hand, my father, a Black Muslim, condemned whites and looked upon them as being the chief source of evil in this world. After my mother and father divorced, my sister and I attended an all-black elementary school in a suburb of Ohio. There, whites were considered the minorities, but everything was fine; everyone treated everyone equally and with respect. I never would have imagined that things would be different the other way around.

As a freshman, I attended the University of Buffalo. Moving all of my belongings into my room, I did not see one black face. As soon as I opened the door, there were my two roommates—Carla and Julie. It must have been the first time either one of them had been in the same room with a black person, because they both did the same thing; they stopped and looked, without saying a word. I then took the initiative to speak first and introduced myself to both Carla and Julie. Carla, who seemed friendly, spoke back with no hesitation but I felt that Julie only spoke to me because she was forced to.

As the months progressed, we became friends. It was then Parent's Day Weekend at my school. Of course my mother was unable to attend, due to work, but my roommates' parents showed up. While sitting on my bed doing absolutely nothing, Julie's parents asked me if I wanted to tag along with them and other family members. I could have said no and just hung out with my other black friends but they were willing to take me out to dinner and to a comedy show. Excited to have free food, I joined them. This time I was the only black out of about fifteen whites. I felt like it was all eyes on me. Everything I said to them was funny, they fed me as if I hadn't eaten in years, and they were all interested in my background. Nervous and uncomfortable, I couldn't tell them that my parents were divorced, or that I went to an all-black elementary and middle school, or that my father was practically a Black Panther who hated them, so I lied. I was afraid they would look at me differently and consider me a typical black troublemaker if I had told them the truth.

One day before the year ended, I told Julie about that night. She told me that I shouldn't have felt uncomfortable, but I told her she did not understand and it was hard for me to explain. That night seeing them all together, pronouncing every single word, talking about their jobs and the money they had, the degrees they had received in school, and the use of terms I had never heard in my entire life made feel inferior. I am proud of my mother for raising my sister and me by herself and with the help of God. She has a great job and a master's degree, but she wasn't on the same level as Julie's parents. I guess I was ashamed that night. When I decided to come to Howard, I felt comfortable about being surrounded by people of the same race. However, I found out later that there are some blacks here that act the same way Julie's parents acted that night. So, I shouldn't feel uncomfortable because wherever I go people are just people like my mother said. If my mother can make it in this world without feeling uncomfortable, then so can I.

Nina was born in Mexico and was a student at University of California at Santa Barbara. She was often told that she could not succeed because she was Mexican.

I was born in Michoacan, Mexico and lived there for about seven years. Every girl that you would see on the street was usually dark, short, had black hair, and got married at an early age to start their family. From the first day that I came to the United States I was in complete culture shock because I did not know so many people of different races existed. I did not know that there was a higher school level other than middle school, and I was really excited that I was going to learn how to do different things and get an education. However, all of my dreams were crushed when I heard my grandfather tell my dad, "No sé porque las registrar en la escuela si al final van a salir con su domingo siete. No to das cuenta que nada mas somos Mexicanos, nuestra vida es trabajar en la fresa para los gringos."[1]

After eleven years, I still remember the words of my grandfather and the pain; the feeling of disgust and shame still comes back to me. From the day I heard him say this I got the idea that being Mexican was bad, that we couldn't achieve anything in life and that my only purpose was to get married, have children, and work in the fields. However despite my grandfather and his thoughts, my dad decided to enroll us in school, but that only served to make me feel even worse than I already felt. From the first day that I walked into my classroom, most of the kids would make fun of me because I was short, dark, and didn't know English They would always call me names like "negra" or "mugrosa" and tell me to go back to Mexico. Being brought up in such an environment, I always felt uncomfortable, disgusted, and ashamed of being Mexican. I recall the humiliation and the pity that I felt and how much I regretted belonging to that race. I used to think that maybe what my grandpa told my dad was true and that I would end up getting married and working in the fields.

Throughout elementary, middle, and part of high school I kept on feeling degraded, uncomfortable, and regretted the fact that I was Mexican. It wasn't until I decided to take history classes and join the folkloric group in my high school that I started meeting people with the same background as me who wanted to accomplish "The American Dream" while clinging to their Mexican roots. I also learned that there are a lot of Mexican people who have achieved their goals and now live a good decent life. Now that I had more knowledge about my culture and heritage, I felt proud to be who I was and decided to continue with school and pursue a career.

For so many years I had felt shame, pity, and rejection over who I was and where I come from. I attained the knowledge to see that I was my own person and that only I decided what to do with my life. Why is it that you experience racial discrimination among your own race and even worse, your own family? Why can't we all get along and try to stop racial discrimination? After all, aren't we all equal in the eyes of God?

Colon was a Hispanic student who attended the University of California at Santa Barbara. Growing up, he felt very inferior because of his Hispanic background.

When I was in elementary school my parents would always take the entire family to San Diego, a city bordering Tijuana, practically every weekend. I am originally from South El Monte, in the San Gabriel Valley, in Los Angeles County. This city has a majority Latino population with Asians next in line. Interestingly, our surrounding cities were composed of middle class white people. Coming from such an environment, I constantly felt that I lived in some kind of a bubble, a small world, away from the public eye. San Diego is almost like Los Angeles; it has its nasty and classy parts, Latin and white parts. These excursions into San Diego were never pleasant for me. Immediately after I set my foot out of the car, I was blasted by the sight of nothing but white people. It was so odd to see such a sight, for I never dwelled in a white community. We were all in a very classy plaza with fountains, restaurants, boutiques, and small, well-kept coffee houses. I felt extremely uncomfortable. I felt and still continue feeling uncomfortable when I walk amongst masses of white crowds. I feel that I don't belong in such a crowd. I felt minor, puny, unimportant, dirty, and savage.

After seeing so many beautiful portrayals of the white race in all sorts of media forms (TV, magazines, newspapers), I felt like nothing compared to them. I didn't have the blonde muscular body. I knew that I did not belong in San Diego. It was such a tense atmosphere and it was hard to deal with as a child.

Now that I attend UCSB, I have learned to cope with such environments but I can still recall the past. As I walked through the streets of San Diego, I would look back and forth between the whites and myself. I would see white and see purity, clean, glam. Then I would turn and see myself and observe the dark complexion, the dirtiness, and a low and gloomy feeling. As I felt and observed these feelings, all I could feel was tension, pain, shame, and humility. I felt inferior and looked down upon. Perhaps the whites did not see me like that, but I certainly did. It was my psychological war that I somewhat deal with today. As a Chicano, I am learning to become a border crosser. I am managing to hold my native Mexican roots while continuing to uphold certain aspects of the American life.

Delores was a Hispanic student who attended the University of California at Santa Barbara. She was made fun of because she was dark.

There are many people in the world who have had horrible racial experiences. My worst racial experience may not be life threatening, as many others were, but it was something that happens in everyday life.

Throughout my middle school years and most of high school, other students humiliated me, calling me "dark." My classmates always mistook me for Hindu because of the dark color of my skin. They also commented on my arms, saying that my arm hair was "hairy" and "gross." The comments about the arm hair made me really upset. However, I found a solution to this problem. One day in the eighth grade I decided to shave my arm hair. I felt so much better and confident about showing my arms after this. Unfortunately, I found no solution to lighten the color of my skin. I was ashamed of my heritage and blamed my color on my father. My father has very dark skin, and I assumed that I inherited it from him. Although I wouldn't come home from school crying every time someone made fun of my skin color, it still hurt me a lot. I started to become uncomfortable with myself and I had low confidence. I learned to hate the sun. I would stay away from swimming, or any other outdoor activity for that matter. I couldn't afford to get any darker.

When I entered high school, there weren't many students who made fun of my skin color. The only people who continued to comment on my skin were a few of my close friends. I hung around light-skinned Mexican Americans. I had one friend who made me feel the worst about my skin. She would unexpectedly and for no reason say "You are so dark." Every time we would joke around with each other, she would end with, "Well at least I'm not dark like you." Even though we were joking around, it lowered my self-esteem.

I learned to love the color of my skin through males. I started to get a lot of attention from boys through the three remaining years of high school. Many of the guys I talked to commented on my skin. They would say how beautiful my skin color was, and that it was of caramel color. All the attention I received helped build up my confidence. My friends still commented on my skin and I still felt a little uncomfortable; however I learned to ignore them and get over it quickly.

I feel it is unfortunate that I had to appreciate my skin color through males. I wish I could have learned to love my skin color on my own, but it is not important to me now. The important thing now is that I love myself, my body, my mind and everything else about me. I don't worry about the sun. I actually love the sun now, and I ended up at a campus right off the beach. I believe that my skin color is my best physical trait. When all is said and done, I am not ashamed of myself. I know I'm beautiful, inside and out.

Kai was a Chinese student who attended the University of California at Santa Barbara. She was made fun of as a kid because of her background. For a while she had a bad self-image.

I immigrated to the United States from Hong Kong when I was fourteen. In a suburb town in central New Jersey, I attended high school for a year. The school and the town were not very diverse. With my fashion sense completely different than that of most Americans, I stuck out like a sore thumb. I did not have a lot of friends because of the language barrier. Although most of the students were nice to me, some of them liked to tease me. I felt like I was made fun of mostly in the PE and biology class because all my classmates were freshmen. I guess most upperclassmen were more mature and didn't find teasing vulnerable people amusing. In my geometry class, which consisted of mostly sophomores, I was respected. They even thought I was a genius because I knew most of the material and did very well.

I remember these two boys in my biology class, Chris and Andrew. They were the class clowns. They liked to ask me stupid questions and make offensive comments. I tried to respond to them just to be friendly. One time they asked if I had a boyfriend back in Hong Kong. I told them the truth—yes. Then Chris said, "What's his name? Cheung-Ching-Chong?" I laughed at first, as I didn't realize how offensive it was. The teacher was outraged and told Chris he was rude. I didn't know that the "Ching-Chong" sound is what Americans use to depict Asian languages. Now I know that Chris was stereotyping and was humiliating me.

I know my so-called worst experience is not really that bad and I'm glad that I haven't been victimized too often. However, many of these little incidents have made me ashamed of my background. For a while I tried not to tell people that I was foreign born. I used to hide my Chinese magazines when my white friends came over. Now I understand that all the deceiving did not make me a better person, nor did it make me happy. I am now open about my heritage; all my friends know I was born in Hong Kong and I speak fluent Cantonese. I have many good friends and one awesome boyfriend; my life is satisfying. I have to admit that I am quite assimilated to American culture. The more Americanized one is, the less chance one has to be a victim of racial discrimination. The better you blend in, the less likely you get picked on. Yet, no one can be happy if he is not true to himself. My conclusion is that people of color should assimilate and keep in touch with their culture at the same time.

NOTE

1. "I don't know why you registered her at school if in the end you all are going to leave with your Sunday seven. You don't realize that we are nothing more than Mexicans; our life is to work in the strawberry fields for the white people."

16

Violence

The maiming and murder of people because of the color of their skin is the logical outcome of racism left unchecked. There are few images more chilling than that of whites smiling in the background of a lynching that occurred in the South in the 1930s. The days of community lynchings are gone. However, as the following essays highlight, individual and group acts of violence based upon a person's race still exist. The victims in these essays were both white and minorities. (The best source for hate crimes is the *Intelligence Report* put out by the Southern Poverty Law Center.)

Barnes and Ephross (1994) describe hate crime and violence as violence "against person, families, groups, or organizations because of their racial, ethnic, religious, or sexual identities or their sexual orientation or condition of disability." Hateful acts and violence against other individuals has a long and complicated history in the United States, and although it is difficult to determine the prevalence of hate violence many sources suggest there has been an increase of such violence in recent years, particularly since 9/11. And yet despite the increase in such crimes the research is quite limited. Green, McFalls, and Smith (2001) contend that much of the research on hate crime and violence is focused on attitudes and beliefs (e.g., measures of tolerance, prejudice, racism, and xenophobia) rather than prejudiced conduct.

Numerous explanations as to why hate crime or violence occurs have been offered ranging from psychological causes rooted in prejudice beliefs to macro-economic conditions (Green, Glaser, and Rich 1998). Other scholars have examined small group dynamics as a foundation for white supremacist groups and the role of peer pressure in committing hate crimes (Watts 1996). Some research contends that hate crimes are rooted

in cultural traditions and patterns of behavior as the way in which so-
cieties define and debate hate crime depends on their political-cultural
traditions (Green, McFalls, and Smith 2001). Similar to political-cultural
explanations are sociological explanations that contend that hate crime
results from socially disintegrated individuals who perceive to have lost
out in the midst of rapid social change. For example, economic disloca-
tion, the breakdown of social norms and authority, and greater social
and spatial mobility are found to coincide with an increase in racist hate
crime (McLaren 1999). Another explanation for the occurrence of hate
crimes is rooted in group conflict theory in which perceptions of competition with jobs, housing, and education fuel frustration. If this conflict
is mobilized along group lines, frustration can potentially lead to hate
crimes.

Green, McFalls, and Smith (2001, p. 489) contend that the common
theme interwoven through these theories is the sense of "competition
bred grievance, the salience of group-related discord, and normalization
of violence against out-group." However, the empirical literature testing
these theories is still in its beginning stages. Much of the research rests on
historical narratives, descriptive studies, attitudinal studies, etiological studies, and media analyses. More empirically based studies are limited due to
unreliable or non-existent statistics.

The essays within this chapter show numerous examples of racial violence and the perpetrators of such violence. Donald, an African American,
witnessed the assault of a fellow white student and Pamela had her family
home trashed after moving into a white neighborhood. Green, McFalls, and
Smith (2001) contend that the studies of *perpetrators* of hate crime provide a
portrait of the motives and circumstances that underlie hate crime violence.
White and Perrone (2001) developed a typology of the hate crime perpetrator. The *Thrill Seeker* is motivated by the excitement and rush of engaging
in a crime; these perpetrators are often youth. The *Reactive Offender* is motivated by a sense of superiority and the violence is viewed as a way to protect their way of life and their rights and privileges. And finally, the *Mission
Offender* is most often linked to hate groups. The violence is premeditated
and often based on a political ideology.

Throughout this chapter are examples of the *Reactive Offender* and more
often the *Thrill Seeker*. However, the pain is the same for the victims. The
essays within this chapter provide a glimpse of what it feels like for the
victims of hate crimes. Barnes and Ephross (1994) contend that research is
beginning to uncover the effects of hate violence on victims, but it is still
limited. In their study, they find that a majority of the victims felt anger
toward the perpetrator, as well as fear of injury and fear that their families
would be harmed. Likewise, many of the victims within the study engaged
in a number of behavioral changes that enabled them to cope including

moving out of the neighborhood, decreased social participation, increasing safety precautions for themselves and/or family (e.g., purchasing/using a gun). Some individuals coped by preparing for retaliation. Students within this chapter exhibited similar forms of coping. For example, David, a white student, felt anger after his victimization as he states, "The event was traumatic for me, and left me feeling angry with black people for several years." Claire states that she "felt humiliated and disrespected. I could not believe people could behave that way" after being victimized at the home of an acquaintance.

This chapter highlights the experiences of victims while also providing a glimpse of the perpetrators of the crimes. As the reader will see, the victims *and* perpetrators are from all races and backgrounds.

Denise was a black student attending Howard University. She describes how someone called her a derogatory name and she responded with violence. Were her actions justified? She concluded that even when the person apologized, justice was not served. Is she correct in this interpretation?

I migrated from Kingston, Jamaica about thirteen years ago, and now reside in the United States as a citizen. Several years ago, I was an employee in Rye Playland theme park, in Rye, New York. The theme park had just closed at midnight, and it was time for everyone to vacate the premises. There were two Caucasian security guards at the gate, and I thought that because I was an employee and we were somewhat good acquaintances that we could play around. One of the security guards asked me if I had a car, knowing that I really didn't have a car. My response to his question was yes I do, and at the same time I was standing by a car, and started to playfully insert my keys into the car door. To my surprise the owner of the car, a white male in his mid twenties, approached me. These were his words and I quote "Hey, you black bitch get the %!#@ away from my car! What the hell do you think you are doing?"

Surprisingly, with shock and blood running through my veins, I stood there watching the two security guards laughing hysterically at what had just occurred. Without thinking, I ran and got a piece of board, ran up to the white male, and just started hitting him continuously until I was arrested. When I finally realized what had taken place it was a little too late, and the same security guards that knew what was going on still didn't intervene until I had to give my statement. The case was taken to court, and every time that the case was called the two security guards and the white male would not show up. Finally, after three months of time wasted, the white male came to court, stated that he didn't want to press charges, and said that he wanted to give me an apology. I received the apology, and accepted it, but in the back of my mind I knew that justice was not served.

John was a white student attending Villanova University. While he was a bartender he witnessed a fight between the white lacrosse team and the black football team.

This past year I got a job as a bartender. I work three nights a week at a local college bar. The environment that surrounds bartending forces you to be ready for anything. Once the drinks start pouring, people have been known to get a little carried away. Fights aren't a random occurrence; they happen nightly. Since this is Villanova, you see a strange mix of kids. On one side of the bar you can find the larger-than-life football players. They are all on scholarship, and the majority of them are African American. On the other side, you find the rich white kids. Most of them are on the lacrosse team, some are rather big, but most are normal size. In the beginning everything seems ok; the lacrosse kids keep to themselves, while the football players do their thing. Nothing seems to be wrong.

Then one night out of nowhere a fight broke out. It started on the dance floor. It seems a black guy was dancing, and he came close to one of the white guy's girlfriends. In what seemed like seconds, their argument turned physical. One of the white guy's friends said, "Let's get that nigger." This of course angered the black guy, yet at the same time he was sort of helpless because all his friends were on the other side of the room, unaware of what was going on. They surrounded him and the shouting grew louder and louder. A beer bottle crashed into the head of the black guy. The look on his face expressed his shock.

Within a second, the football team was on the dance floor. They basically approached the lacrosse team as they would on the field. Bodies began flying everywhere. The two who originally started the incident were nowhere to be seen. Everyone was hitting everyone; there were no set teams anymore.

As the fight was breaking up, the white kids kept shouting out the word "nigger." Over and over, they just kept repeating it. As if the beating they received was not enough, they wanted to continue to provoke the football player. Luckily the captain of the team was there and he rounded up his team. He told them to walk away and thankfully they did. They had the ability to walk away from the childish talk of the lacrosse players. It didn't make sense. They had just been visibly beaten, yet they still had so much hate for these black guys. It seemed almost like a jealous rage, if nothing else. The football players went back to their beers and watched the TVs, but that altercation had an effect on me. It gave me some insight into how bitter people can be when discussing race. The thing that confused me even more was why the bitterness existed. Did these rich white kids envy the black kids enough to bring it to this?

Jacob was a white student at the University of Maryland. He was roughed up a little by some black bouncers at a hip-hop concert.

For a long while I have been immersed in hip-hop culture. Since I was around eleven or twelve, I began listening to rap music nonstop. It is simply my thing; it's what I like to do.

About a year and a half ago a few friends and I heard of an upcoming show at the 9:30 Club in Washington DC. The group was called "X" and I had been a fan for quite some time, so I scrounged some money together and got myself a ticket with a few friends. One of these friends had worked at a record store and was able to get us backstage passes for the show. My friends and I now had tickets to the show and backstage passes, so there was little that could take any of us off of "cloud nine."

We went to the show. They put on an amazing performance. Yet throughout the entire show it was blatantly obvious that I was one of easily less than ten white males in the club. I was aware that I was seemingly a little bit out of place. It was obvious in facial expressions of everyone around me—blank stares and curious looks as to why this five-foot-six "wigger" was trying to fit in.

Following the act, I approached the backstage area with my friends that I went to the show with, who happen to be black. My friends were allowed to pass by several large black men. I had my pass on my shirt, and I went right behind the guys I showed up with. I was stopped with a hand on my chest and the pleasant greeting of, "Where the fuck do you think you're going white boy?" I pointed to my pass. My friends came back and said that I was with them. I grew up with two of these guys. They weren't just going to leave me alone in a club in the middle of DC, especially while I was living in Frederick, Maryland, about forty-five miles away. After that things become a little bit hazy. A man that was with the bouncer to the backstage area gave me a quick left hook and knocked me down. My friends tussled with the bouncer and his friend for a second, until several other bouncers came to show us the exit in a manner faster than walking. I heard the two instigators call my friends Uncle Toms, amongst other things, and was outside in the street before I realized what had just happened to me.

At first I was in complete disbelief. There was no way that that could have just happened. Was it a dream? Was it a nightmare? And why the hell did my head hurt so much? But, that's beside the point. I had a pretty long talk with my friends on the way home and that was my first real exploration into a black man's mindset toward racism. I can't claim to understand what it feels like to have thousands of years of persecution behind me, but it was the first step to really understanding at least a little bit. I hold no ill will toward the two men responsible for this. It's not their fault that they had problems with me. For all I know, I may look exactly like someone who owes them money; who knows? But, what I took from this was that it was a completely racist situation.

Candace was a white student at St. Louis University. Her sister was shot by a racist black male gang member.

I grew up in a small town in Missouri where there was not a large number of African Americans, and the people who were black in our community never appeared that different to my family and friends. I also was not raised in a family that ever indicated that there was a reason for me to possess a different attitude toward people of a different color. It was always hard for me to realize that animosity still existed between these two races. Of course as I grew older and progressed through grade school I learned a lot about certain time periods like the 1960s, where racial protests were flying free. To me it was just history and seemed very far away from the life I lived every day. My parents divorced when my sisters and I were still young. During the separation my two younger sisters moved to a larger city with my mother. We didn't see each other a whole lot, and as a result we grew up in two separate worlds. Little did I know at the time how truly different they were.

On September 23, 2001, I received a phone call at approximately 6:00 a.m. By the time the brief conversation had ended, my phone had fallen to the bathroom floor. My younger sister and her best friend had been shot. My family and I made the three-hour drive to the hospital in one hour that morning. When we got to the hospital we found out that her best friend was already dead and they didn't know if my sister would live or not. We entered into a "waiting period" that would last for the next two months to discover the answer. She had been labeled a "victim of domestic violence" with the exact cause still unknown. I began to do serious research on my sister's case. The main reason for this horrific crime was beyond understandable to me at the time.

My sister and her best friend had been shot with a twenty-gauge shotgun simply because they were white. The African American male that shot them was part of an inner-city gang that had strong animosity toward whites. The gang members had two objectives. The first was to date a white girl simply to prove to the white male that they could have "their women." The second was to lose the girl. At times this meant to simply stop dating the girl and at worst it meant the scenario that faced my sister and her friend.

Only by a miracle did my sister somehow survive this terror. Unfortunately, her best friend did not. As I sat through the trial of the case many months later, I felt beyond threatened. I felt angry and confused, staring at a man who could take the stand and feel absolutely no remorse or regret for what he had done or why

How can there be so much division and hatred still in our society? I responded to this at first with an angry attitude. After a few months, however, I realized that it would not help the situation by staying angry. I slowly realized that the people who still express such hatred and hold these prejudices are simply the low and worthless part of our society. My purpose was therefore not to get angry but to continue to work toward eliminating any of the division lines between races that others had drawn. Although I can say that I have personally experienced a very terrible form of racism, I know that I'm not the only one who has. I hope that our society will continue to put these prejudices behind them and progress toward an equal community.

Pamela was a black student attending Howard University. When her family moved to a new home in Texas, the outside was trashed.

My worst racial experience happened to me when I was about seven or eight years old. I live in a small suburb of Dallas with a high concentration of whites and many upper-middle-class families. We had just moved to a new house with a big pool and a slide, a circular driveway, and a doggie door. There was even an upstairs playroom with a great view of the neighbor's backyard. I woke up one morning to let my dog come into the house, when I noticed there was something floating in my pool. It was still dark and I could not figure out exactly what it was, so I turned on the lights. What I saw then still brings tears to my eyes. My pool had been trashed. There were grass clippings, trash, and paint thrown in as well as what I was later told was a highly toxic poison. On the back of our fence in white spray paint were written the words "nigger" just as big and bold. In the front of the house there were toilet paper balls covered in feces. The crowning piece to this whole ordeal was that in the elliptical part of my front yard the letters KKK had been written in gasoline. Now, contrary to the ever-popular "lighting a cross on fire," these sick bastards wrote in gas so that as the weather got hotter and the grass started to get greener, the only part that wouldn't be green is that part. They did this so that the whole world would have a daily reminder of what had happened.

I ran and woke up my parents crying. They looked both heartbroken and furious. My father called the police. I vividly remember that the officer in charge chuckled and said that nothing could be done because this was just a dumb teenage prank. After the officers left, my father disappeared for a couple of hours with strict instructions not to touch anything—period.

Upon his return he had two black FBI agents with him. He had gone downtown and talked to the hate crime division, a unit that wouldn't just pass the destruction off as a "teenage prank." The agents took samples of the grass from the pool and a few other items, and then left and said they'd be in touch. Later my father told me that the grass had been matched to one man's yard from further up the street and that he had actually been a part of it. My father even told me the man and his followers had been "chased out of town."

Claire was a black student at Howard University. She was threatened and attacked by two white kids at the home of an acquaintance.

Most of the racism I have experienced in my lifetime has been very subtle. However, my worst racial experience is something that will always be clear in my mind. This experience made me realize that racism is still a part of America today and it seems it will be for years to come.

In my hometown of Williamsville, New York there are not many blacks. When I was thirteen years old, I went to an almost all-white middle school and I was widely accepted. I was everyone's friend. Outside of school I hung out with the "cool" kids who were friends with the kids who were risk takers and troublemakers. One day a friend of mine asked me if I would go to a boy's house with her. This boy was one of the biggest bullies in our town. She really didn't want to go by herself. We were greeted by the people that we knew. However, we were not so warmly accepted by two guys who we had never seen. They just looked at us with disgusted looks. One of the guys pulled us to the side and warned us to stay away from those guys because they were extremely prejudiced.

After talking to our friends for a while, the two older boys got into their car and began to pull out of the driveway. My friend and I turned away as they started down the driveway, but we were soon startled by the revving engine and realized that they were gonna try to run us over. We moved out of the way quickly as they yelled some racial slurs at us, drove over the grass in the front yard, and left the property. The boy that my friend had originally came to see apologized for his friends and just told us to pay it no attention. We went into the house and hung out for a while. Things were fine until the two boys returned. I heard them outside say, "Are those niggers still here? We have something planned for them. It's gonna be fun." I began to get scared and went to get my friend who had gone somewhere with the boy. I finally convinced her that we were just not in a good situation and we should leave so we tried to call her mom; however, her mom wasn't home. My friend and I walked out the house and were met with menacing looks from one of the boys who was sharpening a stick with his pocketknife. Then the boys began calling us names and threatening us, telling us we don't belong there and saying we had to leave. One of the boys had gone into the house and I saw from the window that he went in the fridge. He returned with some eggs. This is when I became extremely uncomfortable and decided that we should wait at the school down the street, so we began to walk away. I was so scared. We finally started down the driveway but as we walked away the two boys began to yell racial slurs and throw the eggs so we had to run away.

I felt humiliated and disrespected. I could not believe people could behave that way. Although these people made me scared and uncomfortable I did not develop negative attitudes against whites. This experience just taught me that ignorance and bigotry still exists and that I shouldn't be so naïve.

Donald was a black student at Howard University. He was witness to an assault on a white student in high school.

I was in seventh grade in Greensboro, North Carolina and my middle school was predominantly black. The white students were even outnumbered by Asians. I went to the restroom in between classes and there was a young man there who was everything that was plaguing the black youth in America. He had a bad reputation for being very aggressive and had one of the worst attitudes in the school. He was enrolled in remedial classes. Also in the restroom was a white kid who was small and frail. It was obvious that the white kid had said something that made the young black man angry. Then the black kid grabbed this little white kid and started to beat him up. I remember vividly how he slammed his head into the urinal several times, and him falling to the ground bleeding. While the white kid was on the ground the black kid kicked him twice, and mind you he was wearing heavy construction boots. I remember it sounded as if the boy's ribs had cracked. It all happened so fast. By this time other students had begun to arrive in the restroom, causing the black kid to leave before anyone caught on to what was happening.

After he left I helped the white kid up and tried to help him clean up his injuries. I think he realized that I too was black, the same as the young man that had just beat him up, and he started making racial comments to me and the other black kids. He said, "You stupid fucking nigger; I will kill you!" I looked at him as if he was crazy. I understand that he was very upset about getting beat up by someone whose skin was the same color as mine, but there was no reason to lash out at someone who was trying to help. The comments did not stop; he just continued to call us names as if we were all guilty.

I have often thought about that day, and I realize that I could have done more to help the young man, but at the time I was just so taken by the whole situation. I really don't fault the white kid for what he said because of what had just happened to him. Who can really blame him as a fourteen-year-old kid? I just remember how mad I was at the time by what he was saying as I was trying to help him. It was an unfortunate event that taught me a lot about people.

Natalie was a black student attending the University of South Florida. In 1985, some white thugs threatened her because she was shopping in a "white" store. Her university did not support her.

The year was 1985 and it was my junior year of college at the University of West Florida in Pensacola, where I attended school and played basketball. One day I went shopping at the local Piggly Wiggly with my white room- mate. We went shopping to buy goods for a place the university had rented for us until we could move into dorms the next year. It wasn't until we en- tered the door that the 6'3" white guy jumped out with two of his buddies and said "nigger where do you think you're going?" We did not reply. We entered the store only to be looked at by each clerk, customer, and store manager. Finally an elderly woman walked toward us, stating to my room- mate, "We don't shop with niggers in this store." At this time all three guys in the store were making their way toward us. They appeared to have been drinking. The biggest one said "don't you know what happens to niggers in this town? You must not be from here." We did not comment. We left the items and began to exit the store, only to be confronted again. One of the older people had called the police to come, in fear that something would happen when we exited the store. The officer said, "It's best you girls shop in Pensacola; it's different out here." We got into the car only to be followed by these same three individuals.

While we were at the university, these three guys located our place and wrote racial slurs on our front door. When we returned home to this, our other roommate had come home at the same time. She too was upset and angered at this act of racial injustice. She called the coach, who said "just wipe it off the door and go inside." I called back home to inform my family, and so did my roommate. Both of our parents called the coach to inquire about other living alternatives. I was told that the only option was for me to move in with some other basketball player more like me. What does "more like" mean? Well Negro, black, African American, or just nigger, I felt. I had not only been told I was a nigger by perfect strangers, but had those feelings of inequality reinforced by a university with which I agreed to spend my next two years playing collegiate sports. This left a bitter taste in my mouth and soul. I still feel the hurt and pain of this. I left that spring.

I tried to bury these feelings. It took years of internal therapy to come to terms with that situation. I guess that's just how some things were back then.

Sarah was a Jewish student who attended the University of South Florida. When she lived in Boston, a cross was burned on her black neighbor's lawn.

When I was young I equated racism with anti-Semitism. I assumed that because I was Jewish I had some idea of what it felt like to be hated for something beyond my control. As I got older I came to understand that there are inherent differences between the two experiences. My religion is something internal and only obvious if I care to share, whereas race is something that is usually obvious just by looking. Additionally, both forms of hatred carry their own set of stereotypes and tragic pasts. Racism's violent history in this country still reverberates today.

I grew up in the Northeast. I was not raised in a home where issues of race were discussed at the kitchen table, but I knew early on that the color of someone's skin was simply a piece of the puzzle of their life, not their definition.

One day, an African American family moved onto our street. They had a son named Bill who was just my age and I was thrilled to have a classmate living so close. We walked to and from school together every day for several months and became great friends. Late one night, I woke up startled by something outside my window. Looking out I saw black smoke filling the night sky and wondered what caused it, but I was so tired that I fell back to sleep. The next day when I came down for breakfast, I remembered the image and told my parents about it. I sat down in our den and watched as my parents struggled for the words to describe what I had witnessed. I remember feeling badly for their discomfort even as I wondered why they seemed so awkward. My dad told me that there were people, filled with hate, that spend their time being cruel to others based on their prejudices. He explained how they had erected a cross and burned it as a warning for the family to get out. And they did. I never saw Bill again, but his face, our friendship, and the smoke-filled sky have stayed with me. It was only later that I learned that the same fate could have touched our lives. But again, it was different because we did not have a Semitic name. This placed us in the position of blending in with everyone else. It is this concept of blending that I have always found troubling.

Mary was a white student at the University of South Florida. In seventh grade there was frequent interracial violence at her school. She began to fear blacks because of this.

I grew up in a predominately white middle-class community. In all the schools I attended there was always a fair mixture of white and black students. In the schools that I attended in elementary and high school, every student, no matter the color, was treated the same. However, seventh grade was a different scene.

In the mid 1990s, the Hillsborough County School system decided to integrate the schools in west Tampa with the schools in south Tampa. This meant the students in the middle-class areas were to be bussed to the schools in south Tampa, the lower-class areas. I went to a seventh grade school where only seventh graders attended. Blacks were the majority, next were the Hispanics, and then the whites were the minority. The school was separated according to the students' academic level. The honor students, who were mostly white, were placed on the south side of the school and never left that side. If you were an "average" grade point student like me, you were placed in the main campus. In the main campus, the blacks ruled every-thing—the bathrooms, the hallways, and you! The worst racial experience was that year in seventh grade. That experience is called "White Cracker Day."

The Friday before "White Cracker Day" was called "Hell Day." This was the day the black students made their threats to the minority students that they wished to beat up. The blacks would threaten the Hispanics and the Hispanics would threaten the white students. If you were one of the threat-ened students, your accuser would beat you next Monday, "White Cracker Day." I will never forget when "White Cracker Day" arrived. I was one of the few students who never received any threats. That Monday there were only a couple dozen white students who showed up for school. The attendance at school that day was so low that teachers would not teach. All the beatings went down in the bathrooms or in the locker rooms. I did not personally witness any beatings because I knew if I did I would be next. I did know girls who were threatened by other students and they chose not to show up on that particular day of school.

"White Cracker Day" was not the only day in which there was violence but it was the most damaging to many students because people planned what they wanted to do to other students. There were constant fights almost every day between each ethnic group. Toward the middle of the year the school hired a police officer to watch the hallways, classrooms, and bath-rooms. I will never forget seventh grade and luckily the next year my school was only one mile away from home. Two years later, the school system changed school zones and students from the middle-class areas were no longer sent to the south side schools.

I have not personally witnessed a horrible racist event like a fight or a beating. I do believe this is because of my experience in seventh grade. I learned from my middle school years not to test a black person because I would lose in a second. Black people, unlike white people, fight in cliques, not one-on-one. I never underestimate a black man. In fact, I fear some black men. They dominated my middle school years. I do not fear white men because to me they are inferior to black men.

David was a white student at Villanova. Some black kids attacked him when he was in sixth grade.

My worst racial experience was when I was a younger child. I grew up in a shore town in South New Jersey. When I was in sixth grade, I lived near the bay and within four blocks or so of a black neighborhood. One time I was riding my bike into that neighborhood to get some milk for my father as the local Wawa convenience store. On my way out of the Wawa, several black kids were yelling things at me like "Hey white boy, where the fuck you going?" I hopped on my bike, and peddled down the street as fast as I could. Unfortunately for me, I was unable to get away in time.

One of the black kids kicked my bike down, and I went with it. Upon falling, the milk broke open and spilled all over me. The kids proceeded to laugh at me, curse, and beat my bike with their boots, leaving it in shambles. They then proceeded to kick me a few times. I got up and ran home, slightly injured (scrapes and bruises) but was relatively okay. I was so upset and hurt and I was ashamed to tell my father what happened, but I had little choice in the matter, given my battered appearance and the smell of spilled milk all over me.

The event was traumatic for me, and left me feeling angry with black people for several years. Now, in my college days, I realize that events such as this are not isolated to black people, but the event definitely scarred me for a long time. That was the first time I was discriminated against, and it felt awful. I cannot imagine a lifetime of the same feelings.

Donald was a white student attending Salisbury State University. Several African Americans threatened a group that he was walking with.

Over winter break a few of my friends and our girlfriends went to Newark, Delaware to play some pool at the town pool hall. Newark is where the University of Delaware is and the town is usually a very popular place. However, our evening out on the town coincided with the college's winter break so the town was fairly deserted. We played pool for about an hour and ate some pizza. We left the restaurant at around 9:30 p.m. and began to walk the couple of blocks back to the car. About halfway down the street we heard some shouting and glanced across the road to the opposite sidewalk. There, shouting obscenities and yelling catcalls at our girls, was a group of about six African American males. They were all about 6'5" and weighed about three hundred pounds, or at least that's the way it looked at the time. I am a fairly big boy and my friends were all members of the football team too, so we weren't short on size but this was definitely a situation we all wanted to stay out of. We just kept walking. The cursing continued with vulgar language about our mothers and other upsetting things. We heard "chicken," "coward," "cracker," and those sort of derogatory things. We continued walking as they made their way across the street toward us, trying to escalate a verbal confrontation into a physical one.

When the group was about ten yards directly behind us and we were still maybe a block away from the car, I was beginning to feel that we were going to have to confront these men. Moments after I had this thought, an officer pulled up along the sidewalk and asked if there was a problem. The group following us turned around and went in the opposite direction and we, relieved, said there was no problem and made our way to the car and to safety.

I am not sure what would have happened if the police officer hadn't shown up. I don't know if they were trying to scare us or do something worse. I can tell you though if it is the former they succeeded. I wouldn't say the situation was racially motivated per se, but I do think the fact that we were white kids made us more appealing targets. This situation worked out in the end with no one getting hurt but I can certainly say that this was my "worst racial experience."

Walter was a white student at Salisbury State University. When he was at a private school in Baltimore, a verbal exchange between members of his track team and kids from the community escalated. Do you think the school did the right thing by having the fence that is described?

My "worst racial experience" occurred my freshman year of high school. I attended a private school located in Irvington, which is on the outskirts of Baltimore city. At this point in my life I had experienced very little racism and had thought little about the differences between my life and others. This all changed very quickly upon entering my new high school. The school was very nice and had a great reputation for preparing students for college and life. Upon arriving I realized that my school was surrounded by tall fences and barbed wire with security guards at the entrances. After the initial shock, I thought very little about it and trusted that my school was working in my best interest to keep us safe, which it was.

These gates and fences came in use when I was attending my gym class some months later. As the gym teacher instructed us that we were to run a timed mile for today's class, I gazed at the barbed-wire fences and once again pondered the importance of these structures. I soon would know as I was on my third lap, huffing and puffing, when a group of young African American school children no older then eleven or twelve started mocking us and cussing us out for no reason. In response, many of my fellow classmates staring hurling racial slurs back at them as both sides now exchanged racial obscenities. As my classmates and I turned the corner on the last lap, the children were still there waiting with more curses. My classmates were instructed by our teacher to keep quiet as we passed them, so we jogged by as they followed us along the fence when the unthinkable happened. Two of the children picked up glass bottles lying on the street and hurled them over the fence onto the track on which we were running. Everyone quickly turned away from the shattering glass to the safety of our gym. This story was quickly told and further embellished as it made the rounds.

This racial experience was nothing like anything I had ever experienced before. Sure, I had heard racial slurs and jokes about other races, but never had I heard them directly spoken to a person of that race with such hatred. I had also never, ever, seen it result in violence before. From then on we all felt differently toward the local population of the area as we all felt scared to leave our tall walls and barbed-wire fences.

Melissa was a white student attending the University of California at Santa Barbara. There was a race riot at her school.

Norco High is located in a small horse town in Southern California. The town is predominately Caucasian and many of its citizens are very racist or simply not very open-minded toward different people. In my school, there were only seventy-one African American students out of three thousand students. It was a racial time bomb just waiting to explode.

In every school, students and their friends have a specified place they hang out between classes, at lunch, and before and after the school day. There was a wall at the top of the quad where all the popular kids hung out and was called "The White Wall." Almost all of the African American students hung out at the bottom of the quad under the trees, also known as "The Jungle." There were always small problems between students of different races, but it never escalated into what it did one day during my junior year.

One day at the beginning of the quarter, four or five black students came up to "The White Wall" and just sat down. They were not eating and they were not talking; they were just sitting there staring at all the white kids and waiting for someone to say or do something. After about fifteen minutes of taunting them, one of the white kids threw a banana at the table they were sitting at. In retaliation, one of the black kids threw a can of Coke at another student, and when everyone saw this, they came running. The African American students came running up from the trees and all the white students came over to the table that they were sitting at. Without any warning, over two hundred students were throwing punches and jumping all over each other and they weren't holding anything back.

In the end, authorities broke it up. Three African-American students were severely injured and one was killed. It was definitely like nothing I have ever seen before.

In the days that followed, the school made strict regulations for every student and teacher on campus. For example, one was not permitted to wear any clothing that displayed an iron cross or fist on it because it implied a racist attitude. Also, if one was caught using a racist slur, they were suspended and recommended for expulsion. The rules were found all over campus, on the web, and in every school handbook. The authorities were very strict with these rules.

Although I am white, I still felt the impact that racism inflicts on people. I could never imagine myself having to deal with issues like that. The fight at my school made me realize that racism still does exist and people should truly try to fight it. I would never want to see a situation like that, first-hand or second, ever again.

17

Police

No greater difference exists between blacks and whites than the extent to which racism exists in the administration of justice (Smith and Seltzer 2000; Hurwitz and Peffley 1997). Blacks and Hispanics are far more likely than whites to believe that racism pervades the justice system from arrests to prosecutions to convictions to length and type of incarceration (Weitzer 1996). For example, Weitzer and Tuch (2005) find that most whites believe minorities are treated the same as whites by police officers and many whites are skeptical when it comes to police discrimination. African Americans are more likely than Hispanics and whites to perceive police bias against Hispanics and African Americans while Hispanics are less likely to perceive bias than blacks (Weitzer and Tuch 2005). Many perceptions of police discrimination are conditioned by race *and* class. Middle-income African Americans are often more critical of the police and justice system than lower income African Americans (Weitzer and Tuch 1999; Weitzer 1999).

African Americans and Hispanics are more likely to report personal discrimination at the hands of police officers (Weitzer and Tuch 2005). The fact that African Americans and Latinos are more likely to perceive bias is a function of the disproportionate negative interactions experienced by the police. African Americans make up 12 percent of the population yet they account for more than half of all arrests for robbery and murder and just under half of all inmates in state and federal correctional facilities. Police officers are not the only perceived perpetrators of discrimination within the criminal justice system. Prosecutors, judges, jurors, parole officers, and prison officials are also often blamed for racial bias and discrimination in the administration of justice. The perception of racial bias has to lead to mistrust of the criminal justice system and those who administer justice as indicated by the words in David's essay after police broke into his home looking for his brother, "I knew I would never appreciate cops, authority, and white boys who get tough behind badges. Never."

The association of race and criminal justice has permeated the public consciousness and are conflated by the role of the media, particularly with regard to African Americans (Gilliam, Jr. and Iyengar 2000). Research finds that the more "stereotypically black" a person's physical traits are, the more criminal that person is perceived (Eberhardt, Davies, Purdie-Vaughn and Johnson 2006). Such bias exists with sentencing decisions as well, where judges give harsher sentences to defendants who are more stereotypically black than defendants who are not, even when controlling for criminal histories (Eberhardt et al. 2006). The media further distorts the reality of an already biased criminal justice system such that the public is even more likely to accept the myth of black criminality. Dixon and Linz (2000) found that African Americans were overrepresented as perpetrators of crime, while Latinos were underrepresented as perpetrators and as police officers. The underrepresentation of Latinos is attributed to the language barrier. However, whites were overrepresented as police officers and law abiding citizens. As a result, the stereotypic criminal characteristics of African Americans and Latinos often activate stereotypic associations among viewers as well as the news editors and reporters that choose whether or not a story is newsworthy. A different picture emerges in the representation of minorities and whites as criminals and police officers in television entertainment. As crime shows have become a staple of primetime entertainment, Mastro and Robinson (2000) found that although minorities are overrepresented as officers and underrepresented as criminals, *young minority perpetrators* experienced more aggression and force at the hands of police officers than white perpetrators. The authors find that these images of young minority men may create fears of youth violence. Likewise, such images may again feed into the stereotypic associations of minority youth as criminal.

In this chapter we see examples of kids being stopped by the police while they are riding bikes, walking, and jogging. The police are seen as busting through homes, stopping black kids from using a basketball facility, and harassing young blacks at a local restaurant. On the other hand, there is also an essay in which the overreaction of the police in a brawl is placed in the context of the unruly behavior of a group of kids.

Many students wrote about their experiences being stereotyped as criminals and profiled most notably in terms of DWB (driving while black) or SWB (shopping while black). For example, Stephan was pulled over and accused of stealing a truck and John describes how he was pulled over for a crime he did not commit. Profiling is a specific and directed form of social cognition aimed at determining who has or is likely to engage in crime (Dabney, Dugan, Topalli, Hollinger 2006). Police stops of citizens have long been controversial in minority communities as police have been accused of stopping people who fit a certain profile as drug offenders or gang members (Weitzer 1999). Many of the initial studies focusing on traffic stops show Blacks and Hispanics are widely overrepresented while Whites are significantly underrepresented (Petrocelli, Piquero, and Smith 2002). The post-9/11 era has ushered in a "new" kind of racial profiling and studies of racial profiling directed at those of Middle Eastern descent. The targets of racial profiling are no longer just African Americans and Latinos, but other minorities suspected of domestic crime and drug rime such as Arab Americans, Muslims, and others of Middle Eastern origin (Harris 2003).

Students in this chapter describe how they or their parents were pulled over. Many students say they expected their experience to occur. Others characterized their experiences in a variety of ways, including feeling threatened, embarrassed, scared, or just plain tiring.

Terrence was a black student at Howard University. He describes being stopped by the police in Houston, Texas while he was riding his bike.

I have been fortunate throughout my life in that I have not ever really had a blatant negative racial experience. I am sure that I have experienced inherent racism or some sort of "under the surface" racism. However, there is one case in my life, when I was twelve years old, where I had a negative experience that shaped me as a black man.

It was the summer of 1991. I had just moved to Houston, Texas from Atlanta, Georgia the year before. The significance here is that the city of Atlanta is primarily composed of African Americans. I lived in a black neighborhood and went to schools with all black populations. I had primarily grown up around African Americans my entire life. In fact, the only whites that I engaged with were at my church. My church was an incredible environment, a mixture of the black population that lived in the area and the whites who were instrumental in building the church. Everyone got along like family. Several senior-aged whites were instrumental in my development at an early age. As a result I only had the most positive experiences with whites and that influenced my thinking when it came to race relations.

My neighborhood in Houston was a very diverse one, composed of whites, blacks, Hispanics, Asian Americans, and Middle Easterners. I had three best friends at the time—one was Indian American, one Mexican American, and one was white. I stayed at my Indian friend's house a lot. I would ride my bike around the neighborhood a great deal, going from one friend's house to another. One day while I was riding home from a friend's house, I was stopped by what I later found out was a police detective in an unmarked car. He informed me that a couple of kids were vandalizing vacant houses around the neighborhood, and that I "fit the description." I also later learned that the description was a kid on a black bike with a blue hat. I had a black bike and my hat was black. I guess what I failed to realize in all of my innocence was that my skin was black too, and in that neighborhood that could be considered an offense as well.

They kept me in the hot sun for about an hour, during which another detective was called to the scene. I told them that I did not know what they were talking about and that I had been at my best friend's house all morning. They did not believe me, and finally my Indian friend and his mother arrived on the scene. She informed them that I had been at her house for most of the morning, but they did not seem to listen to her either. Maybe it was because her skin was darker than mine. Finally my white friend's aunt showed up and informed the detectives that indeed I had been at my Indian friend's house most of the morning because her nephew was with us. Finally the cops let me go, and I rode home not the same person I was an hour before. I know that I lost my innocence on that day. I went from a black child whom the world looks upon with hope, to a black man many people view with contempt. Now I realize that this experience was my initiation into an order of black men who share the intranational experience of being black in America. All of them have experienced racial discrimination in some manner, and what is sad is that I think all blacks, and people of color, will eventually join this order in their lifetimes.

David was a black student at Howard University. He describes how the police broke into his house looking for his brother.

I would say that my worst experience with race came when I was about sixteen. It was a Sunday morning in Westbury, New York, on Long Island. It is a predominately black and Hispanic neighborhood full of good sides and bad. My grandmother was in her room preparing for church. My mother was in the kitchen in her housedress cooking breakfast. All was quiet and calm for the first few hours until we heard a knock at the door. More like a heavy bang. Bang. Bang.

My mother obviously stopped to address the rudeness of the person on the other side of the door. I slept on the floor peacefully until I heard the voices of two very familiar, authoritative police officers. The officers were looking for my older brother for some old warrant. Nassau County cops in any black neighborhood bring the disturbing mood of sharks looking for prey. They are always these Italian or Irish tough guys looking for some poor idiot's ass. We gave them nicknames like "Superman" and "Puma." Superman relentlessly pursued criminals. Puma, with his older crater-like skin, took guys across the tracks for a bruising before going to his precinct. Some have a Shere Khan [Editor's Note: From the movie *The Lion King*] tone when they need volunteers for a line-up at the precinct. Some brothers gave in to the small change the officers offered as an incentive. I didn't fall for it. I knew their tricks. I didn't want to end up in their database.

My mother kept them at the door as best she could saying, "He isn't here." One officer asked, "Can we look around ma'am?" She repeated that he was not here at the time but his question was directly followed by a forceful step into my grandmother's apartment. The speaking officer disrespected the woman standing in the way of his target. I could hear the heavy steps of the lead cop hit the floor as his handcuffs jingled and his radio bleeped static messages. His steps moved past the kitchen into the living room where I slept. He saw a long figure resting a few feet away from where he stood. I usually pulled my blankets over my head so I can sleep better. He could not see my face. Without hesitation I heard the button snap on the holster to his weapon. I could hear his gun slide out of the holster and rest inches away from my head. "Don't you move boy." The other officer stepped in further. The volume quickly escalated. My mother yelled, "That's not him." They ignored her, "Step back please ma'am. We have a warrant for the arrest of your son." The officer pointing his gun at my head didn't touch me but called me by my brother's name and told me to put my "God damn hands up right now." My grandmother entered from her room to see the events unfold. She screamed a few unholy expletives at the two white cops who typically patrolled the neighborhood. I felt fear, rage, and disgust bubble in my stomach. All of those things raced through my head as I slowly pulled down my blankets to stare down the barrel. I hated their purpose. I hated the disregard of my mother's honesty. I hated that the officer even cursed God on Sunday. I hated that moment. I stared the officer in his eyes until he holstered his gun. He said, "It is just procedure, miss. We have to follow our instinct sometimes. If you see your son, advise him to turn himself in before we get him. Have a nice day." There was no apology. I hated them for that. I knew if they got to him first he would not be driven straight to the precinct. They would serve him somewhere before that. My mother closed the door behind the officers and checked me out. We shared the same emotions at that moment. I knew I would never appreciate cops, authority, and white boys who get tough behind badges. Never.

John was a black male student at Howard University. He describes being stopped by a police officer in North Carolina for a crime he did not commit.

I am from a small, racially divided town in North Carolina called Golds-boro. The population takes pride in the fact that it was the only town in North Carolina that Civil War General William T. Sherman failed to burn on his march to the sea. Later in history there were several billboards along the outskirts of Goldsboro that read, "Niggers go home!" Even during the supposedly progressive 1990s, several Klan rallies were held in the center of historic Goldsboro.

Because Goldsboro is home to a military base, Seymour Johnson Air Force Base, the town's population is actually quite diverse. However, there's always tension between black citizens and the police department.

When I was a senior in high school, I was a model student and citizen; I attended Governor's School, was an honor student, and a star football and basketball player for Goldsboro High School. I was friendly with the chief of police because I helped cement the formation of a Crime-Stoppers Alert Group within my school and sat on the Wayne County Safe School Committee.

But my accomplishments fell on deaf ears to the police officer who drove past me as I walked to a routine basketball practice at 7:30 in the morning. As I came to the end of the street not more than a block away from my house, a white male police officer pulled his car in front of me and jumped out, gun drawn. I stopped and looked at him as he instructed me not to move and to put my hands up. I reluctantly obeyed as he returned his gun to his holster and handcuffed me. He patted me down and told me that I was being detained as a suspect in a robbery that had just been committed thirty minutes before.

According to him, I fit the description the victim gave to police. That description was of a young black male clothed in athletic wear. I was outraged. Apparently, the robber had stolen a Moped.

"Do you honestly think I would be walking if I had stolen a Moped?" I asked him. "You stopped me because I am a black male." He admitted that I was right and then asked me for my name. I refused to give it to him, so he called for a transport unit on his walkie-talkie.

Just then, one of my teammates rode by. He happened to be the individual who had been robbed, and he stopped to ask what was going on. When the officer informed him, he was just as outraged as I was because he never said that the suspect was black.

Needless to say, the officer now looked rather meek and immediately began to apologize and uncuff me. His excuse for stopping me was that he automatically assumed the thief was black because white people in Goldsboro do not ride Mopeds. His excuse would have worked, except for one small detail: white people in Goldsboro *do* ride Mopeds.

I took the officer's name and badge number and continued on to basketball practice with my teammate. I told our assistant coach because he was a member of the police force as well. The next day, Coach told me that he spoke with the officer in question, who was stunned when he discovered who I was. I was content knowing that the man felt like a complete idiot, but I was more angered than anything. It is dangerous to be a black man, whether you are walking, driving, or just minding your own damn business.

Thomas was a Hispanic male student at Villanova University. The police stopped him as he was jogging with a friend.

I am fortunate enough to attend college on a full athletic scholarship. In high school, I excelled at track and field and was recruited by many schools, but opted for Villanova University because of its reputation—both academically and athletically. While on the track team, I met another sprinter who is black and became good friends with him. One night we decided to go out for pizza, and parked the car in a parking lot and walked to a pizzeria restaurant. After finishing dinner, we started to walk back to his car. It was getting late, and it was beginning to rain, so we took advantage of our athletic ability and began to jog toward my roommate's car. Before we could reach his car, we heard a loud voice behind us cry out "Freeze! Hands in the air!" The two of us turned around to see a policeman in pursuit of us with his hand on his holster. We immediately put our hands in the air, at which time the officer ran over to us, grabbed my hands, put them behind my back, pushed me onto the ground and handcuffed me. He then proceeded to do the same to my roommate.

One of the officers began telling me to just let him know what we did and he would let us off easy. I did not have a clue as to what he was talking about, and kept telling him this. His only reply was that I was making things more difficult on myself. He asked where I was fifteen minutes ago, and replied I was eating pizza in a restaurant, and that there were witnesses. He took out my wallet and asked where I was from, I told him New York, that I attended the university, and was here for summer school. He walked over to his car, leaving me in handcuffs, looked up my information, and came back. Once again he asked if I could explain where I was from 10:30 to 11:30, I told him exactly what I did, where I was, and asked him why he had me in handcuffs. He explained to me that someone had called the police claiming that two individuals were attempting to break into a car. There was no description, only that they began to run away, and it was about five blocks away. Apparently the officer saw me and my roommate jogging down Lancaster Avenue and detained us as suspects. He took no notice of our clothing, the fact that we were headed toward a parked car. Later on I found out that we were actually jogging toward the area where the alleged crime took place. As far as I am concerned, he saw a black and Hispanic college-aged kids jogging down the street in a predominately white upper-class neighborhood. After further questioning, they eventually uncuffed my roommate and me and let us go with an apology.

Raul was a Hispanic male attending Villanova University. He lived in an afflu-
ent town and tells how the local police ran a group of black kids off the basketball
court. He describes how he was dumbfounded by the experience. Is there some-
thing else that he could have done?

I am the first son born to immigrant parents—my father is from Cuba
and my mother is from Spain. Spanish was my first language; though my father made sure I spoke English as well. My mother had been part of an anti-
Franco movement in Spain back when that meant serious consequences for
her and her family. Her liberal politics rubbed off on my father and me.

In second grade we moved from a rather diverse blue-collar community
to a town in New Jersey called Allendale. It was a very affluent area—almost
entirely white—with an excellent school system.

One of the most popular activities was playing basketball. My friends and
I would play every day during the summer, against anyone. One day, in my
freshman year of high school, a group of black kids came in from Paterson,
a city about twenty minutes away. Paterson was very black, very urban, and
very poor. However being well aware of the racial makeup of the NBA, my
friends and I were eager to play against them.

Despite any fears or misunderstandings I had about black kids, they were
really nice. The first game was us versus them, and the second game we
mixed it up. I don't really remember who won either game, but I remember
having fun so they must have been competitive.

About halfway through the third game a police car pulled up to the parking lot next to us and a cop walked out. I never saw what happened next
coming. The cop told the black kids that the court was for residents only,
that townspeople had complained, and that they would have to leave. My
friends and I didn't even blink. We were all just numb. Without putting up
any fight at all, the kids just left quietly, shaking their heads. Though this
was my first time, these kids had obviously dealt with this before. After they
left, the cop told us we could stay, and he left.

We all kind of looked at each other then, each of us looking for a lead
from someone else. Despite what our parents might have thought, we
were all extremely nonracist, and had never really experienced anything
quite like it. Finally my friend Jimmy spoke. "I'm going home; I'll see you
guys later." We all followed suit, and quietly departed. When I was about
halfway home, it finally sunk in how the kids were kicked out because they
were black. Looking back, this was pretty obvious, but having never had to
deal with such a thing in my quiet suburban town it took time to accept.

By the time I got home, I was furious. I went to talk to my mother right
away, still looking to sort the whole ordeal out. She explained to me that
intolerance was still very strong, even in the northeast, even then. She had
dealt with it herself after coming from Spain in 1977.

Brian was a black student at Howard University. He was involved in a brawl with the police in Virginia Beach.

A few of us went to Virginia Beach in July, a place known to many Virginians as a racist area. I had been warned about the dos and don'ts of that area. As the temperature rose, so did our need to be intoxicated. As we made our way down the strip we ran into some acquaintances, who rolled with us like tag-alongs. Before we knew it, we moved from a group of seven to a gang of thirty plus! Everyone moved out of our way, with no questions. I remember walking down the strip saying what I wanted. We were laughing at anyone in his or her face, and just being rude and obnoxious. The police noticed as well, and decided to make their move.

They first approached us on horses and began to bother us. A friend of mine had a radio with him, as did many other beach-goers. They told him his music was too loud and that he had to turn it down. As he began, the boys in blue told him he did not do it fast enough, and locked him up. Another friend I was with practiced one of his rights to speak and voiced his opinion of the unfair display. He was dragged down the sidewalk by his arms to the paddywagon. This only increased the tension among us. We came across a small crowd of about ten, and exchanged some words. Large crowds plus liquor could only equate to one thing: violence. I tried to prevent a buddy from fighting by holding him back only to get hit. As the fight ensued, the police, without a warning, began to mace me directly in my eyes. I was smacked in the rear of my knees with a billy club and tackled to the ground. My face was smashed repeatedly, about six times (they said to restrain me). However, both arms were alongside my body during both the tackle and beating. I ended up bruised with some broken teeth. I never heard my Miranda rights, nor was I given a reason for my arrest. I was thrown in the wagon and hosed down like a wild animal. However, just as fast as it began, it was over. I did not do any paperwork. I was just released. I walked back to my hotel the next morning looking like shit; teeth messed up, face full of bruises, and ripped up clothes. It was an experience.

I don't think I acted inappropriately, because anyone who was in my predicament would have tried to prevent their friends from fighting when police were near. Next time I will just walk away. I did not think of filing any complaints, because I did not think I had a good enough case.

These actions were not too new to me. I'm from a place where things like that always happen. The police have always bothered me (chased, patted down, called names, had guns drawn on, pulled over, approached inappropriately in stores, had handcuffs put on me). I feel my actions did come to play here, because I was involved in a brawl. However the excessiveness used to contain me was wrong.

Zenobia was a black student attending Howard University. The police at the Waffle House tried to drive out the black customers by playing country songs on the jukebox.

I am a twenty-year-old black female from Charleston, South Carolina, so I know racism. It was 3:00 a.m. on a Sunday morning. I was with three of my friends. We ran into a couple of our male friends and decided to go to the "after-club spot"—Waffle House. Every black person goes there after leaving the club. We ended up sitting on a ledge of the window right next to a table of four white police. Observing the surroundings, I saw girls with high ponytails, short skirts, and lots of gold jewelry. I saw boys with gold teeth, intricately designed braids, baggy jeans, and tattoos on arms, necks, and legs. Nothing was going on except people walking around greeting friends.

Still the police didn't like the fact that there were so many black people in one place, even though they were the ones equipped with every weapon ever devised. There are jukeboxes in Waffle House. With me sitting right next to him, a police officer said to his coworkers, "Give me some quarters." He collected ten quarters and said, "This should be enough to get them out of here, because there are too many of them here." He walked over to the jukebox, filled it with quarters, and ordered ten country songs. He and his coworkers laughed when he got back to the table and the music started. Everyone in the Waffle House started complaining. The police were happy because they figured we would start to filter out.

Now, I have never been one to sit back and take extreme unfair treatment. I wanted to get everyone to stay. I looked at the policeman and rolled my eyes. His coworker told the officer that he thought I had overheard. I turned to him and told him that he was correct, but it was cool because most cops were no good anyway. The coworker laughed, and told his partner to watch his mouth in the future. I stood up and got all of my friends to join me in country line dancing. More and more people joined in. We had a great time, and the police were livid. We danced through at least six songs.

I was upset about the officer's blatant actions. If the police aren't beating on someone, they are harassing us in ways that won't get them in trouble. I am a southern girl at heart, but racism is alive and well down there, and it still hurts every time I experience it.

Ronald was a black student at Howard University. He describes being pulled over by the police for no reason other than being black. He places this incident in perspective.

My story is one that many black males have probably experienced. I'm from Flint, Michigan. If one knows anything about Flint, they know that it is a rough city to grow up in. From the high crime to having the youngest murderer ever in U.S. history, Flint is depressing. The mindset in Flint is strange. General Motors had a one-hundred-year lease on Flint to produce cars. Once the lease was up, they decimated our downtown buildings. All that is left now is a barren wasteland. It is almost a ghost town. GM went to Mexico for cheap labor and left my city in shambles. When GM closed down, the crime rate went up. People were jobless and hungry. On the documentary *Bowling for Columbine*, Arthur Busch, the county prosecutor of Flint, Michigan, basically said that the police only worry about the kids in mostly white suburbia—not the inner-city youth. Basically they do not care if the mostly black inner-city youth kill each other. With that said, one can imagine how the police treat black kids in the city of Flint.

One day I left basketball practice with my teammates. We drove to the gas station directly down the street from my high school. We got in the store, got our drinks and candy, and then we drove off. Fifteen seconds after we drove off, two white cops pulled us over. One of the cops told me, "I'm pulling you over because you're drinking a beer while riding in an automobile." He said that I could not have open alcohol while in a car. He saw four young black males with du-rags and sweatbands on, which led him to believe that we were thugs. I pulled the brown bag from around the can and showed him it was iced tea. The cop felt stupid so then he asked us if were we smoking weed. I never smoked a day in my life and he had the audacity to accuse me of smoking and carrying weed I did not have. After a long argument in which we told the cops that we did not smoke and they asked us ludicrous, absurd questions, they let us go. They embarrassed and accused us of horrible things just because we were four black males in street clothes. The sweatbands and du-rags were because of basketball practice but we could not convince him of that.

In Flint, I had other bad incidents with police pulling me over or police having to deal with parents, players and referees playing basketball.

Growing up in Flint was tough; to see all of the wrongdoing that occurs in this city has affected me in different ways. In some ways it has helped me because I know how typical white America feels about me. It has also hurt me but it has made me stronger because I know how to deal with the situations when they occur.

In my high school class, only one of the two students who had the grades and financial stability to leave the state for college did so. Everyone else stayed in Michigan. I am not saying that is all bad because there are some good schools in Michigan but many of my friends work menial jobs just to get by. My other friends sell drugs. There is something very wrong here. The government does not care about my city. They just watch us kill each other. Hopefully I can help Flint when I become economically sound. I will try to bring a new mentality to Flint to help people see that there are other things besides death and agony. Flint really needs help and I wish someone would come to the rescue.

Stephan was a black student attending Howard University. He was falsely accused of driving a stolen car.

As a black child growing up in Macon, Georgia, I was faced with many disturbing racial experiences. My last, and probably the worst, racial experience occurred in October while I was a student at Georgia Southern University in Statesboro. My girlfriend and I had just taken a weekend excursion to Savannah after a week of mid-term exams. While driving back to Statesboro from Savannah, I noticed a Georgia state patrol car following every move that I was making on I-75. Being extra cautious of my driving, I made sure that I stayed three miles under the speed limit to avoid any unnecessary speeding tickets. After about ten minutes with the patrol car tailing me I saw another police car speed in front of my truck. All of a sudden both of the cars turned on their lights and flagged me over to the side of the road.

Before I could even put my truck into park, one of the officers had jumped out of his car and demanded that I step outside of the car. Immediately, my girlfriend started having a panic attack. After I made sure that she was all right, I rolled down my window and the cop demanded that I put my hands on my steering wheel. When I asked the police officer what the problem was he told me that I was driving a stolen vehicle and that I was a suspect in a string of auto thefts in Savannah. Before he was finished telling me this he reached in my car, unlocked my door, opened it, and pulled me out onto the side of the road and cuffed me. I was so humiliated. My girlfriend was telling the police officers that we just went down for the weekend and that it was my truck that we were driving. The other police officer took my girlfriend into his car and took her down to the station while my car was towed to the station.

When I got to Bulloch County State patrol station, I was questioned for about an hour before an officer came into the interrogation room and told them that after looking in the glove compartment they found my insurance information and that they had pulled over the wrong person. The only description of the culprit was a black male between the age of sixteen and twenty that was driving a silver SUV. I personally know about four people that fit that description! I was so angry that I immediately started cursing the officers out and crying hysterically. After another half an hour, I was released, but I still had to pay $75 to get my car out of impound.

I was so angry that I called my lawyer and my parents so that we could retaliate with legal action. After my lawyer talked to the state patrol director, I got a letter in the mail a week later from the officers. I was also promised that the officers would receive demerits (which I later learned never happened). Instead of taking legal action, I swore that would never live in the south again and so I enrolled at Howard University. To my dismay, I see the same things happening in Washington, D.C. that I saw in Macon.

Cecelia was a black student at Howard University. She describes a variety of stops made on her boyfriend in one day.

Fortunately, I have not personally encountered many racially motivated incidents; but I have witnessed a few. The incidents that I have witnessed were common cases of "driving while black." My former boyfriend was a frequent violator of this unspoken offense.

One weekend I took a trip to New Jersey to visit my boyfriend. As my bus was making the final turn into the bus terminal, all the passengers turned to watch a person who had been pulled over by the police. The only difference between the other passengers and me was that I knew the driver. It was my boyfriend Ellis.

When his Mazda Millennia pulled around the corner to the front of the terminal, a sour face greeted me. As we were driving along Routes 1 and 9, he began to tell me that what I had observed resulted in no tickets but a waste of time. Ellis also informed me that it was not the first time that day that he was pulled over. Earlier that morning, at approximately 1:00 a.m., he and his friend Jeff were pulled over near Jeff's house in the suburb of Roselle. The officer had offered no explanation about why he had stopped them. After a satisfactory check of the vehicle's tags and his license, Ellis was sent on his way.

Later that evening, Jeff, his girlfriend Alisha, and Ellis and I decided to go out for the evening. When our evening came to an end we decided to make a last stop at an all-night diner for an early breakfast. We noticed a patrol car behind us. Ellis kept driving and signaled to change to the far-left lane to make the left turn into the diner. Before we could reach the intersection, the lights went on, the sirens sounded, and once again Ellis was being pulled over.

At this time Ellis was very agitated. He proceeded to roll down his window, stick his head out as the officer was approaching and said, "What the #@% do you want now?" His response was met by the officer and his partner asking to step out of the vehicle. Another patrol car appeared and then there were four officers talking to Ellis. At this time we were all talking about what was happening and how much we had to offer for bail money. Someone made a joke that resulted in our laughter. This prompted one of the officers to approach the car. He leaned into the window and asked if we had a problem. Jeff replied, "Yes, we are tired of being pulled over and searched and asked stupid questions for no reason." He was then asked to step out of the vehicle. After all the arguing was over, Ellis had five tickets, one for each of us in the car without a seatbelt and one for failure to keep right.

After our breakfast, Jeff and Alisha were taken home and Ellis and I headed home. As we drove, we laughed over failing to keep right while making a left turn. Overall, we were pleased that we managed to salvage what was left of the night. Finally, we approached his house, also in the suburb of Roselle, and attempted to drive along the side of the curb, intending to park in front of the house. As I got out of the car and stood on the curb, Ellis felt along the floor of the car in search of his house keys. A patrol car on park duty drove over and asked what was he doing in the car. As Ellis tried to convince the officer that it was his car, and that he doesn't attach his car keys to his house keys because he doesn't want to lose them both, the state trooper that lives behind the house came out to assist. He then assured the officer that it was Ellis's car and that he did live in the house. The day had come to an end. Finally.

Stacy was a Hispanic student attending the University of California at Santa Barbara. Her father was pulled over and interrogated about his citizenship status.

I have experienced racism throughout my life coming from a small, white, Christian town. My father is Mexican and my mother is Jewish so I understand and have experienced the negative effects of racism and bigotry. One of my racial experiences happened when I was in San Diego with my father. I was about eight years old and we were driving to visit my grandfather. We were driving on the highway and we heard sirens, so my dad pulled over. The officer asked if we were American citizens. My dad said yes. The officer apparently didn't believe him because he asked him to recite his social security number and mine. He asked me what school I went to and what grade I was in. Then he asked my father to show his drivers license and then he asked for his birth certificate. My dad had a copy of his birth certificate because he had been pulled over for the same reason when he was in college. The officer kept asking questions. My father is a smart, highly educated professional and this officer made him feel like a second-rate citizen. After it was made clear that we were not illegal immigrants, the officer threw my dad's birth certificate back into his lap and turned around to walk back to his patrol car. He didn't say anything to us—no apologies, no have a nice day, nothing. The only reason he pulled us over was because we were Mexican. I remember my dad being very calm and polite to the officer. He did not give him attitude or talk back. I remember him saying that the officer was being rude and asking a lot of questions because he wanted my father to react in a negative and maybe violent way. My dad told me that he would not give the officer that satisfaction and would not allow himself to play the game the officer was playing. This experience, although it was not directed at me, made me realize at a very young age that there are people in the world who are racist and will treat you with disrespect. I learned that I could not let them win.

18

Is Prejudiced

Prejudice can be defined as positive or negative attitudes toward an identified social group (Jones 2002). In these essays, we find individuals who find themselves grappling with their own racial prejudice, negative attitudes about a person of color based on generalized beliefs (stereotypes) pertaining to the racial/ethnic group (Castillo, Conley, King, Rollins, Rivera, and Veve 2006). Our attitudes toward social groups are rooted in three sources: cognitive, affective, and behavioral information. Prejudice is often an initial emotional reaction to social groups whereas the cognitive information and behavioral actions are often revealed through our stereotypes and discrimination, respectively.

It is no longer socially correct to admit publicly that you are racist. Most people who hold racist beliefs will either state them with a disclaimer (but, some of my best friends are . . .) or they will attempt to excuse their racism with a story of how they were harmed (they were a victim of a crime or some perceived discrimination). We usually don't know the extent to which the racism preceded the supposed event. Furthermore, many people have been victims of interracial crimes and did not develop prejudice because of this. Seltzer has a white friend who was shot by a white teenager and in another incident was threatened with a gun by a black man. The friend uses the second incident to justify racist statements and conveniently ignores being shot by a white person.

Ralph Ezekiel (1995) wrote a very readable book cataloging meetings and interviews he had with dozens of leaders and followers of different hate groups such as the Klan, Nazis, skinheads, and other "modern" manifestations of racist organizations. The reader develops an appreciation of the structure (or lack thereof) of these organizations and why certain people are attracted to these organizations.

In this chapter the contributors attempt to place their racism and racial prejudice within the context of an experience with crime. Indeed, much of the literature on criminal victimization focuses on the characteristics of individuals that are related to fear, and one such characteristic is most certainly race given the associated stereotypes of race and crime. Research pertaining to black stereotypes shows many whites have a strong association of blacks and crime (Citrin, Green, and Sears 1990; Sniderman and Piazza 1993). St. John and Moore (1996) examined the role of racial prejudice in understanding fear associated with criminal victimization and finds that whites' encounters with black strangers were more likely to evoke fear than encounters with white strangers, and such an effect is conditioned by racial prejudice. Some evidence has shown interactions with young black men in public settings are especially likely to evoke high levels of fear (Anderson 1990). Matthew describes how he has struggled not to be prejudiced despite being the victim of several crimes at the hands of black men; "I have been mugged at knife point, had my house and car burglarized, and two members of my immediate family assaulted—all by black men. Yet again, I try to remind myself that these are only isolated cases."

Many of these essays show demonstrations of guilt regarding feelings of prejudice. Allport (1954) aptly describes guilt as an uneasiness or "inner check" that forces egalitarians to correct their behavior when they sense it deviating from nonprejudiced standards. Amodio, Devine, and Harmon-Jones (2007) suggest that guilt allows one to "make up for past transgressions and behave more appropriately in future situations." Indeed, in these essays we see how guilt affects many writers who recognize their prejudice and seek ways to change. As Tracey describes, "Hopefully, when meeting Hispanic males in the future, I will be able to be open-minded and remind myself that I cannot generalize an entire population based on the way a few people have acted."

Karen was a white student attending the University of St. Louis. Her car was stolen by kids while she was at college and she started to be much more cautious around African Americans.

I grew up in small-town USA, which was a racially segregated town of 13,000 in Missouri. A person's skin color had never been an issue growing up.

When I was eighteen I made the first big decision of my life. I chose to go to school in the city. I looked forward to the people I would meet and the things I would learn living in St. Louis. I was aware that the area was surrounded by the so-called ghetto, but for the first three years the ghetto was just that to me . . . so-called.

In my senior year my boyfriend dropped me off to get my car. There was only one problem—my car was no longer there. My small town naiveté showed at that moment. I knew that my car could not have been stolen. Who would want my early 1990s Buick anyway? I finally called the police.

Hours later my car was found. It had been located in one of the worst areas the city has to offer—a predominantly black area in North St. Louis. We arrived at the all-black police impound to find my car totaled. All my belongings in the trunk had been taken. I had been terribly violated. The journal that was in my trunk had been taken.

The workers at the towing impound did not seem to care much about my possessions. They only wanted our money, a total of $450. How gracious of them to hold my car at the impound for less than twenty-four hours, at a mere cost of $450. They said that my car was most likely stolen by kids in the area. Nonchalantly, they told me they probably just needed a ride home and proceeded to laugh. For the first time in my life I was being filled with anger and an insecurity I could not seem to control.

The days following the theft were, to say the least, terrible. I could not sleep, let alone walk down the street without worrying that someone was watching me. I lost a part of myself the day I found that my car was stolen. I caught myself locking my doors when I was in sight of a black man on the street. I found myself wondering and getting angry at the thought of someone flipping through the pages of my journal. I lost the naiveties that lead me to believe that all people are good and instead of seeing everyone as who they are, I was noticing the color of their skin. It was a terrible feeling knowing that I let myself be burned by this experience. I hated that I started to think of people as different.

Months after the theft now I have slowly recovered. I would not say that I have let my guard down any but I have become a bit more clear-headed again. The day my car was stolen is the worst racial experience of my life, not because the people who stole my car may have been black, but because every presumption I had in my head was telling me that the people who stole my car were black. The small town girl had reacted like a small town girl. I was not as great as I thought I would be in that kind of situation after all. One thing is for sure, I have learned a lot about myself.

Adam was a white student attending St. Louis University. He says he is not a racist, but is merely prejudiced against urban city people. You be the judge.

I would like to begin my essay by first stating that I am from a small rural farming community that is primarily white and Catholic. The worst racial experience has been living in off-campus housing at Saint Louis University (SLU) and hearing all the stories that have happened to everyone else.

My sophomore year started with moving down to school a couple of weeks before school started and being welcomed to the sight of overgrown weeds, trash everywhere, and my favorite—broken glass from car windows. The campus is certainly the rose growing out of a pile of crap. You step foot outside the gates, and you really are rolling the dice. If I am walking by myself at night and I see any black person, besides the few who actually go here, (who are distinctive and actually good people), I will not walk towards them and be (1) robbed, (2) asked for money, (3) have an aggressive move made toward me by some juvenile trying to prove that he is the "alpha" male on this block, or (4) yelled at.

The most common occurrence that I see is some bum who wants money. The solution I have come up with is to just say you do not have any money but give them a cigarette as a consolation prize so they do not cause a scene when you walk past them.

Not everyone that goes to SLU is as lucky as me; my friends have been robbed at gunpoint, had their cars broken into for the premium electronics in them (radar detectors, CD players, and the like) and even bums breaking your window in order to steal things like Kleenex, a change jar, or other cheap things.

Hearing all these stories makes me seem like I am racist, but I feel that I am just prejudiced toward inner-city people. It may sound like the same thing because everyone around me is black, but I do not feel unsafe around any other black people back home.

I feel no sympathy toward these people. I will not give a beggar money; I will not turn around to help the black man yelling at me for directions, or lend a helping hand to anyone in this community. The best way I have heard this put is by my friend who said, "I will never do any community service for these people. I think I've done my part by getting over $2,000 worth of stereo equipment stolen out of my car."

To conclude, I will reiterate that this essay is in no way, shape, or form racist propaganda. I just feel very strongly about this small group of individuals that create stereotypes for the whole race. Racism is for ignorant people. Being cautious is a way of life for the white college kid in a harsh, cruel environment.

Tracy was a white student at St. Louis University. She feels uncomfortable around Hispanics because so many of them whistle and stare at her. She hopes to get over this in the future.

The occurrence that I would describe as my worst racial experience has actually happened multiple times. In my hometown of Barrington, a Chicago suburb, the majority of the landscaping companies were made up of Hispanic men. It seemed that whenever they passed by me in their trucks, whether I was walking down the street or driving in my car, they would all turn and stare at me. They would proceed to whistle and make catcalls at me.

Such situations made me feel uncomfortable and humiliated. I would talk to other girls about it, and they would tell me that they experienced the same thing. It seemed to us that these Hispanic men would turn and stare at any female in sight. Personally, I found it entirely disgusting. I didn't understand why this particular racial population of males insisted on being so outwardly perverted. Such actions by these men were so disrespectful and degrading to all women. Furthermore, there were a large number of Hispanics at my high school, and as a result I began to feel slightly uncomfortable around the Hispanic guys that I knew because I felt like they were having the same ideas as the landscaping men. I may be assuming too much, but I think that these attitudes towards women are more acceptable in their culture, and perhaps that is why the men act this way. And, although I know that I cannot stereotype all Hispanic men to act this way, I sometimes have a hard time looking past my previous experiences. Hopefully, when meeting Hispanic males in the future, I will be able to be open-minded and remind myself that I cannot generalize an entire population based on the way a few people have acted.

Harry was a white student at St. Louis University. His father was ripped off by a black scalper at a baseball game. This reinforced Harry's prejudiced views of African Americans.

I am from a capital city suburb in the Midwest. I am very aware of society and politics, and I am a very conservative Republican.

My family and I were on a vacation in Chicago. Being in a larger, more racially diverse city, I was already on "high alert" to be conscious of my surroundings and to protect the three female family members I was traveling with. The family decided to attend a Chicago Cubs game. Being without tickets, we were forced to deal with scalpers. Having already spoken of my level of distrust for those different from me, I was intent on buying tickets from a white male like myself. We ran into a shortage of tickets, and had little other choice than a black male in his mid-twenties. I was not happy with this situation, and let my father handle the transaction. We paid $250 in cash for five tickets. As soon as the black seller had the cash in his hands, he took off running. The man had one legitimate ticket and four counterfeit tickets in the stack that he sold us. We were out of a great deal of money, and were very embarrassed by the situation. It was humiliating to fall for such a cheap ploy by a dishonest individual. The time he spent fabricating fake tickets should have been spent earning a respectable wage at a real job, rather than ripping off honest and hard-working people. This situation served to reinforce my beliefs and to show my younger and naive sisters a little bit more about what I had talked about.

As a student at Saint Louis University, there are certain places that I will not go in the city because I am outraged by the same blacks loitering and panhandling the general public.

Matthew was a white student at the University of South Florida. He has been the victim of a number of black-on-white crimes, which have affected his views of African Americans.

In my life I have been subject to several "racial experiences" which have all affected me in various ways. With all of the experiences, I have been forced to rationalize the situations and try not to let my emotions lead me to have one blanket view of life in general. I have always been an athlete and through sports I spent quite a bit of time around people of all races and backgrounds. I think at one point in my life I was probably more comfortable around black people than most of the white people I knew. But, this all changed following the Rodney King verdict. I walked my then-girlfriend to her class as I always did and headed to my class, late as usual. Before I got to my class, however, I was stopped in the hallway by five or six black kids. For no reason at all they began pushing me and yelling obscenities at me. It did not take long for the whole group of them to begin beating me unmercifully. I didn't do anything to these kids and I clearly had nothing to do with the case in California, so why was I being beaten? From that day forward I was more likely to prejudge the people I came into contact with. As my mother explained to me, I knew that I should not view all blacks in the same way that I now viewed these particular kids, but it was difficult.

During my senior year I worked at Publix, the local grocery store. We were robbed by five black men wearing masks over their faces. One of the men pointed a gun right in my face and yelled some command at me that I was not able to perform, simply out of fear. For this he punched me in the face and then proceeded to beat up a cashier. She was a pregnant young woman. The men made off with a couple of hundred dollars and then robbed a convenience store just up the road. There they actually shot the clerk. Again, even through all of this I tried to tell myself that these were isolated incidents and these things could have just as easily been committed by white men, but the fact is that they weren't.

In addition to the situations I have described, I have been mugged at knife-point, had my house and car burglarized, and two members of my immediate family assaulted—all by black men. Yet again, I try to remind myself that these are only isolated cases. All of these things happen to people at the hands of white men everyday, but the thoughts still linger in my mind. This is a shame because as a rational person I understand that the media portrays an unfair rendition of the actual crime rates in this country. I also understand that the criminal justice system as a whole is unfairly biased and that blacks are prosecuted at a rate far exceeding their proportion of crimes committed. Still, in my everyday life I find it hard to forget the things that have happened to me.

I feel guilty sometimes for the way I assume people will behave even before meeting them. I do not like that I have prejudiced notions about many of the people I come into contact with. However, I do not know that I will ever be able to fully clear the slate of life experiences enough to ever look at life through colorless lenses again.

Carol was a twenty-five-year-old white student attending the University of South Florida. She was raped by a black man, and that incident has subsequently affected her racial attitudes.

I attended Connecticut College, where I lived on campus. I was extremely open-minded and eager to learn about all the new people that surrounded me. I was so eager to learn about people that most of my friends were not white. I wanted to prove my parents wrong about their attitudes regarding people from other races. (I was born in Poland.)

For the first time in my life I was romantically attracted to an African American man. He lived on the floor beneath me. Upon seeing him at a party where I was highly intoxicated, I made my way through the crowd to grab his attention. By the end of the night, he had raped me in his car. I was extremely disgusted and did not know how to react. For days I blamed myself, and convinced myself that I would never make it in life. I told myself that my parents have always been right and that I was too gullible for my own good. Then I started blaming the "nigger." I convinced myself that only a "nigger" could do such a thing. He denied everything. He yelled that he would never touch a "white girl" because they make him sick. This is when my hate started. For years I despised black men. I didn't despise black girls as much as black men. However, I still had a bias against that race. I no longer wanted to meet more people of different races because my train of thought believed that only an African American could rape a woman, and then make a comment that he would never degrade himself that much to romantically touch a white woman. That statement never left my mind. I still hear that statement and it still makes me angry.

After this incident my grades started dropping and I was on my way to being kicked out of school. Every time I saw a black man, even a man that looked nothing like my rapist, I would still put him in the same category as my rapist, simply because of his skin color.

Throughout my last few months at the school, the support that I received from my friends opened my eyes. At first they were skeptical of what happened because of the amount of alcohol I consumed that night, but in the end they were right there with me. What shocked me more was that the majority of my supporters were African Americans. I assumed that since they were both the same race, the other guys would never believe me and would take his side. I felt like a rock hundreds of feet under the ground. I felt like a stereotypical "white trash" female. Yet, my friends supported me and helped me through this episode of my life. If it weren't for those friends, I would still have that hatred for people of different races to this day.

Currently I am living in a different state and have minimal interactions with people of different races. However, deep down I am still realizing that we cannot put people in separate categories like we have throughout our entire existence. When we do this, we learn how to hate, fear, and dislike the "unknown." Our first encounter with someone of the other race will be biased, therefore making it surreal.

Gabe was a white student who attended Villanova University. When he was thirteen he felt threatened by a Hispanic kid. Because of this he learned how to shoot a gun and has been distrustful of minorities in general.

As a white male living in a mostly suburban town, I did not have much interaction with minorities. My town is about half an hour from Scranton, Pennsylvania. We were able to live with nice spacious lawns and room for large outdoor activities while also being close enough to the city to enjoy ice skating, upper-class malls, and great cinemas. My town began to have a growing Hispanic population when I got to middle school.

In middle school we were finally able to go hang out at the local mall of basketball courts. It was a popular place for our parents to drop us off and just hang out. Once the girls came out regularly, it was only a matter of time before older guys started showing up. A group of fifteen-year-old Hispanics started hanging out there, and I didn't see anything wrong with that situation or them in particular. Nevertheless, they did seem to stick together, and came across as cockier than my friends, who were all white.

The biggest Hispanic had a very loud mouth and his name was Jason. One night, while I was trying to socialize and talk to friends, all of a sudden one of my friends grabbed me and put his arm around me. He then whispered, "Just walk with me; don't look. Just come with me. We have to get out of here." I was completely confused until we were a few yards away. He began talking normally and said, "Jason said he wanted to hit you, he kept thinking about it and was telling people he was about to punch you in the face, just like he did some other kid last week." I then looked back and saw him staring at me as I walked away with my friend. I felt completely powerless. Here I was, barely one hundred pounds, twelve years old, completely shy and having never insulted anyone. I was about to be crushed by a kid three years older, six inches taller, and double my weight for no reason. It was obvious he wanted to do it simply because he could.

For a few weeks I was almost completely alone. I couldn't get myself to go back, and I was terrified of being beat up. (I had never been hit before.) Also, my friends had no desire to get into a fight, or even stick together for that matter. On the other hand, the Hispanic kids were always ready for a fight. They always stuck together and they all would have backed him up in a second, while I was sure my friends would have looked at each other while my nose was being broken.

Eventually some of my older friends talked to him and got him to drop the idea. But, from then on, every time I was around a group of minorities I thought, "These are not my people, I don't fit in," and was fearful. I began practicing with my father's rifle and eventually learned how to use a handgun. I was overwhelmed with the feeling that minorities stick together and majorities don't, and white, academically-urban, suburban kids make terrible friends in a fight. I became better and better with a handgun, and I began to lose my fear, but something replaced it—a distrust of anyone who was not a middle-class white suburbanite. It has taken me many years to overcome that, but still to this day whenever I see a group of black or Hispanic males, I mentally prepare like there might be a fight—all because of a course of events that happened when I was twelve.

Stephanie was a white student who attended the University of California at Santa Barbara. She was accosted by a Chicano man and has feared Chicano men since then.

My worst racial experience happened upon my first visit to California. I am a blonde southern female. At the time of the incident, I was not a day over seventeen. On our first evening in Santa Monica, California, my sister and I were out at around 9:00 on a Saturday evening. It was just the two of us walking along completely mesmerized by the beauty surrounding us.

On our walk home, a Chicano man began to follow us. My sister picked up on his peculiar behavior and instructed me to walk faster. All of a sudden, this man jumped out of nowhere and tried to initiate a conversation with me. He said that I was clearly not from California because I had an accent. My sister had already begun to pick up her pace again. Then, out of nowhere, this man reached over and grabbed my butt. This was not a light brush either. It was a hard, very sexual grab. I screamed and took off running. As I was running off, I could hear this Chicano man laughing and saying, "rich southern bitch."

My sister and I did not stop running until we reached our hotel. We ran in jeans and high heels for over a mile. I truly thought that the Chicano man was going to rape me. I have never been so scared in my entire life. While I know that it could have been a man of any race that could have harassed me that night, the fact that it was a Chicano man has instilled in me a fear of Chicano men. I realize in our society that Chicanos can often times be unfairly discriminated against. Just a few bad apples, like the Chicano man who harassed me, give Chicano men a bad stereotype. That night will remain imprinted in my memory forever. Although, I have become a stronger and more aware person, I will always be a little wary when I'm out at night and I see a poor, Chicano man wandering around on the streets.

19

No Racism

The United States is a far less racist society than it was before the advent of the Civil Rights Movement. In 1958, a majority (53 percent) of Americans said they would NOT vote for a black candidate for president according to the first Gallup Poll in which this question was asked. In 2003, only 6 percent gave this response, and in 2009 Barack Obama is president.

As mentioned throughout this book, the increasing diversity in our society has contributed to greater interracial contact. Today, people are likely to live near someone of another race, work with someone of another race, and have a friend of another race. Indeed, interracial contact or the "contact theory" as developed by social scientists posits that increased interracial contact will nurture greater tolerance and increased positive racial attitudes. However, Emerson, Kimbro, and Yancey (2002) state that in order for true racial tolerance to be achieved it is important to go beyond mere "interracial contact"; the interracial contact experienced in schools and neighborhoods can have the affect of more intimate interracial contact as friends and within social groups.

Branton and Jones (2005) find that living in diverse environments of high socioeconomic status often lead to greater support on racial/social issues. Karen describes the actions of her white neighbor as the most important reason she has not experienced racism, as Binh, a Vietnamese student, describes the diversity of his neighborhood as the primary reason he has not experienced racism.

However, some research shows that greater diversity *does not* lead to greater tolerance and acceptance. For example, Taylor (1998) finds that white antipathy toward blacks increases as the local black population grows within community. Likewise, Emerson, Yancey, and Chai (2001), find that while Asian and Hispanic neighborhood composition does not matter to whites, whites prefer not live with African Americans in their neighborhoods due to their association of African Americans with high crime, low housing values, and low quality education. However, Harris (2001) finds that whites *and* African Americans are averse to African American neighbors due to the association of poverty, crime, and other social problems.

The literature shows that interracial contact may indeed have its limits on our perceptions of others from a different race and indeed, it may be our *willingness* to associate with others of a different race that underlies more positive racial attitudes. As previously mentioned, many individuals do not live in diverse neighborhoods and have had limited contact with others from a different racial or ethnic group. Several essays within this chapter show students who recall the lack of diversity within their towns and therefore experienced no racism. In fact, many of our essayists cannot remember a single racist experience. Some whites, such as Nathan, attribute the lack of negative racial experiences to growing up in segregated communities and had little interactions with minorities. Karla, a Hispanic student, also says she did not encounter racism because she had few interactions with whites.

However, there are also several African American students who indicate that their experience living in segregated, majority African American communities is one reason they have not experienced racism as well. Many of the African Americans within this chapter describe their experience as growing up in neighborhoods that are middle-class regardless of whether or not the neighborhood is racially mixed or predominantly African American. Gay (2004) finds that neighborhood quality and socioeconomic composition affect African American racial attitudes, particularly as they evaluate the quality of their life. Growing up in an environment absent social and economic desperation may have affected how the African American students in this chapter viewed their experience. Roger alludes to the discrepancy in experience when he describes "educated African Americans" and growing up in a predominantly African American community.

Throughout this chapter there are several common themes despite the fact that these students belong to a variety of racial backgrounds. However, what it is perhaps most interesting is that *diversity* and *a lack of diversity* are provided as explanations for why these students have not experienced racism.

Lanie was a black student at Howard University. He believes that racism is used as an excuse by other blacks and can only be combated through education.

I have personally not had any real encounters with racism. However, I may have had such an encounter and just not seen it that way. I am from

Jamaica and we have a different way of looking at life. I am not saying that it does not exist, but I personally have not been exposed to it.

In Jamaica we have a strong class division but not racism. The concept of not speaking to someone of another race and acting "white" or "black" is very foreign to me.

I have been living in the United States now for about nine or ten years and I can honestly say that I have never really been in a racist situation. However, others may look at things differently and what I would view as normal behavior another may view as racism. I try to live my life free of unnecessary stress, and I believe if you go out looking for something you will find it. I know that the blacks of this country have been through a lot of struggles, but as far as my generation goes, I do not believe that they have. For them to constantly call racism seems to be an excuse to me. This is not to say that it does not happen, but maybe not as much as it seems. For example, there have been discussions of how blacks can't buy homes in certain neighborhoods. It may simply mean that they are not financially qualified.

I believe that the African American communities of the United States tend to go too far at times with the race issue. Being an immigrant in this country is very hard and if immigrants can come to this country, be black, still find jobs, and live their lives without going on welfare or other forms of government help, then I do not see why African Americans cannot. I understand they have been through much but like many nations of the world, the people of Jamaica were also slaves and we have overcome that. The country is not in the best financial state but it is working to improve itself. The country is not looking for reparations from England.

I also believe that the racism in this country is not just against blacks but I believe that blacks are also racist toward whites. I believe that the reason for that is fear. Both groups have shared this country for years but are still plagued with stereotypes on both sides. I am not saying that stereotypes are not all over the world but this country seems to dwell on them. Each side is unaware of how the other side truly operates and I believe that there is ignorance on both sides. I also believe that because the African American community seems to dwell on race so much, it becomes an even bigger issue. It seems as if it is the only problem this community faces.

Once again, I know that racism exists, but it is an ideology and is like the War on Terrorism. One cannot win through extensive laws and political intervention; it can only be combated with knowledge.

Denise was a black student at Howard University. She believes her lack of racial experiences is due to her gender and the environment where she grew up.

Despite my knowledge of other people's numerous negative racial encounters, I am unable to recall any significant racial experiences of my own. After taking a considerable amount of time to think about why this is so, being a young woman of color, I can conclude that environment and gender are the main factors.

I was born and raised in the Bronx, New York in a middle-class, racially mixed neighborhood. I attended private and Catholic schools all of my life, most of which were racially diverse or predominantly African American and Latino. During the nineteen-year span of my life, I have not witnessed or been subject to racism.

Gender, I trust, plays a significant role in one's racial experience in America. Being a woman is beneficial, I believe, when it comes to actual racist action. For example, "DWB" (driving while black), although applied to both genders, commonly refers to black men who are pulled over because they "fit the profile" of a criminal. (This has happened to my father numerous times). More recently, black men are also usually victims of hate crimes (i.e. Abner Louima and Amadou Diallo). I believe this to be true because throughout American history, the black man, being the (allegedly) more powerful and dominant sex of the race, has been the main target of racially motivated abuse.

Unfortunately, my lack of direct racial experiences does not dissuade my skepticism about race relations in America. I am still very much aware of the racism that exists today, due to either personal accounts of racial experiences from friends and family or from images in the media, as well as current events. However, I hope that I will continue to avoid any traumatizing and racially motivated incidents for the duration of my life, and I wish the same for future generations.

Nathan was a white student at Villanova. He had very little interactions with blacks.

I have not been able to think of a single—not one—bad racial experience. I think the reason why I have not been able to think of a single bad experience is not because America is getting less racist, but rather the lack of diversity or exposure in my life. I can only recall one black man who has ever lived in my neighborhood during the twenty years that I have called that house my home. That one black man was an English boxing promoter who I seem to recall had a white wife. The black, or for that matter nonwhite, overall population of my hometown is negligible. I did not attend the local public high school. In fact, the private high school I attended probably had less than fifteen black students in my graduating class, and not too many more Hispanics or Asians.

My university is not much different. Villanova is not diverse. One of its nicknames, after all, is Vanillanova (and that's not just because it's not a big party school).

Do I feel like I have been cheated because I have not had significant interactions with people of other races? Not really. I, like most Americans, am content to live within the life I have come to know and love, not willing to risk stepping out of my comfort zone to see what else is out there.

Martin was a white student at St. Louis University. He feels very uncomfortable around minorities and has never had a really bad racial experience because he has little contact with minorities.

I have pondered this question several times throughout the previous semester, and I remain unable to label an experience as being my "worst racial experience." I believe this is because I have never experienced anything particularly out of the ordinary when it comes to interracial confrontations and experiences. Certainly there have been instances where I have felt uncomfortable, but I am ashamed to admit that the discomfort I experienced was most likely unwarranted or a function of the negative stereotypes that I have adopted. Instances that come to mind include simple things such as riding on the subway and other forms of transportation where minorities are simply present. I found myself feeling agitated, nervous, and paranoid just by the presence of people who were not white. Being educated about the stereotypes and misconceptions that have plagued our society in the past, I have felt guilty and remorseful about my negative stereotypes, yet I remained unable to curtail the feelings I was experiencing. The main reason that I am unable to produce a story about my worst racial experience is probably because the first fourteen years of my life were spent without having any nonwhite persons in any aspect of life. My only contact with nonwhites before high school was the information I gathered about them from watching sports and television. Upon entering high school, I was fortunate enough to be exposed to minorities who I would work with, attend classes with, compete in sports with, and generally spend time with. Still, my view of African Americans and Hispanics in general is a bit distorted.

Andy was a white student attending St. Louis University. He never had any racial experiences before college and in retrospect is upset that he lived in such a bubble.

I grew up in southern Missouri—the Bible Belt Midwest. My parents and teachers preached equality; they preached tolerance and acceptance—and I listened.

Where I grew up and went to school there were only four nonwhites. My friends and I were the same, and our parents were the same.

After graduation I moved to St. Louis to attend St. Louis University. Here I have already gained a vast knowledge of other cultures. Two of my best friends are black. I eat lunch with some of my Indian friends. One of my pledge brothers is a great friend of mine and he is Filipino. What is weird-est of all is that I thought by coming here I would not be familiar with these other races, that perhaps things would be awkward because I had no contact with someone of another race all of my life—but I quickly realized that it does not matter. Race is just a physical bond and friendship is much deeper than that. I am proud that I do not see race for "race" and instead look upon these new friendships as a chance to get closer to different hu-man beings.

My worst racial experience then would have to be my entire upbring-ing. The fact that I was rarely introduced to someone of a different race or culture is appalling to me now. It makes me sad that I never got to become familiar with people of a different culture until my collegiate years.

Roger was a black student at Howard University. He gives a variety of reasons why he has not had a bad racial experience.

I believe that I have not had a bad racial experience because of the so-ciety in which I grew up. The city in Pennsylvania in which I grew up was a predominately black city, yet I attended what started out as a predomi-nately white school. I say that my school started out predominately white, because by the time I graduated from the school, it was a predominately black student body with a predominantly white faculty. I think that my school has a lot to do with my lack of a bad racial experience. The members of the faculty in the school were very open-minded toward black people and treated us as fairly as they treated the white students. I also feel that the length of time that I spent at the school also had a hand in why I was not discriminated against in the school. I attended the school from kinder-garten to twelfth grade. The staff, for the most part, consisted of the same people that worked there for all the years that I attended the school, so they became accustomed to me and I was "accepted" by them. I believe that this is a factor because I have seen new people come into the school and I have seen them treated differently than those that had been at the school for a longer amount of time—including myself.

Though my school is a factor, I feel that my community was another factor. I lived in a community and a society that had about a 70 percent black population. The small number of white people that did live in my community were of my age group and my generation. I have found that younger white America is much more open-minded about other races than the elderly people in white America. I feel that this is the case because once a person has reached a certain age, it is very hard to change their view point on certain issues—racial prejudice being one of those issues. The younger generation has been exposed to racial "equality," interracial marriages, and blacks and whites standing side by side for a common cause (i.e., the months following September 11).

Finally, I feel that the third, and probably most influential cause for my lack of a bad racial experience is my parents. My parents have raised me in such a way that I would not put myself into a situation that could possibly become a bad racial situation. My parents have taught me to be open-minded about other races. From a very young age I was always surrounded by people of other races that were open-minded. They put me in a school where all that mattered was the education of the students and not the color of the students' skin.

I feel that at times we bring the bad racial situations on ourselves. We go into establishments operated by people of other races, and act as if we do not have common sense. We're loud, obnoxious, and rude, and then we get upset when the workers use racial connotations such as "you people" and "those niggers." I know that we cannot change everyone, but I do believe that some people would be open minded if we blacks acted correctly, showed them that there are many educated black people, and that we all do not act like ignorant niggers.

Thomas was a student at Howard University. He believes he has not had bad racial experiences because of the way that he carries himself.

I am proud to say that I have not had a bad racial experience. This is a great surprise because I grew up in a county in the mid-Atlantic, where the population is about 85 percent white. I went to a high school where in my graduation class of three hundred students, about twenty-four members of that class was nonwhite. Even though there were some degrees of racial animosity, it never came to point of total discomfort on my part.

The reason for my success against any racial animosity is the way I carried myself as a young black man. I was a student government president and had a job that gave me the chance to be exposed to many prominent older white people of the community. Many people knew that I was not wasting my youth on foolish practices, so they had no reason to ever judge me because of the color of my skin. I was one of the few members of my graduating class to go to a college outside of the state. Also, when traveling to places which may be considered "white," I am usually the only black person, or I should say, the only black person of my generation. Of course, I get looks of shock and surprise when I go downtown to an expensive restaurant, when I am looking for a suit in Brooks Brothers, or when I am in Bethesda or Tyson's Corner. With the looks I receive, I simply give them right back and the person who is overlooking me feels it and simply stops looking.

In conclusion, if a man carries himself in a certain matter, which is of pride and success, people have no reason to approach him with any discomfort. Throughout my life, I have done this to the best of my ability, and the payoff has been very satisfying. A racial experience is something that unfortunately, all black people in the United States will have to go through. The degree of the experience can be avoided sometimes, but some people will still hate you because of minor things like skin color. The only hate you should give back is the one to fight ignorance.

Lynn was a black student attending Howard University. She has had a variety of experiences that others in this book described as racist. However, she does not believe they compare to the experiences of others in the past. Do you think she is correct?

I have experienced racism a lot in the nineteen years that I have been on this earth. One thing I haven't experienced yet is my "worst racial experience." Yes, I have been called the "n" word and I have been discriminated against because I'm an African American. I have come across people who thought they were superior to me because I am a young, intelligent, African American female. Although I have experienced these things, they aren't anything compared to the racism that went on during slavery and the Civil Rights Movement. One would think that by growing up in a predominately white west suburb of Chicago (one of the most segregated cities in the United States), that I would have plenty to tell. Well, I don't.

Now don't get me wrong. I'm not blinded. As a matter of fact, I'm well aware that the racial experiences I have had don't compare to the experiences of my parents, my grandparents, Rosa Parks, Dr. King, Medger Evers, Malcolm X, and many more of my African American ancestors. I feel like being called the "n-word" is nothing compared to being called the "n-word" while being beaten. I feel like being watched while I shop in a store is nothing compared to not having a choice about what store I would like to shop in. By no means am I justifying the racial experiences that I have had—I'm in some way grateful for them. I'm grateful for the era in which I was born because I don't know if I would have the strength to deal with that kind of racism or the courage to take a stand because of it.

I think one of the main reasons why I can't think of a bad racial experience is that racism is not done in the same form. There is no doubt in my mind that racism still exists. It's just that people aren't being as bold anymore. People have realized that there are now consequences for their actions such as serving time in jail or having to pay money. People are not so willing to beat up a person just because they are of another race.

Kate was a white student at Villanova. She has never had a bad racial experience but has had to struggle with her own thoughts.

My professor told us to think about our worst racial experience and write about it. I have racked my memory for an intense, outraging story, but cannot think of one. I cannot recall a horrific racial experience because for most of my life, race has never been a big factor.

It kills me to admit that I now, after three years of college-level political science, ethics, and sociology classes, feel much more educated and well-informed about racial issues than I did when I graduated high school. I am involved in peace and justice organizations, and advocate for the rights of people who are oftentimes people of a different race than me. My friends and I talk about racial reconciliation on a regular basis. We read about it, meditate on it, and even pray about it. We hope to someday form a Christian community in the inner city and live in an integrated society. I do not want my children to grow up only knowing African Americans through volunteer work. I consider myself a progressive white.

With as much study as I have done on the issue of race, I have never been personally affected by it. I have never felt discriminated against because of my race. I have rarely felt out of place because of my race, even if I was a minority in the situation. I have never truly resented my race or another race.

Even through all my efforts in understanding the black predicament and promoting racial equality, I still find myself thinking negative thoughts about other races. I scorn myself for thinking that way. Subconscious thoughts of white superiority still sneak on me, despite my efforts to curb them. This makes me feel ashamed, and truly bothers me. I meditate on why these unfair thoughts sometimes enter my mind, and my only answer is because I have not been exposed to very many people of different races yet, and am too accustomed to whites having the upper hand.

I do not want to notice when I am talking to a person who is not of my race. I don't mentally think, "Oh, this person is white" when I talk to most people at Villanova, so why should I think, "Oh, this person is black" when I talk to an African American person? I don't want to notice race in the way that I do now.

Thinking about the future, I have decided that I want to live in an integrated community, send my kids to an integrated school, and worship in an integrated church. I want to further racial reconciliation and understanding. I do not want my children to think twice about dating or befriending a person of a different race. I pray that I do not seek out and live in an all-white suburb just because it is easy and the norm.

I want to see no color, and if I do, I want to see a mix of colors, and not continue to be surrounded by a dangerous blanket of white.

Janice was a black student at Howard University. She grew up in areas where racism was not prevalent. Her mother instilled in her the view to not overanalyze anything.

I don't think that I have ever been a victim of racism. I thought back to when I lived in southern Virginia and my family was the only African American family in the gated community where we lived. My siblings and I made friends pretty quickly, all of whom were white. Growing up in Philadelphia, I was always surrounded by other blacks, and when I did come in contact with members of other races, it was as if we were all the same person. Maybe I am just lucky to have grown up in areas where racism is not prevalent and everyone is treated as equals. There is no one incident that sticks out in my mind to make me think that I was a victim of racism. I think that this may be because of the nonchalant attitude my mother has instilled in me since I was a child. I was taught to never take anything too deeply because overanalysis can prove detrimental to a person's growth. In that, I have always made it a point to push others to treat me as their equal, no matter their race or gender. I'm sure that as I excel further in my career and in life, I can continue to keep this attitude.

Ken was a white student attending Salisbury State. He came from a town with a history of racism. However, he has not seen any sign of that today. He would prefer less diversity and have everyone treated the same.

I grew up in Mardela Springs, Maryland, which is a town that touches the Mason-Dixon Line corner marker, between Delaware and Maryland. This town is twenty minutes, on the highway, from Cambridge, Maryland, which was the scene of major violence only weeks before Martin Luther King Jr. gave his famous speech on the Mall in Washington, D.C. I should mention that in that famous "I Have a Dream" speech, he mentions that "there is rioting in the streets of Cambridge." The town was near Atholoo Landing, which was a major slave trading area and is about five miles from the birth place of Harriet Tubman, who was of course the finest conductor of the Underground Railroad.

All this history exists in my area and yet I, as a youth, had never experienced a real racial experience. I am blind because I have grown up next to racists. Every couple years or so there is a newsflash that someone has written KKK on the side of a barn or something, but there is no active Klan anywhere around. In middle school and high school, my friends and I would constantly hear that there are racists around and that we just don't see them or pay attention or want to pay attention. Interestingly, the teachers and parents were the "concerned" ones in the community. I have friends that are of another race and culture, and have had these friends for some time. The teachers wanted the students to be aware that the area was, at one time, a moderately active hotbed of race conflicts. We, as students, insisted that there was little to no racism in our generation and that the only way that racism was perpetuated was through the older members of society insisting that there was racism in our community. The time in which I grew up had a lot of tolerance and celebration of diversity. It seemed that the theme of our culture at that time was, "Be whatever you want to be, regardless of what that is, and society has to accept that."

Now, in the year 2005, I would prefer that society be less liberal in its acceptance of diversity. I, being the product of a former hotbed of racism, and being raised in an extremely liberal time where acceptance was drilled in to our minds, would rather not see the celebration of diversity. I think we are all people that face the same conflicts and questions in life and that the past is less important. I am a white male that has North American Indian, Irish, German, Nordic and English blood. I am a mutt by any standards and I don't think race should play a part in any determination about me. My neighbors and I are mostly mutt (we have no real nation behind us or a belief that we are superior). I think racism is on the decline and that the melting pot has cooked up a realization that the only clear thing that separates us from one another is religious outlooks or social standing, and even that has become much more blurry. I believe that in the future, racism won't be nearly as common, and that religious persecution and turmoil, if anything, will be the racism of the past.

Esperanza was a Hispanic student attending the University of California at Santa Barbara. She attributes her lack of negative racial experiences to the fact that she grew up in a Latino community and has become Americanized.

Fortunately, racism has not played a significant role in my life. I have yet to knowingly be a victim of its harsh cruelties. I am aware of its existence and despise it greatly, but have not experienced it first-hand. I believe that my lack of an encounter with racism is due to the fact that I lived in a predominantly Latino community, attended generally Latino schools, and have become Americanized.

My whole experience with education prior to attending the University of Santa Barbra has been shared with Latino peers. With Latinos as the majority at all my schools, I felt right at home and never experienced discomfort or inequality with others. I was an honor/AP student and with that came many privileges. I was praised and supported by my teachers and by the whole administrative staff. My comfort and confidence level were just as high when it came to interacting with my peers. I was an active student who participated in many of my school's clubs and organizations. Never did I encounter a peer or teacher who made me feel less because of my race. I believe that this is solely an outcome of attending schools with Latinos as the majority race. Had this been different, I am sure that my short life would be filled with a number of shocking and traumatizing racial encounters.

My community also consisted of other minorities in addition to Latinos. There are cities that are adjacent to Pomona that do not have many minorities but I never really interacted much with these communities. I would pass through them at most.

Even after I moved to the Santa Barbara area, which consists of mostly Anglos, I found myself associating and seeking out people of the Latino race. Surrounding myself with people of my race has certainly worked as a shield against racism.

My Americanized personality can be seen as another cause for my inexperience with racism. I am a second-generation Latina and have grown up in the American way. I know and follow many of the Latino traditions but I have also accepted many of the American ways and developed a few American qualities. Consequently, I do not exactly come off as a very Latino-cultured individual. I am sure that if I fit the Latino stereotypes more, I would experience unwanted racism. I am sure that my Americanized ways have played a part in sheltering me from major racism.

Altogether I have been fortunate enough to not come across a great racial experience; I strongly believe that being surrounded by Latinos and becoming more Americanized has caused me to experience minimal racism.

Karla was a Hispanic student attending the University of California at Santa Barbara. She has never felt discriminated against because she knew few Anglos before college and since attending college, she has had a very accepting roommate.

I have been fortunate enough to avoid racial humiliation because I was born and raised in East L.A. I am one of those people who feel most comfortable inside their box. My box was East L.A. and I very rarely had to go outside my box. That is, until I got to Santa Barbara, where the majority of my peers are now Caucasian.

Here I was forced to interact with people outside my box for the first time. I was raised to not judge others before I got to know them. I have tried to live my life this way, although at times it has been challenging. Until now, the only white people I was forced to interact with were my teachers. Knowing this, it is easy to imagine how shocked I was when I found out that the person I was going to be rooming with was a white girl from a small town.

When I first read her name on my housing application it scared me, not knowing how she would react to having a Mexican from East L.A. living with her. Then I realized she and I both had to get used to the idea that we were going to be living with people outside our norms. I got over my fear and decided to give her a call in order to get to know her better and not be completely shocked when we first saw each other. Our conversation over the phone was very comforting. I realized we were both very different people but that we had many things in common that would hopefully allow us to build a friendship, or at least respect one another.

We shared pictures of one another to give ourselves a better idea of what we were getting into, but nothing had prepared me for our meeting. Everything about the way we looked was different, not only our skin color but the way we dressed and carried ourselves. Although we are very different from one another, I am very glad we are roommates. She has taught me a lot and has never at any point in time alienated me. On the other hand, she has always tried to incorporate me into her life and activities. She does this although I am at times resistant. UCSB is known to be a party school and like every college there is definitely partying. I like to go out and have fun which is one of the reasons why teachers advised me not to attend this school. However, I have partied only one weekend since I came here eight months ago. I came to the conclusion that I just did not feel comfortable. I have made very few Hispanic friends at UCSB and all of those whom I have made go home often, or for some reason or another, we do not go out or socialize with each other. My roommate on the other hand does not go home so when I decide to go out, I go out with her and her friends, who also happen to be white. This is something that I am not used to and that is why I find myself often rejecting invitations from my roommate to go out on weekends. Lately however, I have found myself being more interactive and in general being myself.

What often helps me be more accepting is just thinking how I would not want my roommate to feel alienated if she ever went to East L.A. I need to give others the opportunity my roommate has given me.

Karen was a Hispanic student who attended the University of California at Santa Barbara. She says she was not discriminated against because of the great actions of her white neighbor.

My mom was born in Mexico and I was born in California. We have always lived in my current house, next door to Deborah, a white woman. It's because of her that I have never really felt discriminated against. I don't have a typical Chicana life because I don't have personal experiences of feeling discriminated. I believe that I have not been discriminated against because of my relationship with a white woman.

Deborah is like my second mother; that is how close she is to my family. She has always been there for me and helped us in anyway she could. Whenever I needed help with my homework, she would help me, which is why I was able to do better in school. Deborah would do whatever it took to make sure I was ok and that I was on track to go to a university. She knew that I was capable of going to a university; she knew how good of a student I was. She respected me and how well I was doing in school.

Deborah would take me everywhere with her. She mainly took me to dinner, but when I was at dinner with her or just at her house, she would have
some of her coworkers there or family. They all knew about me through
Deborah and when I met them they were pleased to meet me. They didn't
treat me differently just because I was the poor little Mexican girl. When I
would talk to them about my future plans they were really proud of me. It
was really nice hearing these things from them, especially because they were
white. I thought they would be shocked to hear that I had plans of going
to college. My relationship with Deborah is what, in a way, prevented me
from being hurt by discriminating words. All the other white people that I
have associated with were through her. They were all really supportive and
I could tell that it was genuine.

*Binh was a Vietnamese student attending the University of California at Santa
Barbara. He grew up in a very diverse community.*

I have been very fortunate to not have a bad racial experience. I was
"lucky" enough to be raised in a city with great diversity and great individuals to help me along the way.

I grew in San Jose, California, in an area where individuals of all races,
shapes, and colors were right next door. Trying to fit in or make friends
was not a very difficult task to achieve as a child. The most common issue
that was discussed among friends was what kinds of foods we ate and what
types of games we played. Racial slurs or any forms of racism were not even
mentioned; let alone talked about with us. We all shared the commonality
of being different in a good way.

My parents enrolled me in very diverse schools starting from elementary
school and on. In addition, I also grew up with the same childhood friends
that shared my experiences. Growing up in the same area with the same
friends gave me the advantage of not feeling uncomfortable and alone. All
throughout school, I pretty much knew everyone at school because of my
current friends and my older sister's friends. Because of the fact that San
Jose is such a diverse city, it gave me the advantage of diversity itself. It is
the reason why I have not had a bad racial experience yet. I believe that if
I grew up in a different city without a strongly diverse group of people, I
would have most likely had a bad racial experience.

*Neena was a Hispanic student who attended the University of California at Santa
Barbara. She has not experienced racism because she looks white.*

Growing up as a Mexican American in Santa Barbara, California, I cannot
recall having a particularly negative racial experience. Despite the fact that I
witnessed other Latinos being discriminated against, I never felt as though

I was being singled out and attacked because of my race or ethnicity. I feel that this is due to the fact that my physical appearance is not typical of most other Mexicans and Mexican Americans.

My parents are from the state of Jalisco in Mexico. This state is in the central region of Mexico and is known for having a large number of fair-skinned, light-haired, and light-eyed people. Since the European colonizers wiped out most of the indigenous population in the state, it is fairly common to encounter blonde-haired, blue/green-eyed people when you visit Jalisco. My sister, in fact, fits this description, as do my cousins who live in Jalisco. Although I am not blonde and blue-eyed, I am fair-skinned, on the tall side compared to Mexican standards, and have hazel eyes and medium brown hair. According to many of the people that I have met, I do not "look Mexican." Because of my looks, I am able to "blend in" with mainstream American society.

My unique appearance has often evoked interesting reactions from individuals when I tell them that I am Mexican American. When I began high school, I met some Mexican American girls in P.E. class and decided to play basketball with them. When one of them made some offhanded joke about white people, they all quickly apologized to me, saying that they had nothing against whites. When I told them that I was Mexican, none of them could believe it, so they asked me to say something in Spanish in order to "prove my ethnicity."

My physical appearance has prevented me from being humiliated in many social aspects, including my schooling. For example, in high school, even though I was often one of the very few Latino students in honors classes, I never felt like an outsider because I was a minority. This was because many of the other students thought I was white. Only when they heard my Spanish surname did they realize I was Latina. My strong academic record and unaccented English also made it relatively easy for me to become friends with many of the white students at my school. Overall, I feel that my atypical Mexican appearance has spared me from having to endure any unpleasant, irritating, or humiliating moments on account of my ethnicity or race. I suppose that my interesting features will continue to inspire more amusing theories about my origins in the future.

Vanessa was a white student attending the University of California at Santa Barbara. She gets along with her friends of other races because everyone has a sense of humor.

I have had the privilege of growing up in a diverse community of the San Fernando Valley. The majority of my friends were Chicanas. Being a Caucasian female in a white-dominated society, I have not experienced any particularly harmful racially discriminatory experiences. Because my hometown is so diverse, there were teachers of many races. White students were the minority at my high school and associating with people of other backgrounds was for the most part practiced and acceptable.

My friends and I find that we can make jokes about other races and our own without causing offense. Through humor we are able to diffuse the significance of their meaning. The intent behind them is not to denigrate a race or subordinate one to another but to make light of our differences and realize that although we are somewhat different in cultural behaviors and ideologies, we can be united by humor.

Tracy was a white student who attended the University of California at Santa Barbara. Her hometown was rural, equally divided between white and Hispanic, and had little conflict. She believes it was the culture of her town that created a lack of racial tension.

In preparing for this essay, I realized that I couldn't think of a single incident that could be considered a "bad racial experience." My family moved to Hollister, California when I was in the third grade. It once functioned solely as an agricultural town with an abundance of orchards, vineyards, and cattle. Now, it struggles to find a balance between its ranching roots and its growing identity as just another commute town for nearby Silicon Valley workers. Another dichotomy that Hollister has always dealt with is its racial identity. The population is almost exactly split in half between people who are of Mexican descent and those who are white. In my opinion, this should be the ideal situation for high racial tension. Have I missed it?

The congregation of the church I attended was, admittedly, almost entirely comprised of white people. There was never any indication of racial prejudice, however, even among the older, very conservative members. We participated in outreach programs in partnership with other churches in the community, many of which had mostly Latino congregations. The school I attended in elementary and middle school also consisted of mainly white students but this was because we lived in a rural part of town and my neighbors (and, consequently, my classmates) were predominantly white farmers whose families had been working on their land for generations. There were only three people in my graduating class in middle school. In this white, rural section of the community, there could (and maybe should) have been tensions between the three Chicano kids at our school and the rest of us. That was never the case, though; none of us ever even considered the difference.

Other activities that I was involved in were somewhat different. I played eight seasons on different soccer teams within the city-sponsored league. The league and my teams were racially even, mirroring the city's ethnic ratio. More often than not, Latino kids outnumbered the white kids. Still, there were never any problems (at least not on my teams) between players, parents, or coaches that arose because of racial issues.

When I reached high school, and racial proportions evened out considerably, race was still not an issue. It seemed like there was a complete balance between white and Latino students in the classroom (both in honors and nonhonors classes), sports, and clubs. Along with our Modern American Literature class, our school offered a Spanish Literature class that was aimed at fluent Spanish speakers. Along with dance and Interact clubs, we had Club Folklorico, McChA, and LULAC.

As I was jotting down these ideas to brainstorm for this essay, I realized something—I had never really considered the cultural diversity of my school and community to be unusual in any way. That's just how our town functions. We, members of both races, have ceased to see ourselves solely in terms of race. We embrace our own cultures, as well as the cultures of our friends and neighbors. There undoubtedly were racial tensions and bad occurrences. But, if in twelve years I managed to miss it, maybe it is because my community promotes a great sense of understanding and tolerance that others could learn from.

Conclusion

The twenty-first century marks a number of changes in racial experiences. Under the new rules of civil discourse, it is not proper to mention the person's race when describing him or her to another person or in an article in the newspaper.[1]

The virulent racism of the 1850s, 1890s, 1930s, and 1960s is gone. Slavery no longer exists, the Ku Klux Klan is not terrorizing large numbers of people, people of color can drink from any water fountain, tremendous progress has been made in reducing discrimination in employment and education, and overt manifestations of racist attitudes are no longer tolerated by most Americans. However, the essays in this book clearly show that racism is still alive in the United States. Only by understanding the manner in which racism still exists can we work for its elimination.

Is the glass half-empty or half-full? For those who think the glass is half-empty, it clear that racism still has a tremendous negative impact on the lives of many Americans. For those who say it is half-full, it is equally clear that we have made tremendous strides in reducing racism in the United States. For those who are victims of a far more virulent racism in Darfur or Bosnia or Rwanda. . . , the example of how America has changed offers a lot of reason for hope.

Racism is a changing phenomenon. Sears and Kinder (1971) started an ongoing discussion about whether or not overt racism has been replaced by symbolic racism. In essence, many whites will not admit to being racist because it is no longer socially correct. However, in private they still hold racist attitudes and publicly oppose policies that promote racial equality under the ruse of "treating everyone the same."

Another change in racism concerns the targets of racism. Hispanics, Asians, and Native Americans are far more vocal than they were in the past in pointing to the special racism to which they are subjected. Furthermore, many whites feel discriminated against in employment, education and access to city services while others feel physically threatened in public spaces.

In an earlier era, there was less contact between people of different races because of de jure segregation. However, with the integration of public spaces, sports teams and schools, people of different races have new ways to interact in both positive as well as negative ways. Most people find these interactions enlightening and positive. Many people have realized that diversity is something to be treasured and not avoided. Nevertheless, tensions sometimes arise in these new types of interactions.

WHAT IS RACISM?

People sometimes have very different interpretations of what constitutes racism and what constitutes harm.[2] Lynn believes her experiences of being called the "n-word" are relatively trivial compared to the racism that occurred during slavery and the civil rights movement. Similarly, Hazel [essay not included] was not easily offended when hearing anti-Hispanic jokes. Ralph, a white growing up in a Hispanic neighborhood, was not particularly upset by being called "Wonder Bread" or "White Devil." On the other hand, when someone at a softball game yelled at Tiffany's dad, "Shut that fucking nigger up," he looked stricken and his daughter began to weep uncontrollably. Similarly, when Brad [essay not included], a popular kid in a mostly white high school, found some racist graffiti in the restroom at school, he said it changed his life and he stopped all friendships with whites. The intensity of the statement yelled at Tiffany's dad likely had some role in how Tiffany and her dad received it. In addition, the fact that Tiffany's mom had recently died also made them particularly vulnerable at the time. People's reactions to these kinds of incidents are affected by the intensity of the statement, how the incident is placed in the context of history and location, and the personality of the victim.

The actual events are also subject to various interpretations. Several contributors mention being followed in stores by store clerks. Sometimes the following was blatant. Other times it was not always clear that they were being followed. And, if they were being followed, was it because of their race, their age, their gender, or the appearance of their economic class? Janet, who was passed up numerous times when trying to hail a cab, commented, "Indeed, every experience is subject to personal interpretation and this interpretation is often colored by past experiences, stereotypes and social construction."

Several contributions come from people whose actions could have been interpreted as being racist. Lynn was very distraught when she had to deny a table to two black gentlemen at a restaurant because the kitchen was backed up and the men did not have reservations. She was convinced that they would think she was racist. We would have loved to interview the two gentlemen she discusses to get their perception of what happened.

It is perhaps useful to distinguish between racist events that occur "spontaneously" and those that are planned. Some of the bad incidents discussed in this book occurred in the heat of anger. When Miguel [essay not included] made the all-star baseball team, he was called a "little 'spic" by the father of a player who did not make the team. The father later apologized and Miguel accepted because he realized it was an isolated experience. Rick was called a "nigger" by another student in fifth grade as he was walking up the staircase. The student immediately apologized. Olivia called one of her black friends a "nigger" in the "heat of the moment." The next day her friend hit her in the legs with a 2 × 4 because of the incident. However, they were able to remain friends.

Clearly, many of the "spontaneous" acts described in this book resulted from a person's general racist tendencies. However, it is important to recognize that people do change. When people do things in the heat of anger or the under the haze of alcohol or drugs, they should probably be understood in a different context.

CHANGES IN RACISM

There has been a massive generational shift in attitudes toward race. In May of 1944, The National Opinion Research Center asked the following two questions in a nationwide survey:

Do you think Negroes should have as good a chance as white people to get any kind of job, or do you think white people should have the first chance at any kind of job?

| As good a chance | 42% |
| White people first | 51% |

Do you think some restaurants in this town should serve both Negro and white people?

| Yes | 46% |
| No | 47% |

Over half the populace supported overt discrimination in employment and services. Any similar question asked today would find support in the low single digits. Today, the populace is divided not over the principle of equality, but over how to implement it.

Several contributors said they never experienced a racial incident because times have changed. Others compared their racial incidents with the much worse incidents that occurred in the past. In addition, many contributors interpreted the actions of older friends or family members in terms of how they were socialized before the 1960s.

Andy was called a "nigger" at a Mardi Gras parade in Alabama when he was nine. Although he was very upset, his mother and aunt told him that it was much worse for them during the age of busing. Jonathan [essay not included] tells the story of how his white grandfather walked out of the Christmas dinner when given a Christmas card depicting a black Santa. Andy interpreted the family fight as generational as his grandfather was raised in the Deep South.

THE EFFECTS OF RACISM

Racism has ended quite a few friendships. Monica heard her best friend say that the only reason why Monica got into a certain university was because she is black. When Rashe's [essay not included] best friend called her a "nigger" during a fight in the third grade, their friendship essentially ended even though her friend apologized.

Sometimes it was the racism of a parent or another third-party that ended the friendship. Elena stopped associating with Lisa because Lisa's mother would not let Elena ride in her car. Lisa's mother said that Elena would get hair grease on the car window. Mary slowly ended her friendship with her best friend Anna, who was Jewish, because so many of her classmates called her names like "Oreo" as well as more hurtful and severely derogatory names.

The racist acts have sometimes caused major psychological damage. When Vanessa [essay not included] was called a "nigger" in elementary school, she said, "I began crying hysterically [in front of my parents] and screaming that I was sorry for being a nigger and that I would do anything to change it." Similarly, when Donelle was called "dirty" in elementary school, she scrubbed her body so hard at bath time that her skin started to bleed. Ellen asked her daddy if she could get painted white because the kids would not play with her in kindergarten.

Racism has also engendered a variety of violent actions. Pamela's house was trashed with racist graffiti when her family moved into a new house in Texas. John describes a brawl between the black football team and the white lacrosse team when someone made a racially derogatory statement. Mary describes how in high school, blacks beat up Hispanics and both blacks and Hispanics beat up whites. Several other contributors also talked about racial violence in the schools. Violence generated by racism is not simply an artifact of the past.

Racism is so pernicious that it also divides families. Robin confronted her uncle for making racial slurs about a black man on the street. Her uncle told her father, "Your no-good daughter chose to bad mouth her uncle for a black man!" Similarly, Tracy, a Hispanic student, had numerous arguments with her stepdad about his descriptions of blacks. Carlos was so embarrassed by his mother's lack of English that he allowed his classmates to make fun of her during a class trip. His mother was extremely disappointed in him.

The fear of "miscegenation" has been and remains one of the major causes of racial antagonism. Numerous contributors tell tales of being harassed for dating someone of another race. Dating a person of another race is a common source of friction within families. Fran tells how her mother was dating a black man and her mother's brother abused her for dating a "nigger." Physical confrontations almost occurred between Fran's brother and Fran's uncle when Fran's uncle said the mother was a whore for dating a "nigger." Bree was virtually disowned by her father for many years because she dated a black man.

BEING BIRACIAL

Contributors who are the offspring of biracial couples sometimes faced a special type of discrimination.[3] Daniel's mother was from Tonga and his father was a first generation Hungarian-Jew. His Tongan relatives belittled him for not being physically strong and he heard far too many anti-Semitic comments. Carmen had a German father and a black mother. Students and teachers in North Carolina thought she was white until her mother came to school for the first time. After that she was treated very differently. Jan had a Creole mother and a black father. The Creole side of her family subtly put her down because of her African American roots. Karen personally struggled with who she was because she has one parent from Guatemala and another from Spain.

HISPANICS AND RACISM

Hispanics face racism for two additional reasons: language and citizenship. Raul describes the experiences of a new Chicana student at his high school. An African American student told her to go back to her own country because she did not speak English. Stacy's father was pulled over so many times by police officers that he kept his birth certificate in the car in order to prove his citizenship. Paula describes the horrible experience of how some of her white classmates in Florida treated some of the Hispanic students in school following an immigration raid that affected many of their parents. Paloma vividly describes the problems her mother experienced when dealing with a hospital billing issue. Paloma's mother experienced these problems because she did not speak English well. Isabella stopped speaking in public when the mother of another student in first grade told her that she should not speak Spanish during recess.

INTRARACIAL RACISM

Intraracial racism took several forms. Some minorities acted in a racist manner toward minorities of their own race. Shelly was denied a job by the black owner of a restaurant because they already had too many blacks. Danielle was passed up by numerous black cab drivers because she was black. Sarah, a Hispanic student, was falsely accused of shoplifting by a Hispanic salesworker. Karen was convinced that the black police officer who pulled her over did so only to impress her white partner.

Another type of intraracial racism consisted of people being mistreated for being the "wrong" hue. Tammy was denied a date by another student because she was too dark and Antoinette's boyfriend was extremely upset with her when she got darker after a vacation in Jamaica. Ken was called "darkie" and "Nightman" because he was so dark. Delores was humiliated by other Hispanics because she was too dark. She was sometimes called a Hindu.

On the other hand, Chantelle was treated badly by her classmates because she was too light-skinned and Lauren [essay not included] was called a "red-boned Negro" for having fair or light skin.

Similarly, being from another country could also be a source of prejudice. Sarah was from Trinidad and was made fun of because she was "dark" and had an accent. Jabari from Nigeria felt he was treated with more respect by white students than by black students. Amir was also from Nigeria and was treated badly by other blacks.

"Acting white" was also considered a crime by some. Dina was told that she was not black because she got good grades. Cara [essay not included] was often accused of "acting white" because she was well-spoken, as was Caroline who also liked the alternative rock group The Smashing Pumpkins. In the Latino community Karen was called a "white-washed bitch" because she did not speak Spanish and Belinda was often told she was not Mexican because she did not speak Spanish.

REACTIONS TO RACISM

The reactions to the racial incidents varied extensively. A variety of contributors thanked the perpetrators for teaching them a lesson.

Aisha's prom plans were cancelled when her prom date's Filipino parents would not let their son go out with an African American. She concluded, "I will never forget the loneliness and disappointment I felt when I received that phone call. I draw from that incident hopes that I never create the same feelings in anyone I come in contact with. I thank Terry's parents for teaching me a lifelong lesson."

Kelly was called a rich white kid in junior high school. It was the first time she had been confronted by racial tension and she saw it as a good learning experience. Emanuel, from Nigeria, was treated miserably by his mostly white classmates in Texas. He states, "Now I can go into any social situation knowing that nothing can happen that I haven't already experienced."

A number of contributors told stories of how their parents used the experience as a learning tool and treated it as a "rite of passage." When Rasche's [essay not included] childhood friend called her a "nigger" in the middle of an argument, Rache's mother sat both of them down to give them a black history lesson. Similarly, when Ellen was called a "nigger" in kindergarten, her father showed them photos depicting slavery and lynchings in order to give a black history lesson. Belia's [essay not included] parents gave her "the talk" when her family was harassed by their white landlord. Belia said:

> I think it's a conversation every black parent has with their child when their child experiences racism. They explained the use of the "N" word and the other comments that made my parents so angry, and why it was so offensive. I learned about slavery and how we are no longer slaves, nor inferior to any race.

Some of the other common reactions to the negative racial experience included:

- *Getting the issue out into the open.* Cary felt she was on display by being the only African-American student at a summer science program in Colorado. She finally called a meeting for everyone and told the attendees about her frustrations. After that, she was treated with more respect.

- *Standing up to the racist behavior.* Anica, a Hispanic student, told off some white students who were telling racist jokes. Others chimed in and the "jokesters" finally realized what they did was wrong. In a different context we see Robin, a white student, who stood up to her uncle's racist statements, which precipitated a major family argument. However, since the argument, her uncle has stopped making such statements.
- *Acting out in violence.* When Darcy was called a "nigger" on the first day of kindergarten, she smacked the boy with a stick, using all her might. When Denise was called a derogatory name while working at an amusement park, she started hitting the man with a board until she was arrested.
- *Acting out in long-term anger.* Geraldo was called a "wetback" by an older man in second grade. Since then he refused to salute the flag at school or take part in the Thanksgiving celebration. Kimberly was still angry many years after she was wrongfully accused of being a racist. She worked at a CD store, which in its store policy, required people to leave their bags at the register. She instructed a black man to leave his backpack at the register and was subsequently accused of being a racist. Elena does not have any white friends today because of an incident that happened when she was in third grade. In this incident, the mother of one of her classmates would not let her ride in the car to go to an event because she would get hair grease on the car window.
- *Getting frustrated because the victim is unable to react.* This occurred a lot during bad interactions with the police, whose power makes it almost impossible for the victim to react.
- *Being fearful.* When Ethan was pulled over by the police for possibly having a stolen bicycle, he started crying when the policeman pulled out his revolver. Claire was scared when she was attacked by two white kids at the home of an acquaintance. Mary still fears black men because of fights that happened while in seventh grade.
- *Issues dissipated over time.* Jabari was mistreated for being Nigerian. However, by the time he started college he started to be more accepted. Delores, a Hispanic student, was made fun of because she was too dark and had a lot of arm hair. She was so stigmatized that she shaved her arms. Only in college did she begin to love the color of her skin.
- *Being so surprised that one does nothing.* Doris was harassed by a white customer because Doris spoke Spanish to another store clerk. Doris was so surprised and perhaps fearful that she did nothing. Ken did not know how to respond when being called a "nigger" at a soccer game, so he did nothing. Since the incidents, both Doris and Ken put a lot of thought into how they should have acted.

- *In retrospect, a person who witnessed someone else being harmed wishing they would have done something to help.* Paula saw kids in her school in Florida being horribly mean toward Mexican students whose parents were just busted by the immigration police. She says that she hopes that in the future she would overcome how scared she was and stop that type of behavior. Similarly, Pricilla regrets that she did not speak up when a patient at the hospital where she worked began spewing racist comments. Donald has often thought about the day he did not do enough to help a white kid who got beat up by a black kid in seventh grade.
- *Talking to one's parents.* Jessica was a white student who was offended by her grandmother's racial comments. She asked her father to talk to her grandmother and her grandmother has since stopped. Stephan was wrongfully stopped by the police for auto theft, humiliated in front of his girlfriend and brought to the police station in handcuffs. When he told his parents they got an attorney involved and eventually got a formal letter of apology.
- *Talking to school administrators.* Gwendolyn was a white student who was harassed by a black student on the bus. When she got to school she complained to a school administrator and the harassment stopped. Randy's talked to the school administrators when Randy's teacher made a racist comment during a film presentation. The teacher made some type of apology. Talking to school administrators did not always help. Sarah's mother complained to the school when several of Sarah's classmates made a variety of anti-Semitic statements. Apparently, the school did nothing.

LACK OF RACISM

Approximately 5 percent of the contributors said they never had a bad racial experience and provided a range of reason for this. As discussed above, several people said that times have changed.

Binh, a Vietnamese student, said he never experienced racism when he grew up because her community was extremely diverse. The makeup of the community also had a positive effect for Roger and Tracy because the community was open-minded. Tracy said:

I had never really considered the cultural diversity of my school and community to be unusual in any way. That's just how our town functions. We, members of both races, have ceased to see ourselves solely in terms of race. We embrace our own cultures, as well as the cultures of our friends and neighbors. There undoubtedly were racial tensions and bad occurrences. But, if in twelve years I managed to miss it, maybe it is because my community promotes a great sense of understanding and tolerance that others could learn from.

More contributors gave the opposite reason for lack of racial tension—they grew up in homogeneous communities. Nathan, a white student, grew up in an all white area and Esperanza experienced no racism because she grew up in a mostly Hispanic community.

Communities are made up of individuals. Several contributors referred to special individuals who helped them. Karla, a Hispanic student, referred to the help of her college roommate. Similarly, Karen believes she was not discriminated against because of the great actions of her neighbor.

Several students said their lack of racial experience was due to the fact that they were assimilated into the American mainstream. Esperanza, a Hispanic student, said her family was assimilated. A few black and Hispanic students who were accused by their peers of "acting white" said they did not encounter racism from whites because they were good students and liked mainstream American culture.

Other personality characteristics also played a role in why some contributors said they lacked a racial experience. Janice, a black student at Howard, was taught by her mother not to overanalyze anything. Vanessa said her friends got together because they had good senses of humor, and Thomas carried himself as someone who was a success.

CLOSING COMMENTS

When we first wrote this conclusion, the story of Don Imus calling the Rutgers University women's basketball team "nappy headed hoes" on his nationally syndicated radio program was prominent in the news. The story has complexity. Is the glass half-empty or half-full? His horrific comments point to the existence of racism in America (the glass is half-empty). On the other hand, he apologized and the advertisers pulled the plug on the program. This would not have occurred before the 1960s (the glass is half-full).

Another part of the complexity is Imus himself. It was noted that he had previously also made racist and anti-Semitic statements. However, he has also given substantial sums of money to charities that help people of color.

One more contradictory part of the story was the reaction to other radio hosts, hip-hop singers, and other entertainers who use equally offensive language against people of color as well as whites. How should they be judged?[4]

Many of the essays in this book detail horrific experiences. However, there is also much room for hope. Many contributors inferred that racism is far less virulent then it was in the 1960s. In addition, many contributors told stories in which their friends came from many different backgrounds and they looked forward to living with diversity. Another positive finding was how many contributors were willing to confront their family members, friends and acquaintances when these people exhibited racist behavior or racist attitudes. Nevertheless, only by exposing situations where racism is still prevalent can we start to end it once and for all.

NOTES

1. Similarly, because it is argued that the United States is (or should be) color-neutral, it is difficult to conduct research on some racial issues because asking a person's race is discouraged. The catch-22 is that it becomes almost impossible to gather data to examine racial discriminations because racial discrimination does not exist, by definition. Seltzer has conducted several jury composition challenges where potential jurors are told on the jury qualification questionnaire that answering the race question is voluntary. Hence in some situations, over 80 percent of jurors did not answer the race question.

2. People often define social problems very differently from one another. Over the years Seltzer has conducted dozens of studies on jury behavior. A common question asked of potential jurors is whether or not they had ever been a victim of a serious crime. In several studies they were then asked to discuss the serious crime. It became apparent that some people considered having a ten-dollar item stolen from their office to be a serious crime while other people would not even mention being robbed at gunpoint because no shots were fired.

3. It is particularly difficult to measure what percentage of Americans are multi-racial. In the 2000 Census, the first census in which respondents could choose more than one race, 2.4 percent of Americans said they were multi-racial. However, as Harris and Sim (2002) note, how people respond to questions which measure race depends a lot on question wording, question context, and mode of survey.

4. For a thoughtful piece on the controversy see Frank Rick, "Everybody Hates Don Imus," *The New York Times*, April 15, 2007.

References

Aboud, Frances E. and Virginia Fenwick. "Exploring and Evaluating School Based Interventions to Reduce Prejudice." *Journal of Social Issues* 55, no. 4 (December 2002): 767–85

Aboud, Frances E., Morton J. Mendelson, and Kelly T. Purdy. "Cross-Race Peer Relations and Friendship Quality." *International Journal of Behavioral Development* 27 (March 2003): 165–73.

Alba, Richard D. "Immigration and the American Realities of Assimilation and Multiculturalism." *Sociology Forum* 14, no.1 (March 1999): 3–25.

Allport, Gordon W. *The Nature Of Prejudice.* Reading, MA: Addison-Wesley, 1954.

Alvarez, Michael R. and John Brehm. "Are Americans Ambivalent Towards Racial Policies?" *American Journal of Political Science* 41, no. 2 (April 1997): 345–74.

Amodio, David M., Patricia G. Devine, P.G., and Eddie Harmon-Jones. "A Dynamic Model of Guilt: Implications of Motivation and Self-Regulation in the Context of Prejudice" *Psychological Science* 18, no. 6 (June 2007): 524–30.

Anderson, Elijah. *Streetwise: Race, Class, and Change in an Urban Community.* Chicago: University of Chicago Press, 1990.

Ansalone, George. "Schooling, Tracking, and Inequality." *Journal of Children and Poverty* 7, no. 1 (March 2001): 33–47.

Arriagada, Paula A. "Family Context and Spanish-Language Use: A Study of Latino Children in the United States." *Social Science Quarterly* 86, (2005): 599–618.

Aveling, Nado. "Hacking at Our Roots: Rearticulating White Racial Identity within the Context of Teacher Education. *Race, Ethnicity, and Education* 9, no. 3 (September 2006): 261–74.

Banks, James A. "Improving Race Relations in Schools: From Theory and Research to Practice." *Journal of Social Issues* 62, no. 3 (2006): 607–14.

Barnes, Arnold and Ephross, Paul H. "The Impact of Hate Violence on Victims Emotional and Behavioral Responses to Attacks." *Social Work*, 39 (May 1994): 247–51.

Bertrand, Marian. and Sendil Mullainathan. "Are Emily and Greg More Employable than Lakisha and Jamal? A Field Experiment on Labor Market Discrimination." University of Chicago School of Business, 2003.

Benson, Janel E. "Exploring the Racial Identities of Black Immigrants in the United States." *Sociological Forum* 21, no. 2, (June 2006): 219–47.

Bijlani, Jagdish J. "Neither Here nor There: Creating a Legally and Politically Distinct South Asian Racial Identity." *Berkeley La Raza Law Journal* 16, (2005): 53–69.

Birzer, Michael L. and Juanita Smith-Mahdi. "Does Race Matter? The Phenomenology of Discrimination Experienced Among African Americans." *Journal of African American Studies* 10, no. 2 (Fall 2006): 22–37.

Blascovich, Jim, Natalie A. Wyer, Laura Sart, and Jeffrey Kibler. "Racism and Racial Categorization." *Journal of Personality and Social Psychology* 72, no. 6 (June 1997): 1364–72.

Bobo, Lawrence. "Race, Public Opinion, and the Social Sphere." *Public Opinion Quarterly* 61, (1997): 1–15.

Bobo, Lawrence and James Kluegel 1997. "Laissez–Faire Racism: The Crystallization of a Kinder, Gentler, Antiblack Ideology" Pp. 15–44 in *Racial Attitudes in the 1990s: Continuity and Change*, edited by Steven Tuch and Michael Hughes. Westport, CT: Praeger.

Bond, Carolyn and Richard Williams. "Residential Segregation and the Transformation of Home Mortgage Lending." *Social Forces* 86, no. 2, (December 2007): 671–98.

Bonilla–Silva, Eduardo and Forman, Tyrone. "I am not Racist but . . .: Mapping White College Students' Racial Ideology in the United States." *Discourse and Society* 11, no. 1 (2000): 50–85.

Bonilla–Silva, Eduardo. *Racism without Racists: Color Blind Racism and the Persistence of Racial Inequality in the United States, 2nd edition.* Lanham, MD.: Rowman & Littlefield, 2000.

Branton, Regina P. and Bradford S. Jones "Reexamining Racial Attitudes: The Conditional Relationship Between Diversity and Socioeconomic Environment." *American Journal of Political Science* 49, (April 2005): 359–72.

Brown, Tony M., James S. Jackson, Kendrick T. Brown, Robert M. Sellers, Shellye Keiper, and Warde J. Manuel. "There's No Race on the Playing Field: Perceptions of Racial Discrimination Among White and Black Athletes." *Journal of Sports and Social Issues* 27, no. 2, (May 2003): 162–83.

Brunsma, David L. "Public Categories, Private Identities: Exploring Regional Differences in Biracial Experience." *Social Science Research* 35, (September 2006): 555–76.

Byrd, C. E. and Ross, S. M. "The Influence of Participation in Junior High Athletics on Students' Attitudes and Grades," *Physical Educator* 48, no. 4 (1991): 170–76.

Cameron, Jessica A., Jeanette M. Alvarez, Diane N. Ruble, and Andrew J. Fuligni. "Children's Lay Theories About Ingroups and Outgroups: Reconceptualizing Research on Prejudice." *Personality and Social Psychology Review* 5, no. 2 (2001): 118–28.

Campbell, Mary E. and Lisa Troyer. "The Implications of Racial Misclassification by Observers." *American Sociological Review* 72, (October 2007): 750–65.

Carter, J. Scott, Lala Carr Steelman, Lynn M. Mulkey, and Casey Borch. 2005. "When the Rubber Meets the Road: Effects of Urban and Regional Residence on Principle and Implementation Measures of Racial Tolerance." *Social Science Research* 34:408–25.

Castillo, Linda G., Collie W. Conoley, Jennifer King, Dahl Rollins, Saori Rivera, and Mia Veve. "Predictors of Racial Prejudice in White American Counseling Students." *Multicultural Counseling and Development* 34, (January 2006): 15–26.

Chatman, Celina and William von Hippel. "Attributional Mediation of Ingroup Bias." *Journal of Experimental Social Psychology* 37, (May 2001): 267–72.

Chen, Zhuojun. "Chinese American Children's Ethnic Identity: Measurement and Implications." *Communication Studies* 51, no. 1 (Spring 2000): 74–95.

Citrin, Jack, Donald P. Green, and David O. Sears. "White Reactions to Black Candidates When Does Race Matter?" *Public Opinion Quarterly* 54 (Spring 1990): 74–96.

Clay-Warner, Jody. "Perceptions of Procedural Injustice: The Effects of Group. Membership and Status." *Social Psychology Quarterly*, (2001): 224–38.

Clotfelter, Charles T. "Interracial Contact in High School Extracurricular Activities." *Urban Review* 34, (March 2002): 25–46.

Comeaux, Eddie. and C. Keith Harrison. "Labels of African American Ballers: A Historical and Contemporary Investigation of African American Male Youth's Depletion from America's Favorite pastime, 1885–2000." *Journal of American Culture* 27, (September 2004): 67–80.

Comer, James P. "Racism and the Education of Young Children." *Teachers College Record* 90, (1989): 352–61.

Condor, Susan G. "Public Prejudice as Collaborative Accomplishment: Towards a Dialogic Social Psychology of Racism." *Journal of Community and Applied Social Psychology* 16, (2006): 1–18.

Constantine, Madonna G. and George Gushue. "School Counselors' Ethnic Tolerance Attitudes and Racism Attitudes as Predictors of Their Multicultural Case Conceptualization of an Immigrant Student." *Journal of Counseling and Development* 81, (2003): 185–90.

Cowan, Gloria. "Interracial Interactions at Racially Diverse University Campuses." *The Journal of Social Psychology* 145, no. 1, (February 2005): 49–63.

Croll, Paul R. "Modeling Determinants of White Racial Identity: Results from a New National Survey." *Social Forces* 86, no. 2, (December 2007): 613–42.

Cross, William E., 'The Thomas and Cross Models of Psychological Nigrescence: A Review." *Journal of Black Psychology* 5, (1978): 13–31.

Dabney, Dean, Laura Dugan, Volkan Topalli, and Richard Hollinger. "The Impact of Implicit Stereotyping on Offender Profiling: Unexpected Results From an Observational Study of Shoplifting." *Criminal Justice and Behavior* 33, (October 2006) : 646–74.

Dawson, Michael. *Behind the Mule: Race and Class in African American Politics*. Princeton, N.J.: Princeton University Press, 1994.

de la Garza, Rodolfo O., Louis DeSipio, Christopher Garcia, John Garcia, and Angleo Falcon. *Latino Voices: Mexican American, Puerto Rican, and Cuban Perspectives on American Politics*. Boulder, CO.: Westview Press, 1992.

Demas, Lane. "Beyond Jackie Robinson: Racial Integration in American College Football and New Directions in Sports History." *History Compass* 5, no. 2, (2007): 675–90.

Derman-Sparks, Louise, Carol Higa, and Bill Sparks. "Children, Race and Racism: How Race Awareness Develops." *Interracial Books for Children Bulletin* 11 (1980): 3–9.

Dinnerstein, Leonard. *Anti–Semitism in America.* New York: Oxford, 1995.

Dixon, Travis L. and Daniel Linz. "Overrepresentation and Underrepresentation of African Americans and Latinos as Lawbreakers on Television News." *Journal of Communication*, Spring (2000): 131–54.

Dixon, Jeffrey C. and Michael Rosenbaum. "Nice to Know You? Testing Contact, Cultural and Group Threat Theories of Anti-Black and Anti-Hispanic Stereotypes." *Social Science Quarterly* 85, no. 2, (2004): 257–80.

Dovidio, John F. and Samuel L. Gaertner, eds. *Prejudice, Discrimination and Racism: Theory and Research.* Orlando, FL: Academic Press, 1986.

Dubois, W. E. B. *The Souls of Black Folk.* New York: Alfred A. Knopf, [1903] 1993.

Dutton, Susanne E., Jeffrey A. Singer, and Ann S. Devlin. "Racial Identity of Children in Integrated, Predominantly White, and Black Schools." *The Journal of Social Psychology* 138, no. 1, (February 1998): 41–53.

Eberhardt, Jennifer L., Paul G. Davies, Valerie Purdie-Vaughn, and Sherri L. Johnson, "Looking Deathworthy: Perceived Stereotypicality of Black Defendants Predicts Capital–Sentencing Outcomes." *Psychological Science* 17, no. 6, (2006): 383–86.

Emerson, Michael O., George Yancey, and Karen J. Chai. "Does Race Matter in Residential Segregation? Exploring the Preferences of White Americans?" *American Sociological Review*, 66 (December 2001): 922–35.

Emerson, Michael O., Rachel T. Kimbro, and George Yancey. "Contact Theory Extended: The Effects of Prior Racial Contact on Current Social Ties." *Social Science Quarterly* 83, (December 2002): 745–60.

Ezekiel, Ralph E. *The Racist Mind: Portraits of American Neo-Nazis and Klansmen.* New York: Viking, 1995.

Farkas, George. "Racial Disparities and Discrimination in Education: What Do We Know, How Do We Know It, and What Do We Need to Know?" *Teachers College Record* 105, no. 6, (2003): 1119–46.

Feagin, Joe R. "The Continuing Significance of Race: Antiblack Discrimination in Public Places." *American Sociological Review* 56, (February 1991): 101–16.

Fein, Steven and Steven J. Spencer. "Prejudice as Self–Image Maintenance: Affirming the Self through Derogating Others." *Journal of Personality and Social Psychology* 73, no. 1, (1997): 31–44.

Figlio, David N. Testing, "Crime, and Punishment." University of Florida, Department of Economics; National Bureau of Economic Research (NBER), working paper W11194.

Frankenberg, Erica, Chungmei Lee, and Gary Orfield. *A Multiracial Society with Segregated Schools: Are We Losing the Dream.* The Civil Rights Project, Harvard University, (2003).

Franklin, Sekou and Richard Seltzer. "Conflicts in the Coalition: Challenges to Black and Latino Political Alliances." *The Western Journal of Black Studies* 26, (2002): 75–88.

Frazer, Ricardo and Uco J. Wiersma. "Prejudice versus Discrimination in the Employment Interview: We May Hire Equally, but Our Memories Harbour Prejudice." *Human Relations* 54, (February 2001): 173–91.

Frederickson, George M. *The Arrogance of Race: Historical Perspectives on Slavery, Racism, and Social Inequality.* Middletown, CT: Wesleyan University Press, 1988.

Gabbidon, Shaun L. "Racial Profiling by Sales Clerks and Security Personnel in Retail Establishments." *Journal of Contemporary Criminal Justice* 19, (2003): 345–64.

Gallagher, Charles A. "Researching Race, Reproducing Racism." *The Review of Education/Pedagogy/Cultural Studies* 21, no. 2, (1999): 165–91.

Gatz, Margaret, Michael A. Messner, and Sandra J. Rokeach. *Paradoxes of Youth and Sports.* Albany: State University of New York Press, 2002.

Gay, Claudine. "Putting Race in Context: Identifying the Environmental Determinants of Black Racial Attitudes." *American Political Science Review* 98, (November 2004): 547–62.

Gilens, Martin. "Race and Poverty in America: Public Misperceptions and the American News Media." *Public Opinion Quarterly* 60, (January 1996): 515–41.

Gilliam Jr., Franklin D., and Shanto Iyengar. "Prime Suspects: The Influence of Local Television News on the Viewing Public." *American Journal of Political Science* 44, (July 2000): 560–73.

Goto, Sharon, Gilbert C. Gee, and David T. Takeuchi. "Strangers Still? The Experience of Discrimination Among Chinese Americans," *Journal of Community Psychology* 30, no. 2, (January 2002): 211–24.

Graham, James A. and Robert Cohen. "Race and Sex as Factors in Children's Sociometric Ratings and Friendship Choices," *Social Development* 6, (1997): 355–72.

Green, Donald P., Lawrence McFalls, L. H., and Jennifer K. Smith. "Hate Crime: An Emergent Research Agenda." *Annual Review of Sociology* 27, (August 2001): 479–504.

Green, Donald P., Jack Glaser, and Andrew Rich. "From Lynching to Gay Bashing: The Elusive Connection Between Economic Conditions and Hate Crime." *Journal of Personality and Social Psychology* 75, no. 1, (July 1998): 82–92.

Greenhoot, Andrea F., Monica Tsethlikai, and Beth Wagoner. "The Relations Between Children's Past Experiences, Social Knowledge, and Memories for Social Situations." *Journal of Cognition and Development* 7, no. 6, (August 2006): 313–40.

Gullickson, Aaron. "The Significance of Color Declines: A Re-analysis of Skin Tone Differentials in Post-Civil Rights America." *Social Forces* 84, (September 2005): 157–80.

Hallinan, Maureen T. and Richard A. Williams. "The Stability of Student's Interracial Friendships." *American Sociological Review* 52, (October 1987): 653–64.

Hallinan, Maureen T. and Richard A. Williams. "Interracial Friendship Choices in Secondary Schools." *American Sociological Review* 54, (February 1989): 67–78.

Hamilton, David L. and Trolier, Tina K. "Stereotypes and Stereotyping: An Overview of the Cognitive Approach." Pp. 127–63 in *Prejudice, Discrimination and Racism: Theory and Research.* edited by John F. Dovidio and Samuel Gaertner. Orlando, FL: Academic Press, 1986.

Hanchard, Michael. "Black Memory versus State Memory: Notes Toward a Method." *Small Axe* 26, (June 2008): 45–62.

Harris, David. "Flying While Arab: Lessons from the Racial Profiling Controversy." *Civil Rights Journal* 6, (Winter 2002): 8–13.

Harris, David R. "Why Are Whites and Blacks Averse to Black Neighbors." *Social Science Research* 30, no. 1, (March 2001): 100–16.

Harris, David R. and Jeremiah J. Sim. "Who is Multiracial? Assessing the Complexity of Lived Race." *American Sociological Review* 67, (August 2002): 614–27.

Helms, Janet E. "Toward a Methodology for Measuring and Assessing Racial as Distinguished from Ethnic Identity." Pp. 143–92 in *Multicultural Assessment in Counseling and Clinical Psychology* edited by Gargi R. Sodowsky and James C. Impara. Lincoln, NE: Buros Institute of Mental Measurements, 1996.

Helms, Janet E. and Regine M. Talleyrand. "Race is Not Ethnicity." *American Psychologist* 52, no. 11, (November 1997): 1246–47.

Henderson, Jacob and Gerald Baldasty. "Race, Advertising, and Prime-Time, and Television" *The Howard Journal of Communications* 14, no. 2 (April–June 2003): 97–112.

Henry, P. J. and David O. Sears. "The Symbolic Racism 2000 Scale." *Political Psychology* 23, no. 3 (June 2002): 253–83.

Hewstone, Miles, Alexander Hantzi, and Lucy Johnston. "Social Categorization and Person Memory: The Pervasiveness of Race as an Organizing Principle." *European Journal of Social Psychology* 21, no. 6, (November/December 1991): 517–28.

Hill, Mark E. "Skin Color and the Perception of Attractiveness among African Americans: Does Gender Make a Difference." *Social Psychology Quarterly* 65, no. 1 (2002): 77–91.

Hill, Patricia C. *Black Feminist Thought: Knowledge, Consciousness, and the Politics of Empowerment*. London and New York: Routledge Press, 2000.

Hochschild, Jennifer L. *Facing up to the American Dream: Race, Class, and the Soul of the Nation*. Princeton, N.J.: Princeton University Press, 1995.

Hochschild, Jennifer L. and Vesla Weaver. "The Skin Color Paradox and the American Racial Order." *Social Forces* 86, no. 2, (December 2007): 643–69.

Hodge, Michael E., Mark C. Dawkins, and Jaxk H. Reeves. "A Case Study of Mortgage Refinancing Discrimination: African American Intergenerational Wealth." *Sociological Inquiry* 77, no. 1, (February 2007): 23–43.

Hughes, Diane and Lisa Chen. "When and What Parents Tell Children About Race: An Examination of Race-Related Socialization Among African American Families." *Applied Developmental Science* 1, (December 1997): 200–14.

Hunt, J. S. (2007). "Implicit Bias and Hate Crimes: A Psychological Framework and Critical Race Theory Analysis." Chapter to appear in R. L. Wiener, B. H. Bornstein, B. Schopp, & S. Wilborn (Eds.), (Eds.), *Legal Decision Making in Everyday Life: Controversies in Social Consciousness* (pp. 247–65). New York: Springer.

Hunter, Margaret L. "If You're Light You're Alright: Light Skin Color as Social Capital for Women of Color." *Gender and Society* 16, no. 2 (April 2002): 175–93.

Hurwitz, John, and Mark Peffley. "Public Perceptions of Race and Crime: The Role of Racial Stereotypes." *American Journal of Political Science* 41, no. 2, (April 1997): 375–401.

Hutchings, Vincent and Nicholas Valentino. "The Centrality of Race in American Politics." *Annual Review of Political Science*, 7 (May 2004): 383–408.

Jackman, Mary R. and Marie Crane. "Some of My Best Friends are Black . . ." Interracial Friendship and Whites' Racial Attitudes." *Public Opinion Quarterly* 50, no. 4, (Winter 1986): 459-86.

Johnson, James D., Carolyn Simmons, Sophie Trawalter, Tara Ferguson, and William Reed. "Variation in Black Anti-White Bias and Target Distancing Cues: Factors That Influence Perceptions of Ambiguously Racist Behavior" *Personality and Social Psychology Bulletin* 29, no. 5, (2003): 609-22.

Jones-Correa, Michael. *Between Two Nations: The Political Predicament of Latinos in New York City*. Ithaca, N.Y.: Cornell University Press, 1998.

Jones, Rachel. and Ye Luo. "The Culture of Poverty and African American Culture: An Empirical Assessment." *Sociological Perspectives* 42 (Autumn 1999): 439-58.

Jones, Michael. *Social Psychology of Prejudice*. Upper Saddle River, N.J.: Prentice Hall, 2002.

Joyner, Kara and Grace Kao. "School Racial Composition and Adolescent Racial Homophily." *Social Science Quarterly* 81, no. 3 (September 2000): 810-25.

Joyner, Kara and Grace Kao. "Interracial Relationships and the Transition to Adulthood" *American Sociological Review* 70, (August 2005): 563-81.

Kahn, Lawrence M. "Discrimination in Professional Sports: A Survey of the Literature," *Industrial and Labor Relations Review* 44, no. 3 (April 1991): 395-418.

Keith, Verna M. and Cedric Herring. "Skin Tone and Stratification in the Black Community." *American Journal of Sociology* 97, no. 3 (November 1991): 760-78.

Kinder, Donald. and Lynn M. Sanders. *Divided By Color*. Chicago: University of Chicago Press, 1996.

King, Rosamond S. "Sheep and Goats Together: Interracial Relationships from Black Men's Perspectives." *Journal of African American Studies* 8 (2004): 108-25.

Kouri, Kristyan M. and Marcia Lasswell, M. "Black-White Marriages: Social Change and Intergenerational Mobility." Pp. 241-54 in *Families On the Move: Migration, Immigration, Emigration, and Mobility* edited by Barbara Settles, Daniel E. Hanks, and Marvin B. Sussman. Binghamton, N.Y.: Haworth Press, 1994.

Kowalski, Kurt. "The Emergence of Ethnic and Racial Attitudes in Preschool-Aged Children," *The Journal of Social Psychology* 143, no. 6 (December 2003): 677-90.

Kramer, Roderick M., and Marilyn Brewer. "Effects of Group Identity on Resource Use in a Simulated Commons Dilemma." *Journal of Personality & Social Psychology*, 46, no. 5 (May 1984): 1044-57.

Krysan, Maria. "Prejudice, Politics, and Public Opinion: Understanding the Sources of Racial Policy Attitudes." *Annual Review of Sociology* 26 (August 2000): 135-68.

Lahelma, Elina. "Tolerance and Understanding? Students and Teachers Reflect on Differences at School." *Educational Research and Evaluation* 10, no. 1 (2004): 3-19.

Lampe, Philip E. "Toward Amalgamation: Interethnic Dating Among Blacks, Mexican Americans and Anglos. *Ethnic Groups* 3, (1981): 97-109.

Lease, Michele. and Jamilia Blake. "A Comparison of Majority-Race Children With and Without a Minority-Race Friend." *Social Development* 14, no.1 (January 2005): 20-41.

Lee, Jennifer and Frank Bean. "America's Changing Color Lines: Immigration, Race/Ethnicity, and Mulitracial Identification." *Annual Review Sociology* 30 (August 2004): 221-42.

Lewis, Richard and George Yancey. "Bi-Racial Marriages in the United States: An Analysis of Variation in Family Member Support of the Decision to Marry." *Sociological Spectrum* 15, no. 4 (December 2001): 443–62.

Levine, Jeffrey, Edward G. Carmines, and Paul M. Sniderman. "The Empirical Dimensionality of Racial Stereotypes." *Public Opinion Quarterly* 63, no. 3 (1999): 371–84.

Lien, Pei-te, M. Margaret Conway, and Janelle Wong. *The Politics of Asian Americans: Diversity and Community.* New York and London: Routledge, 2004.

Lindemann, Stephanie. "Who Speaks 'Broken English': U.S. Undergraduates Perceptions of Non-Native English." *International Journal of Applied Linguistics* 15, no. 2 (June 2005): 187–212.

Lippe-Green, Rosina. 1997. *English with an Accent: Language, Ideology, and Discrimination in the United States.* Routledge Press: New York.

Locke, Don C. *Increasing Multicultural Understanding: A Comprehensive Model.* Newbury Park, CA: Sage Publications, 1992.

Maddox, Keith B. "Brown Paper Bag Syndrome: Dark-Skinned Blacks Are Subject to Greater Discrimination." *Journal of Blacks in Higher Education* 37 (October 2002): 46.

Maddox, Keith B. "Perspectives on Racial Phenotypicality Bias." *Personality and Social Psychology Review* 8 (2004): 383–401.

Maddox, Keith B. and Gray, Stephanie. "Cognitive Representations of Black Americans: Reexploring the Role of Skin Tone." *Personality and Social Psychology Bulletin* 28, no. 2 (2002): 250–59.

Margie, Nancy G., Melanie Killen, Stefanie Sinno, and Heidi McGlothlin. "Minority Children's Intergroup Attitudes About Peer Relationships," *British Journal of Developmental Psychology* 23, no.2 (June 2005): 251–70.

Marshall, B. 2001. "Working While Black: Contours of Unequal Playing Field." *Phylon,* 49: 137–50.

Martin, Judith N., Bradford, Lisa J., Drzewiecka, Jolanta A., and Anu S.Chitgopeka. "Intercultural Dating Patterns Among Young White U.S. Americans: Have They Changed in the Past 20 Years." *The Howard Journal of Communications,* 14, no. 2 (April–June 2003): 53–73.

Masko, Amy L. "I Think About It All the Time": A 12-year-old Girl's Internal Crisis with Racism and the Effects on Her Mental Health." *Urban Review* 37, no. 4: (November 2005): 329–50.

Massey, Douglas S. and Nancy Denton. "Racial Identity and the Spatial Assimilation of Mexicans in the United States." *Social Science Research* 21, (1992): 235–60.

Mastro, Dana E., and Amanda L. Robinson. "Cops and Crooks: Images of Minorities on Primetime Television." *Journal of Criminal Justice* 28, (2000): 385–96.

Mauer, Mark and Ryan S. King, *Uneven Justice: State Rates of Incarceration by Race and Ethnicity,* The Sentencing Project, 2007.

McClain, P. and Tauber, S. (1998). "Black and Latino Socioeconomic and Political Competition: Has a Decade made a Difference?" *American Politics Quarterly,* 26, 237–52.

McCormick, Albert E. and Graham C. Kinloch. "Interracial Contact in the Customer-Clerk Situation." *The Journal of Social Psychology* 126, no. 4 (1986): 551–53.

McDermott, Monica and Frank L. Samson. "White Racial and Ethnic Identity in the United States." *Annual Review of Sociology* 31, (2005): 245–61.

McDermott, Monica. *Working Class White: The Making and Unmaking of Race Relations.* Berkeley: University of California Press, 2006.

McDonald, Steven J. "How Whites Explain Black and Hispanic Inequality" *Public Opinion Quarterly* 65 (Winter 2001): 562–73.

McGlothlin, Heidi, Melanie Killen, and Christina Edmonds. "European American Children's Intergroup Attitudes About Peer Relationships," *British Journal of Developmental Psychology* 23, (2005): 227–49.

McLaren, Lauren M. "Explaining Right-Wing Violence in Germany: A Time Series Analysis." *Social Science Quarterly* 80, no.1. (March 1999): 166–80.

Mercer, Sterett H. and Michael Cunningham. "Racial Identity in White American College Students: Issues of Conceptualization and Measurement." *Journal of College Student Development* 44, no. 2 (March-April 2003): 217–30.

Miller, Tom (ed.). *How I Learned English: 55 Accomplished Latinos Recall Lessons in Language and Life.* Washington, D.C.: National Geographic Press, 2007.

Monteith, Margo J. and C. Vincent Spicer. "Contents and Correlates of Whites' and Blacks Racial Attitudes." *Journal of Experimental Social Psychology* 36, no. 2 (March 2000): 125–54.

Moore, Valerie A. "The Collaborative Emergence of Race in Children's Play: A Case Study of Two Summer Camps," *Social Problems* 49, no. 1 (February 2002): 58–78.

Nesdale, Drew, Maass, Nancy, Durkin, Kevin, and Griffiths, Judith. "Group Norms, Threat, and Children's Racial Prejudice," *Child Development* 76, no. 3: (May 2005): 652–63.

O'Bryan, Meagan, Harold Fishbein, H. D., and P. Neal Ritchey, P. D. "Intergenerational Transmission of Prejudice, Sex Role Stereotyping and Intolerance." *Adolescence* 39, (Fall 2004): 407–27.

O'Neil, John. "A New Generation Confronts Racism." *Educational Leadership* 50, no. 8, (May 1993): 60–63.

Pagano, Maria E. and Barton Hirsch. "Friendships and Romantic Relationships of Black and White Adolescents" *Journal of Child and Family Studies* 16, no. 11 (June 2006): 347–57.

Panagapolous, Costas. "Arab and Muslim Americans and Islam in the Aftermath of 9/11." *Public Opinion Quarterly* 70, no. 4 (2006): 608–24.

Park, Kyeyoung. "The Re-Invention of Affirmative Action: Korean Immigrants Changing Conceptions of African Americans and Latin Americans." *Urban Anthropology* 24, no. 1, (Spring 1995): 59–92.

Peterson, Karen S. "Interracial Dating: For Today's Teens, Race 'Not an Issue' Anymore," *USA Today*, November 3, 1997.

Pettigrew, Thomas F. and Roel W. Meertens. "Subtle and Blatant Prejudice in Western Europe Evidence." *Journal of Experimental Social Psychology,* 25 (1995): 57–75.

Petrocelli, Matthew, Alex Piquero, and Michael Smith. "Conflict Theory and Racial Profiling: An Empirical Analysis of Police Traffic Stop Data." *Journal of Criminal Justice* 31, no. 1 (January–February 2003):1–12.

Phinney, Jean S. "Understanding Ethnic Diversity: The Role of Ethnic Identity." *American Behavioral Scientist* 40, no. 2 (1996): 143–52.

Phinney, Jean S. and Victor Chavira. "Parental Ethnic Socialization and Adolescent Coping with Problems Related to Ethnicity." *Journal of Research on Adolescence* 5, no. 1 (January 1995): 31–35.

Picca, Leslie H. and Joe R. Feagin. *Two-Faced Racism: Whites in the Backstage and Frontstage*, New York: Routledge, 2007.

Porter, Judith R. and Robert Washington. "Minority Identity and Self-Esteem." *Annual Review Sociology* 19 (August 1993): 139–61.

Price, Joseph and Justin Wolfers, (2007). Racial Discrimination Among NBA Referees, National Bureau of Economic Research, Working Paper 13206.

Quillian, Lincoln. "New Approaches to Understanding Racial Prejudice and Discrimination," *Annual Review of Sociology* 32, (August 2006): 299–328.

Reid, Karla S. "Survey Probes Views on Race." *Education Week* 23, no. 36 (May 2004): 1–16.

Reiter, Michael E., Jaimie Krause, and Amber Stirlen. "Intercultural Dating On A College Campus." *College Student Journal* 39, no. 3 (September 2005): 449–54.

Rockquemore, Kerry A. and David L. Brunsma. "Socially Embedded Identities: Theories, Typologies, and Processes of Racial Identity Among Black/White Biracials" *The Sociological Quarterly* 43, no. 3 (2002): 335–56.

Romano, Renee. *Race Mixing: Black-White Marriage in Post-War America*. Cambridge, MA: Harvard University Press, 2003.

Sarkisian, Natalia and Naomi Gerstel. "Kin Support Among Blacks and Whites: Race and Family Organization." *American Sociological Review* 69, no. 6 (December 2004): 812–37.

Schuman, Howard, Charlotte Steeh, Lawrence Bobo, and Maria Krysan. *Racial Attitudes in America-Trends and Interpretation*. Rev. ed. Cambridge, MA: Harvard University Press, 1997.

Sears, David, Colette van Laar, Mary Carillo, and Rick Kosterman. "Is it Really Racism? The Origins of White Americans' Opposition to Race-Targeted Policies." *Public Opinion Quarterly* 61, no. 1 (Spring 1997): 16–53.

Sears, D. O., and Kinder, D. R. Racial tensions and voting in Los Angeles. In W. Z. Hirsch (Ed.), *Los Angeles: Viability and prospects for metropolitan leadership*. New York: Praeger, 1971.

Seltzer, Richard and Robert C. Smith. "Color Differences in the Afro-American Community and the Differences They Make". *Journal of Black Studies* (1991) 21 (3): 279–86.

Sherman, Richard L. "Intergroup Conflict on High School Campuses." *Journal of Multicultural Counseling and Development* 18, no. 1 (January 1990): 11–18.

Sigelman, Lee, Timothy Bledsoe, Susan Welch, and Michael Combs. "Making Contact? Black-White Social Interaction in an Urban Setting," *American Journal of Sociology* 101, no. 5 (March 1996): 1306–32.

Sigelman, Lee and Susan Welch. 1991. *Black Americans' Views of Racial Inequality: The Dream Deferred*. New York: Cambridge University Press, 1991.

Sigelman, Lee and Susan Welch. "The Contact Hypothesis Revisited: Black-White Interaction and Positive Racial Attitudes." *Social Forces* 71, no. 3 (March 1993): 781–95.

Smith, Robert C. and Richard Seltzer. *Contemporary Controversies and the American Racial Divide.* Lanham, MD.: Rowman & Littlefield, 2000.

Smith, Robert C. and Richard Seltzer. *Race, Class and Culture: A Study in Afro-American Mass Opinion,* Albany: SUNY Press, 1992.

Smith, Tom W. "Ethnic Images." *National Opinion Research Center,* University of Chicago, General Social Survey Topical Report No. 19, 1990.

Smith, Tom W. "Measuring Racial and Ethnic Discrimination." *National Opinion Research Center,* University of Chicago, General Social Survey Methodological Report No. 96, 2002.

Sniderman, Paul M. and Thomas Piazza. *The Scar of Race.* Cambridge, MA: Belknap Press/Harvard University Press, 1993.

Solsberry, Priscilla W. "Interracial Couples in the United States of America: Implications for Mental Health Counseling." *Journal o f Mental Health Counseling* 16, no. 3 (July 1994): 304–18.

St. John, Craig and Tamara Heald-Moore. 1996. "Racial Prejudice and Fear of Criminal Victimization by Strangers in Public Settings." *Sociological Inquiry* 66, no. 3 (July 1996): 267–84.

Strum, Charles. "Schools, Tracks and Democracy." *New York Times,* section B1, 1 April 1993

Tarman, Christopher and David Sears. "The Conceptualization and Measurement of Symbolic Racism." *Journal of Politics* 67, no. 3 (August 2005): 731–61.

Tate, Katherine. *From Protest to Politics: The New Black Voters in American Elections.* New York: Russell Sage Foundation, 1992.

Tatum, Beverly D. "Teaching White Students About Racism: The Search for White Allies and the Restoration of Hope." *Teachers College Record* 95, no. 4 (Summer 1994): 462–76.

Taylor, John and R. Jay Turner. "Perceived Discrimination, Social Stress, Depression in the Transition to Adulthood: Racial Contrasts." *Social Psychology Quarterly* 65, no. 3 (2002): 213–25.

Taylor, Marylee C. "How White Attitudes Vary with the Racial Composition of Local Populations: Numbers Count." *American Sociological Review* 63, no. 4 (August 1998): 512–35.

Todd, Judith, Jeanice Mckinney, J.L., Raymond Harris, Ryan Chadderton, and Leslie Small. "Attitudes Toward Interracial Dating: Effects of Age, Sex, and Race" *Journal of Multicultural Counseling and Development* 20, no. 4 (October 1992): 202–8.

Tuch, Steven and Marylee C. Taylor. "Whites' Opinions About Institutional Constraints On Racial Equality." *Social Science Research* 70, no. 4 (1986): 268–71.

Tucker, B. M. and Kernan, C. "Trends in African American Family formation: A Theoretical and Statistical Overview" Pp. 3–16 in *The Decline of Marriage among African Americans: Causes, Consequences, and Policy Implications,* edited by Beverly M. Tucker and Claudia Mitchell–Kernan. New York: Russell Sage Foundation, 1995.

Turner, Margery, Fred Freiburg, Erin B. Godfrey, Carla Herbig, Diane Levy, and Robin E. Smith. "All Other Things Being Equal: A Paired Testing Study of Mortgage Lending Discrimination." The Urban Institute, 2002.

Tyson, Karilyn, William Darity, Jr., and Domini Castellino. "It's Not a Black Thing: Understanding the Burden of Acting White and Other Dilemmas of High Achievement." *American Sociological Review* 70 (August 2005): 582–605.

Vail, Kathleen. "What's in a name? Maybe a Student's Grade!" *American School Board Journal* 192, (August 2005): 6–8.

Vaquera, Elizabeth and Grace Kao. "Private and Public Displays of Affection among Interracial and Intra-Racial Adolescent Couples." *Social Science Quarterly* 86, no. 2 (June 2005): 484–506.

Verma, Rita. "Dialogues about 9/11 the Media and Race." *Radical Teacher* 74, (September 2005): 12–16.

Virtanen, Simo and Leonie Huddy."Old-Fashioned Racism and New Forms of Racial Prejudice" *The Journal of Politics* 60, no. 2 (1998): 311–32.

Wakefield, David W. and Cynthia Hudley. "Ethnic and Racial Identity and Adolescent Well-Being." *Theory into Practice* 46, no. 2 (April 2007): 147–54.

Wallace, Michael. "Labor Market Structure and Salary Determination among Professional Basketball Players," *Work and Occupations* 15, no. 3, (August 1988): 294–312.

Walls, Richard, Rayne Sperling, and Keith Weber. "Autobiographical Memory of School." *The Journal of Educational Research* 95, no. 2 (November 2001): 116–27.

Wang, Hongyu and Grace Kao. "Does Higher Socioeconomic Status Increase Contact Between Minorities and Whites? An Examination of Interracial Romantic Relationships Among Adolescents" *Social Science Quarterly* 88, no. 1 (2007): 146–64.

Washington, Robert E. and David Karen. "Sports and Society." *Annual Review of Sociology* 27, (2001): 187–212.

Waters, Mary C. "Immigration, Intermarriage, and the Challenges of Measuring Racial/Ethnic Identities." *American Journal of Public Health* 90, no. 11 (November 2000): 1735–37.

Watt, Sherri K. "The Story Between the Lines A Thematic Discussion of the Experience of Racism." *Journal of Counseling and Development* 77, no. 1 (Winter 1999): 54–61.

Watts, Meredith. "Political Xenophobia in the Transition from Socialism: Threat, Racism and Ideology Among East German Youth." *Political Psychology* 17, no. 1 (1996): 97–126.

Wies, Lois and Hall, Julia. "I Had A Lot of Black Friends Growing Up that My Father Didn't Know About": An Exploration of White Poor and Working Class Female Racism." *Journal of Gender Studies* 10, no. 1 (2001): 43–66.

Weitzer, Ronald J. and Steven Tuch. "Racially Biased Policing: Determinants of Citizen Perceptions." *Social Forces* 83, no. 3 (March 2005): 1009–30.

Weitzer, Ronald J. and Steven Tuch. "Race, Class, and Perceptions of Discrimination by the Police." *Crime and Delinquency* 45, no. 4 (1999): 494–507.

Weitzer, Ronald J. "Citizens' Perceptions of Police Misconduct: Race and Neighborhood Context." *Justice Quarterly* 16 (1999): 819–46.

Weitzer, Ronald. "Racial Discrimination in the Criminal Justice System: Findings and Problems in the Literature." *Journal of Criminal Justice* 24, no.4 (1996): 309–22.

Weitzer, Ronald. "Racial Prejudice Among Korean Merchants in African American Neighborhoods." *Sociological Quarterly* 38, no. 4 (Fall 1997): 587–606.

Welch, Susan and Lee Sigelman. "The Politics of Hispanic-Americans: Insights from National Surveys, 1980–1988." *Social Science Quarterly* 74, (1993): 76–94.

White, Ismail K. "When Race Matters and When It Doesn't: Racial Group Differences in Response to Racial Cues." *American Political Science Review* 101, no. 2 (May 2007): 339–54.

White, Rob and Santina Perrone. "Racism, Ethnicity, and Hate Crime." *Communal/Plural: Journal of Transnational and Crosscultural Studies* 9, no. 2 (October 2001): 161–81.

Williams, Jerome D., Geraldine Henderson, and Ann Marie Harris. "Consumer Racial Profiling: Bigotry Goes to Market." *The New Crisis* (November/December, 2001): 22–24.

Wilson, William J. *The Truly Disadvantaged: The Inner City, the Underclass, and Public Policy.* Chicago: University of Chicago Press, 1987.

Wilson, Thomas C. "Whites' Opposition to Affirmative Action: Rejection of Group-Based Preferences as well as Rejection of Blacks." *Social Forces* 85, no. 1 (September 2006): 111–20.

Wittenbrink, Bernd, Charles Judd, and Bernadette Park. "Evidence for Racial Prejudice at the Implicit Level and Its Relationship with Questionnaire Measures." *Journal of Personality and Social Psychology* 72, no. 2 (1997): 262–74.

Wong, Carol, Jacquelynne Eccles, and Arnold Sameroff. "The Influence of Ethnic Discrimination and Ethnic Identification on African American Adolescents' School and Socioemotional Adjustment" *Journal of Personality* 76, no. 6 (December 2003): 1197–1232.

Yancey, George. "Who Interracially Dates: An Examination of the Characteristics of Those Who Have Interracially Dated." *Journal of Comparative of Family Studies* 33, no. 2 (March 2002): 179–90.

Yancey, George. "Experiencing Racism: Differences in the Experiences of Whites Married To Blacks and Non-Black Racial Minorities." *Journal of Comparative Family Studies* 38, no. 2 (March 2007): 197–213.

Yancey, George and Richard Lewis. "Biracial Marriages in the United States: An analysis of variation in family member support." *Sociological Spectrum* (15): 443–62.

Zirkel, Sabrina. "What Will You Think of Me? Racial Integration, Peer Relationships and Achievement Among White Students and Students of Color." *Journal of Social Issues* 60, no. 1 (2004): 57–74.

Zubrinsky, Camille L. and Lawrence Bobo. "Prismatic Metropolis: Race and Residential Segregation in the City of Angels." *Social Science Research* 25, no. 4 (1996): 335–74.

About the Authors

Richard Seltzer is professor of political science at Howard University.

Nicole E. Johnson is an independent researcher in urban and minority education.

Breinigsville, PA USA
23 February 2011
256175BV00001B/5/P